# The New Evolutionary Microeconomics

NEW HORIZONS IN INSTITUTIONAL AND EVOLUTIONARY
ECONOMICS

**General Editor:** Geoffrey M. Hodgson
Research Professor, University of Hertfordshire Business School, UK

Economics today is at a crossroads. New ideas and approaches are challenging
the largely static and equilibrium-oriented models that used to dominate
mainstream economics. The study of economic institutions – long neglected
in the economics textbooks – has returned to the forefront of theoretical and
empirical investigation.

This challenging and interdisciplinary series publishes leading works at
the forefront of institutional and evolutionary theory  and focuses on cutting-
edge analyses of modern socio-economic systems. The aim is to understand
both the institutional structures of modern economies and the processes of
economic evolution and development. Contributions will be from all forms of
evolutionary and institutional economics, as well as from Post-Keynesian,
Austrian and other schools. The overriding aim is to understand the processes
of institutional transformation and economic change.

Titles in the series include:

# The New Evolutionary Microeconomics

## Complexity, Competence and Adaptive Behaviour

Jason Potts

*Lecturer in Economics*
*University of Queensland*
*Australia*

NEW HORIZONS IN INSTITUTIONAL AND EVOLUTIONARY
ECONOMICS

**Edward Elgar**
Cheltenham, UK • Northampton, MA, USA

Published by
Edward Elgar Publishing Limited
Glensanda House
Montpellier Parade
Cheltenham
Glos GL50 1UA
UK

Edward Elgar Publishing, Inc.
136 West Street
Suite 202
Northampton
Massachusetts 01060
USA

A catalogue record for this book
is available from the British Library

**Library of Congress Cataloguing in Publication Data**
Potts, Jason D., 1972—
    The new eveolutionary microeconomics : complexity, competence, and
adaptive behaviour / Jason D. Potts.
    p.cm. — (New horizons in institutional and evolutionary economics)
Includes index.
1. Microeconomics. I. Title. II. Series

HB172 .P68 2001
338.5—dc21                                          00–056009


ISBN 1 84064 543 1

Printed and bound in Great Britain by Biddles Ltd, *www.biddles.co.uk*

# Contents

# Figures and tables

## FIGURES

## TABLE

There was a passionate craving among the intellectuals of his age for a means to express their new concepts. They longed for philosophy, for synthesis. The erstwhile happiness of pure withdrawal each into his own discipline was now felt to be inadequate. Here and there a scholar broke through the barriers of his specialty and tried to advance into the terrain of universality. Some dreamed of a new alphabet, a new language of symbols through which they could formulate and exchange their new intellectual experiences. . . .

(Herman Hesse, *The Glass Bead Game* 1969: 36)

# Preface and acknowledgements

By the term 'heterodox' schools of thought, I wish to be understood as referring to Austrian, Behavioural, Evolutionary, Institutional, Post-Keynesian and Neo- and Post Schumpeterian economics, as well as the resource-based theories of the firm, information economics and ecological economics. So that I might offer a theorem to obviate the need to actually read this book, let us represent this rubric as **H**. Let **E** represent evolutionary microeconomics. Lemma 1: **H** → **E**. Now let **S** represent complex systems theory, and **G** graph theory. Lemma 2: **S** → **G**. It can be shown that **E** → **S** (Schumpeter's last theorem . . .), and therefore **E** → **G**. *Modus ponens*, it follows that **H** → **G**. For the formalists among you, that ought to be sufficient.

Of the readers now remaining, I imagine you are three.

The first will be the purebred Walrasian economist, for whom this book will perhaps at best seem meaningless—with its unfathomable discussion of a non-problem—or at worst offensive, with its posture of superseding generality. Or perhaps in my conjectures on the foundations of economic theory I am just plain wrong. Either way, this examination presents the opportunity for dialogue, and you will find my opening gambit in Chapter 2.

The second reader will be the heterodox economist of any stripe, and this book is addressed principally to you. I shall make an offering, thereby, of what I regard as some fundamental truths of your intellectual environment. I hope you will consider these critically, because if my argument is substantially correct and does withstand close examination then a unified heterodox microeconomics is surely imminent.

The third reader will be, more or less, any economist or graduate student for whom the standard theoretical apparatus is sometimes a rather blunt tool. Of course, these tools can be sharpened. Yet the problem is that this process tends to become an end in itself, as research problems are selected on their fit with the sharpest tools, rather than the other way around. The thoughtful economist will inevitably be visited by moments of doubt that will thereby admit the possibility of alternatives. Different tools, perhaps? This will induce mildly exotic behaviours, the surreptitious reading of, say, the *Journal of Post-Keynesian Economics* or some such literature of doctrinal otherness. Such acts will seldom usher forth immediate enlightenment; more often, the reader will find him or herself estranged within the hermetic seal of heterodox economics, where the various points of theory, empiricism and critique that define each school circle impenetrably and self-referentially. Each article presumes that you have read and understood all the others. Even for self-confessed heterodox economists, this rugged aspect of the landscape carries with it in many cases an unwanted and unnecessary sense of isolation. And for students and economists with orthodox training, the absence of clear points of entry, of soft progression and navigational charts, does certainly make for tough going. To paraphrase someone who knew only too well, why would anyone outside of a mental institution willingly become interested in heterodox economic currencies of thought, given the clear and present opportunity costs of doing so?

My own experiences here began as a student who had crash-landed, so to speak, in the heterodox territories after having departed on what was an otherwise orthodox flight through economic theory. My first impressions were indeed of a rough vertiginous landscape, a parochial wash of noisy confusion with rivulets occasionally turning to cascades of powerful insight. What was the nature of this anomalous world? Was it all perhaps merely a mirage of refracting logic? Where were the landmarks? Where were the thoroughfares? Why the tribalism and simmering insurgency?

Slowly, a crucial insight dawned upon me. The differences between the respective heterodox schools of thought are much less than they themselves make out. There is, as I shall argue in this book, an overarching relationship that connects all of the heterodox economics as different manifestations of the same fundamental principle. Genetically, as it were, they are all the same species. This is perhaps a controversial thesis, although I think an intriguing one. For it implies that the unorthodox status of the heterodox schools accrues not because they are misinformed extremists of some sort, but rather because they proceed from a different starting point. Is this starting point ill-conceived or just plain wrong? No. It is nothing other than recognition that *connections* exist, that they are incomplete, and that this matters enormously to structure and dynamics (it does not matter much to statics). That is it. Evolutionary microeconomics, which I propose as a synthesis of the collective heterodox economics, is the study of connections in the economic system.

One might then wonder where and how the term 'evolutionary' is to fit into this scheme. This is an important question and one that can be answered immediately. In this book, I do not much refer to principles of selection or random variation or replication; hardly at all, in fact. Does this mean that I aim to purge all Darwinian heritage from the evolutionary transmutation into microeconomics? No, I certainly do not. The key point to grasp is that evolution is not uniquely, or even necessarily, a biological phenomenon. This book, along with all of evolutionary economics, makes or requires no basis of biological determinism in human behaviour. All we require is bounded rationality, which is simply the statement that human beings make use of abstraction in the navigation of their environment. That is the sum of the direct import, and it comes from psychology, not biology anyway. Rather, the point is that evolution is a statement about a dynamic logic of self-transformation, and it was an idea that in fact preceded Darwin and originated from the Scottish moral philosophers of the mid-eighteenth century who included, incidentally, Adam Smith. And I follow this path. I accept Darwinism and Neo-Darwinism (the modern synthesis) as well as the theory of punctuated equilibria and autocatalytic sets and all of the variations and twists that have woven the fantastic tapestry that is evolutionary biology. I accept all of it, except biology.

Evolution does not depend upon a specific substrate. It is a logic that can be generally expressed as an algorithmic process of emergence. Evolution is as much within the realms of language, or culture, or mathematical solutions, or ideas, or technologies and preferences. The subject domain of evolution spans cosmology to computer science, and it is this perspective on the deep nature of evolution that I shall work with in this book. I shall presume that the reader will be able to cope with this shift of abstraction. The best bridging literature into this domain of universality is, in my opinion, Daniel Dennett's (1995) *Darwin's Dangerous Idea*, Richard Dawkins's (1999) classic *The Extended Phenotype*, and Robert Pirsig's (1991) excellent philosophical novel *Lila*.

When the evolutionary metaphor is released from the biological substrate it then becomes, ultimately, the study of information acting upon itself. As such, the role of substrate is only to hold the information, which may be as DNA, but equally as grammar or syntax, as skills or behaviours, as structure or organization, as symbolic or logical expression. All that matters is that information be capable of acting on itself, which moves the emphasis from the substrate through which the message is carried (such as DNA) to the message itself. We refer then, in the economic context, not to a general allocation problem but to a general coordination problem. In the context of evolutionary economics, we refer to the processes by which a complex system such as an agent or firm, or population of such systems, is able to transform itself by endogenous reconfigurations of that information.

Connections define information. Changes in connections affect a different structure or organization or technology or whatever. Connections by their specificity define systems, and thereby changes in connections represent the micro-processes of evolution. Hence, evolutionary microeconomics is a study of the micro- and macrodynamics of connections. Perhaps the early progenitors of the neoclassical economics had much the same sense of awakening when they first comprehended the notion of equilibrium freed from a celestial or mechanical substrate.

There is so much that we are yet to understand about the nature of the economic system and its highly complex dynamics. The evolutionary project begun by Herbert Spencer, Thorstein Veblen and Joseph Schumpeter is still a long way from completion. It has many pillars but no real sense of architecture (and perhaps, to continue the metaphor, too little heavy moving equipment, cranes in particular). There are of course many facets to such an enterprise—empirical, statistical, methodological and the like—all of which require attention to detail. But there are some brute lifting tasks to perform as well. Specifically, to fit appropriate technical methods onto appropriately refined conceptual constructions. My sincere hope is that the approach developed herein, and the strength of the platform it expresses, might then further encourage students and researchers to make stronger connections between a unified heterodox economics—an evolutionary microeconomics—and the burgeoning research fields of complex systems theory. There is surely much interesting and profitable research to be done here as we attempt to raise a platform to further our understanding of the principles of economic evolution.

## Acknowledgements

My warmest thanks to Peter Earl, Paul Dalziel, Stan Metcalfe, Tim Hazledine, John Woods, Kurt Dopfer, Brian Loasby, Esben Andersen, Richard Nelson and Geoff Hodgson, all of whom have made useful and insightful comments on earlier versions of this book. Special thanks also to John Foster, Tom Mandeville, Rodney Beard, Stuart McDonald, Mirko Draca, Shelton Brown, and other participants of the Emergent Complexity in Economics Group at the University of Queensland for helpful advice and critique. Needless to say, they are all in no way responsible for any sins of omission or distortion that I have subsequently perpetrated upon their fine ideas.

Special thanks also to the International Joseph A. Schumpeter Society and their anonymous referees for the joint award of the Schumpeter prize, and to the good people at *WirtschaftsWoche* for their generous sponsorship and promotion. Vielen Dank. Thanks also to the team at Edward Elgar Publishing for their excellent and efficient work in the preparation of this manuscript.

# 1. Introduction

*Look abroad through nature's range,*
*Nature's mighty Law is change.*
(Robert Burns)

## 1.1 Context, Subtext, Pretext

Metaphysics is the branch of philosophy that attempts to understand the fundamental nature of reality. It asks 'what is . . .' questions, and seeks answers that reveal what anything must be like in order to be at all. This book is not about metaphysics.

Rather, it is about *ontology*, which is the science of being or reality. It is about *economics*, which is the study of what people then do with that being and reality. And it is also about *evolution*, which is a dynamic link between being and reality. This book, then, is about the ontology of economic evolution. It is a study on the nature of economic reality from an evolutionary perspective.

The objective is to lay the foundations for an evolutionary microeconomics and this involves confronting a number of ontological questions. What is an economic system? What is an economy made of? When an economy grows, what grows? When an economy evolves, what evolves? When there is technological change, what changes? When there is uncertainty, what is uncertain? Where is the information in the so-called new information economy? Where exists the capital in human and social capital? What are institutions made of? In what sense is an economic system a complex system? Such questions may perhaps sound like the disillusionment of defunct academic scribblers and certainly do not tend to break the stride of serious, practical economists whose professional task is . . . is to what?

What do economists do? We are scientists and therefore like all scientists we tell stories. There are of course strict rules about what constitutes a good story, or rather what constitutes a bad story, and woe is the career of any economist who does not tell at least a few stories every few years. Our job is to tell stories, and by this activity we learn about our stories, and so come closer to the deep aspects of the phenomena they represent. This book is merely a story about some common elements of all economic stories, and a proposal to distinguish two overarching narratives—an evolutionary microeconomics and a Walrasian

1

microeconomics—by the sorts of interactions between the characters that are permitted in the respective stories.

What do we require to tell economic stories? Clearly, our minimum requirement is a set of objects or events and a set of relationships between them, so that we can tell stories that have identifiable characters and meaningful adventures. The common form of these stories, the familiar characters and the sorts of adventures they might have—or rather, the basic elements and the permitted relationships between them—we refer to as a microeconomics.

The character and logic of any system of microeconomics derives ultimately but completely from the way in which these two primary classes of existence are defined. All theories and models developed within the system of microeconomics will automatically inherit this foundational ontological form. The archetypal expression is something like $\{x \text{ in } R^n\}$, which refers to a set of things (x) and the way they are related (operators defined over the field $R^n$). Both of these are ontological constructions. Concepts such as commodity, input or agent can be fitted within the class of things. But concepts such as technology, preferences, or market refer to the relationship between the things. If we think about the possible forms that these relationships can take, it is apparent that there are two: each-with-all or each-with-some. It follows from this that there are two corresponding general systems of microeconomics.

The neowalrasian (including the neoclassical) microeconomics is a high-level synthesis of orthodox thought constructed upon two ontological primitives: a set of elements and a field. That much is well understood (see Mirowski 1989). What I shall add to this is the proposition that we may define a further system of microeconomics, an evolutionary microeconomics, as a high-level theoretical synthesis of heterodox thought constructed also upon two ontological primitives. But now we refer to a set of elements and a set of specific connections between them. Elements and connections construct a system. The economy, then, is a system of these systems. The evolutionary microeconomics is a framework in which dynamics occur over the space of connections. When connections change, so too does the structure of the system. When structure changes, the dynamic properties of the system change also. This changes the conditions under which connections exist; new ones may form, existing ones may fail or may even become strengthened. This total process linking microstructure with macrodynamics and macrostructure with microdynamics is what I mean by economic evolution, and the evolutionary microeconomics is the framework capable of describing it.

How do you create such an evolutionary microeconomics? The strategy I pursue is eclectic heterodox fusion filtered through network, graph and complex systems theory. The underlying ideas come from Tony Lawson, Robert Clower, Axel Leijonhufvud, Nicolai Foss, Philip Mirowski, John Foster, Stan Metcalfe, Paul Krugman, Edith Penrose, Peter Earl, Brian Loasby, Alan Kirman, Friedrich von Hayek, John Holland, Richard Nelson and Sidney Winter, Stuart Kauffman, Nicholas Georgescu-Roegen, Herbert Simon, Joseph Schumpeter, John Maynard Keynes, Thorstein Veblen, George Shackle, Brian Arthur, and many others as well. Disparate as some of these theorists may seem to one another, and indeed to the schools of thought they represent, they all share common ground in recognizing the existence of connections and the importance of connective structure in dynamics of the economic system. By centring upon the concept of a connection we can synthesize the heterodox schools of economic thought into a unified evolutionary microeconomics.

And what are connections? The abstraction I achieve is that they are usefully thought of as a hyperstructured set $E = (E_1^n, E_2^n, ..., E_k^n)$. But that might not mean much at the moment. Generally, connections are specific direct relationships between elements, and are ubiquitous in the economic system. They exist in the structure of interdependence and interactions between agents. They exist in the modalities of technology and the forms of organization and competence. They exist as contracts. They exist in the structure of decision rules and the way that information is processed. In all such events, the dynamics of economic systems can be seen to occur mostly in the space of connections.

Consider chocolate cake. It has inputs: eggs, flour, butter, oven, labour and suchlike. It is a technology defining a commodity and so exists as a point in multidimensional space, its coordinates given by the quantities of each input required. This is how the economist understands chocolate cake. But even abstract chocolate cake is richer than this. It involves a recipe too, a specific and sometimes very specific way of combining these ingredients (consider, smash eggs into chef then coat with flour, place butter in oven . . . chocolate cake is not an inevitable outcome). These relationships are connections, and it is apparent that only some connections will produce chocolate cake. So before we begin to wrestle with market imperfections or technological trajectories and other such serious subject matter, let us just first ensure that we have understood chocolate cake.

Technological change, for instance, may occur when the relationships between elements change or when new relationships are established. This might be a new design concept or product. (It might be a new recipe.) It may equally be a reconfigured organizational structure or a new distribution network. The phenomenon we refer to as technological change envelops a vast space of possible forms of change. Obviously, experimentation with these connections is what inventors, innovators and entrepreneurs do. (And chefs too.) Institutions change when connections change, forming new behaviours, routines and social structures. Concepts relating to information and coordination are essentially about the connective geometry of the economic system; they are about who is connected to whom, what is connected to what. We are increasingly coming to understand how different sorts of connective structures have markedly different dynamical properties (for example, Kauffman 1993, Watts 1999). Densely connected systems are highly chaotic, sparsely connected systems are typically highly ordered, if not frozen. The complex states of being that so characterize the realms of life, cognition, economy and society are intermediate. Connections matter because the specifics of how and where they exist determine the dynamic properties of the systems that they comprise.

I shall endeavour to catalogue where connections exist in the economy and how they matter as examples along the way. These are important ideas in their own right, because what we refer to are the primary dynamic objects of society. These webs of connections continually form and reform human society and, by implication, economic activity. Joseph Schumpeter wrote in *Capitalism, Socialism and Democracy* (1954: 82) that '[t]he essential point to grasp is that in dealing with capitalism we are dealing with an evolutionary process'. But an even more fundamental point to grasp is that in dealing with human society (which envelops all of capitalism, socialism and democracy) we are also dealing with an evolutionary process. This brings into focus an important question: are the 'things' that change in the evolution of human society the same 'things' that change in the evolution of economic systems? The premise of this book is that in abstract they are. These things, these dynamic objects, are connections. It is the dynamics of connections and the emergence of higher-level structure and pattern (as systems) that is the essence of a generalized evolutionary framework for economics. The beauty of this approach, as many economists who are thinking about these matters have come to understand, is that it moves easily into a dynamic process-orientated argument. The addition of the concept of a connection to the set of descriptive categories we use in economics leads to a strong foundation for the theory of a complex system and the concept of self-organization. This then provides a framework to study economic evolution as the dynamics of these connections.

Why do we need such a retooling of the conceptual apparatus? In essence, the defining characteristic of the modern economy is extremely rapid technological, organizational and institutional change, all embedded within broader patterns of social change. It is as simple as that. Change happens, it happens broadly and deeply, and we require a framework for analysis of its economic aspects. We do not have one. What we have, rather, is a microeconomics geared to study equilibrium and stationary states. That would be fine if we lived in an economy characterized predominantly by stable equilibria. We do not. It would also be sufficient if the role of theory was limited to benchmarking null states. It is not. Some say we are in the midst of an economic revolution from an industrial to an information-based economy. Many economists have expressed vexation about what this actually means, if anything. One thing is apparent though, our standard tools of economic analysis are doing a rather poor job explicating what is occurring. The reason for this is clear, as I shall show. The essential problem is that the standard model does not actually represent (at all) the quantity that is actually changing! It is connections that are changing, and this demands a formal framework that makes connections the prime variables.

Economic theory has come under increasing criticism for its perceived irrelevance and methodological values driven solely by mathematical aestheticism. But it is not just outside snipers who pass these comments; there is a growing body of dissatisfaction and occasionally vehement critique issuing directly from the theory elite themselves. (On this matter, see Bell and Kristol 1981, D'Autume and Cartelier 1997, Lawson 1997 or Louçã 1997.) Criticism is easy enough to ignore, especially if it is perceived to be ill-tempered or fused with agenda. But by and large this has not been the case (excepting much ill-conceived critique of the use of mathematics per se). Rather, it has come in waves, ever gathering in energy and repeatedly hitting the same point. This book attempts to express this as a statement about *the geometry of economic space* as manifest in the conceptual and analytical treatment of 'dynamic objects'. In other words, proper concern about the development of economic theory ought not be directed at the more elliptical points of methodology, or towards suspicion of neoliberal imperialistic tendencies or whatever, but at something far more mundane. In the midst of all the apparent change percolating through modern economic systems, what is actually changing?

Economists have, for instance, long known that by far the most significant factor in explaining the growth of output is improvements in technology. But what has not been apparent is the answer to a seemingly metaphysical question: what is technology, and what changes when it changes? In the neoclassical scheme of things, a technology is a particular bundle of inputs (a quantity of labour and of capital, say) and that technological change is the ability to produce more output by using this same quantity of inputs. This tells you that technological change has occurred, but it does not tell you how or why. It does not tell you what has actually changed. Some economists have been moved to criticize this lack of explanatory content as signalling that the theory project is in some important way incomplete. I stand among them. But I also believe there is a general solution. In the case of technological change, the answer lies in recognizing that a technology is not just a quantity of things (inputs), but also the particular way in which they are combined (descriptive of physical, human and social capital alike). Technological change occurs when new combinations are discovered, which then gives rise to new outputs, which provide further possibilities for recombinations, and so on. Technological change begets economic evolution by complex recombinant means over partially organized distributed networks. Economic growth, it would seem, is perhaps better understood as a side-effect of this evolutionary process.

How do you do evolutionary microeconomics? The approach I develop is geared explicitly towards the development of multiagent simulation modelling, which is much inspired by artificial intelligence/artificial life and theoretical biology. This is in contrast with representative agent modelling, as inspired by nineteenth century physics. The multiagent framework that I shall outline here[1] enables the study of coordination processes, self-organization and distributed processing, microdiversity and structural determination, all in a way that is fundamentally beyond the capabilities of any representative agent model. These are obviously important topics, so why have we not made use of such a framework previously? It is tempting to suggest that multiple heterogeneous agents have not been used simply because of the enormous computational costs involved. But the defences of representative agent methods make little reference to this. Instead, there is an endless tirade of 'it is as if . . .'; or charges of 'ad-hocery' are levelled against any other presumption; or cabalistic incantations of *natura non facit saltum* or *de gustibus non est disputandum* are cast about. Something is clearly fishy. The fact of the matter is that representative agent models are consistent with the use of the space $R^n$. But multiagent models are not; their interactions are predominantly local and invariably partial. They require a network space. So it is the analytical space that determines the character of the agents and therefore of the analysis, not the other way around. The defence, as I shall explain in Chapter 2, was not of representative agents at all but of integral spaces.

Once this is recognized we can move to consider the practicabilities of building and working with such models. Until relatively recently, the computational costs of building multi-agent models was generally prohibitive and the support networks needed to build and interpret them was rather limited. This is no longer the case. Computers have become faster and software better. The internet, that most marvellous of tools, has been developed and there are now freely accessible platforms (including program libraries) such as *Swarm* or *LSD* that make multiagent simulation a viable possibility for researchers that do not have access to, say, defence-department budgets. All of this is good, or at least has the potential to be good, because new tools and techniques also means new ways of looking at the economy and new questions to be asked of it.

For these reasons, this book is intended as a kind of 'first principles' of the new evolutionary microeconomics. It considers how we can reconstruct a framework for evolutionary analysis in terms of first principles. It begins at the beginning. It is evolutionary in the sense that evolution is the mode of dynamical process under investigation. It is a study of open, complex, self-organizing, self-transforming systems with institutional threads woven along the seam of history. It is an attempt to understand many forces at once as a causal logic of local interactions. And it is a microeconomics because it is attempting to describe fundamental building blocks of analysis with atomistic metaphors. More specifically, I shall be arguing that artificial-life simulation is to be considered a proper addition to the core of microeconomic theory and analysis.

In sum, this book communicates just a single idea—that connections matter—and that as such we should re-focus our intellectual energies to understand these dynamic objects. This is already being done in many distinct places and especially within the heterodox schools of economic thought, but the point is that we will be able to do this better if we clearly understand that this focus upon connections is actually what is being done.

Economic reality is a dance of connections, forming and reforming, and by this process, structuring and restructuring the nature of the economic system. What follows is an analytical framework that can describe this structure in terms of the underlying dynamics, and can be used to study the internal structure of the agent, the evolutionary dynamics of the technology and institutions that agents create, the structure of firms, households and other agent complexes, and the interactions between agents over the dynamic network that is the object of our science, the market economy.

## 1.2 Text

The map of this text is as such. We begin with a critique of the general applicability of the real field $R^n$ as a universal logical space for economic analysis. $R^n$ is one of an infinite number of mathematical spaces, and the one that has worked so spectacularly well in physics and engineering. But is it appropriate for economics? Are its ontological implications consistent with what we know empirically of economic systems? In its algebraic and topological expression, the real space $R^n$ underpins a large component of the advanced state of modern economics, that much is clear. The point, rather, is that other spaces, such as network spaces, might also usefully cohabit. This would be uncontroversial and relatively straightforward except for one problem. In short, most fundamental economic concepts—choice, efficiency, technology, preferences, information and suchlike—have acquired a formal meaning that is quite inseparable from $R^n$. These concepts are incommensurable across conceptual spaces. What, for instance, is the meaning of efficiency outside of field theory? (I address this specific question in Chapter 4.) From this distinction between classes of mathematical and analytical spaces, and specifically between what I term *integral* and *non-integral* spaces, we may distinguish plainly the essential difference between the orthodox and heterodox economics. They are ontologically different, and therefore express different conceptual and mathematical spaces. The tension between the orthodox and heterodox economics stems from the fact that both still use the same economic concepts, but these have very different meanings in their respective analytical spaces.

A significant implication follows. The fundamental critical advance of the heterodox schools, as they have done and as they continue to do, is to challenge the concept of an integral geometry of economic space by constructing theories that are fully explicable only in combinatoric or network spaces. The synthesis I propose is simply to turn this outward critique around to focus the development of such 'heterodox' theory towards a general and coherent system of evolutionary microeconomics.

In Chapter 3, I develop the basic mathematical unit that unfolds from this critique and synthesis—a complex system. I describe this abstract object with graph theory, which is a branch of mathematics that recognizes the existence of elements (vertices) and connections (edges) as two distinct sets. This defines, for each possible combination, a *graph* as an ontologically complex object. I then take licence to call this a complex system, a position I shall justify at length. The powerful consequence is that we can use this apparatus (as a kind of calculus of simulcra) to represent the microeconomic events that form the basis of a theory of economic evolution.

In Chapter 4, I extract the major implication for dynamics. Following Kauffman (1993), I propose that a state of network complexity—which is a particular sort of relation between the set of connections and the set of elements—represents dynamic efficiency. Complexity is one of the faces of efficiency. The method of analysis is to consider the lattice representation of the system (somewhat analogous to a Poincaré section) and to infer how different classes of connective structure reveal distinct dynamical potential.

In Chapter 5, I construct an algorithmic model of the economic agent— *hetero economicus*. This object, designed to fly *in silico*, is a learning and interacting artificial agent that will represent individual economic agents (that is, people) as well as higher-level agencies such as firms, institutes or governments. Both preferences and technologies are realized as fully endogenous features of the theoretical framework. By this stage we shall have entered the world of economics as a branch of computer science. It is notable that the term 'evolution' is currently being reworked so as to refer to a generalized information dynamic that overarches both artificial and natural computation. The life and the social sciences have found a deep commonality in the phenomenon of a computation as a primitive object that bisects mathematics and logic. The vanguard of expression for an evolutionary microeconomics, is, I suggest, multiagent simulation modelling of distributed computation with feedback. This is known as a 'bottom-up' or 'process-based' approach and contrasts with the 'top-down' method of general equilibrium theory (see Epstein and Axtell 1996, Gilbert and Troitzsch 1999).

Yet these designs deal with the frontiers of the research programme, not its hard core. The heart of the matter are some simple but fundamental questions— how does the extent and distribution of connections within and between agents matter? How do connections grow into webs that thread together an economy? What are the basic principles of economics that apply to these connections and to the systems they construct? I am of the opinion that the use of the real field $R^n$ has seriously misled us in our thinking on these matters. To illustrate how the evolutionary microeconomics works as a theoretical model, several applications are considered. In Chapter 6, I examine the theory of the firm. This proceeds about the notion of the firm as a *production system* (compare, a production function) and is centred about the interplay of competence and complexity. To demonstrate the generality of this framework, it is applied to the theory of the household (*pace* Becker 1976). In Chapter 7, I consider how the evolutionary microeconomics applies to the theory of expectations. This is a consideration of the evolutionary microeconomic foundations of macroeconomics, and considers the role of probability concepts and the coordination of information. The broad implication is that a deeper understanding of the nature of expectations, which are effectively models of the economy within the economy that are used to create the economy (like cells in organisms), will be a key component of further research in economic evolution. Finally, some conclusions are drawn in Chapter 8 on the present and ongoing nature of the evolutionary microeconomics research programme.

## Note

[1] The reader should perhaps be forewarned that this book will not, in the standard manner, define and report the results of an incrementally modified but otherwise well-known model. I shall propose a new generation of model, but this first requires new theories and systems of microeconomics. Respecting the well-known benefits of division of labour, I have concerned myself only with the latter. The multiagent models I refer to are, at the time of writing, architectural plans and nothing more.

# 2. The Geometry of Economic Space

## 2.1 Introduction

Underpinning all neowalrasian[1] economic theory is the concept of a real field: $R^n$.[2] This is the logical space in which the mathematical operations that define the theory are constrained to operate, and when economic theorists and other such practitioners do acknowledge the existence and primacy of this space it is done so in the neutral context of necessary rigour (for example, Mas-Colell 1985: xiv–xvi). Artists do not often critically speak of the canvas upon which they paint, and similarly the neowalrasian theory has not given much critical attention to its own canvas, as it were, the real field. The reason, it would seem, is essentially that the concept of the real field is the underlying architectural principle of modern science. Indeed, in mathematics the real field is the generalization of arithmetic and the foundation of the integral and differential calculus; one simply cannot do analysis without this concept. From the early part of the twentieth century onwards, it has fully transpired that the driving paradigm of modern physics is to represent the whole of physical reality as a generalized field expression (Harman 1982). Such testimony from mathematics and physics indeed makes for a phenomenal pedigree; a point that was not lost on the pioneers of the then newly emergent neoclassical microtheory. And so from the marginal revolution onwards economics has appropriated this concept and, in a seeming flourish of blind faith, cemented it into the very foundations of the theoretical edifice. The result is that what passes for modern economic theoretical orthodoxy is a special application of field theory. In this chapter I shall unpack the full implications of this for evolutionary economics.

The task ahead requires a reinvestigation of a number of primitive concepts. We begin with the concept of a field, which, I suggest, is analogous to a canvas, in that a painter needs something whole, defined and bounded upon which to paint but once painted it disappears beneath the surface, neutral but necessary. And so it is with mathematical operations and theories, they are necessarily defined over a logical space. But a canvas is not neutral in itself; the artist makes it neutral by covering it completely. Similarly, the real field is not neutral but contains in itself a requirement that the entire 'space' be covered. What, then, is the 'space' of equilibrium theory? I shall show that the deep logic and

11

fundamental character of the theory underpinning the orthodox microeconomics, and, moreover, all of the major points of criticism that have spawned the heterodox schools of economic thought can all be framed, so to speak, in terms of the 'canvas' upon which the theory is constructed. This canvas is the concept of a field and neowalrasian economics is field-theory economics.

This is not a completely new line of critique, as Nicholas Georgescu-Roegen (1971), Philip Mirowski (1988a, 1989) and Robert Clower (1994, 1995), in prime instance, have all examined and argued this point of identification. Still, it is not obvious that an act of identification is actually a critique. Indeed, for Mirowski and Clower (also Clower and Howitt 1997) this proceeds mostly as an exercise in unmasking,[3] in revealing that the theory is not what it claims to be, which would be a theory of how market interaction between firms and consumers determines prices and coordinates economic activity. As Clower (1995: 314) correctly observes,

> In the language of Debreu's formal theory: There are excess demands, but there are no trades; there is a price system, but there are no markets; there are agents and actions, but no events are observable; there are shares in production, but production does not occur. I have been told that these and other 'anomalies' in neowalrasian theory are 'just a matter of semantics'. I do not disagree; but I am bound to reflect that science is concerned with little else.

Clower (1994: 808) publicly began this exposé in the Presidential Address to the Southern Economic Association, where he laid bare the following (slightly edited for brevity). 'In neowalrasian theory:'

> (i) There are no markets. (ii) There is no communication between prospective trading agents. (iii) Agents generate no observable data. (iv) There are no endogenous institutions. (v) No agent announces bids or asked prices. (vi) There is no competition amongst agents. (vii) No agent voluntarily holds inventories or buffer stocks. (viii) There is no money or other medium of exchange. (ix) There is no trading.

This being so, what does the neowalrasian microtheory then consist of? As I have begun to indicate, it is an expression of field theory, and the only things that are 'in' the theory are those things that can be defined in terms of a field. This begs the question of what, then, is a field? In short, and prior to systematic consideration in Section 2.3, a field is a space in which all points are connected to all other points in the space. So the only things that can be 'in' the theory are those things that can be defined in terms of generalized actions over the complete space. Thus the well-recognized characteristic of general equilibrium theory—that everything is a function of everything else—must be understood to be literally true. The total set of demand functions of each agent map to every supply function of each firm: every point in economic space is directly connected to every other point in economic space. In abstract, this is not such a strange idea. For this is how the field concept is expressed in algebra: any two points on a continuum can be mapped by a single operation (by addition or subtraction, say). Furthermore, this is how the field concept is expressed in physics: in a gravitational field, everything with mass affects everything else with mass. Strictly speaking, it is this complete set of interactions that *is* the field (see Mirowski 1989: 66–8). And underlying all such treatment—algebra, physics and economics alike—is the universal analytical canvas $R^n$. The question we must face in economics, however, is whether this universality has any conceivable basis in the reality of an economic system, or whether it is only a reified artifact of the mathematics. What is the real nature of this supposed total connectedness that is axiomatized by $R^n$?

The argument of this chapter, although of very wide compass, ultimately expresses a single, simple point. While acknowledging that the field concept is the rudimentary basis of arithmetic and algebra (logical–deductive space), and further admitting that it has been enormously successful and useful in the natural sciences (physical space) to the extent that all physical theory is ultimately expressed in terms of fields, it is argued that for both ontological and analytical reasons $R^n$ is not an appropriate basis for economic microtheory, at least not in the general sense in which it has been presumed. Field theory does not apply generally to the domain of economic agent interactions (economic space). Moreover, the most conspicuous failings of the paradigm, such as Frank Hahn's (1984: 175) assessment 'that general equilibrium theorists have been unable to deliver one half at least of the required story: how does general equilibrium come to be established?' can, as I endeavour to show, be understood entirely from the perspective of the fallacious analytical basis of a field.[4] Indeed, once it is recognized that the essence of the neowalrasian microtheory is the field construct it becomes readily apparent that all major points of heterodox critique reduce to this single criticism. In Section 2.4, I make this the basis for a unified heterodox economics, in the sense that all extant schools have developed different aspects of the same underlying point of departure.

This point of synthesis is the motive for critique. My argument is not criticism of the neowalrasian microtheory for the interior purposes of improving upon that theory, as is the usual nature of critique. The subject of this chapter and indeed this book is not ultimately neowalrasian microtheory. Rather, the reason for my express concern is purely one of delimitation. To clear the ground for a new system of microeconomics, the neowalrasian theory must first be circumscribed. And I achieve this by introducing an abstract axial concept that I term 'The Geometry of Economic Space'. Within this concept, a field in $R^n$ is an extreme form of a specific geometry, and the geometry of physical space, it seems, is well represented by such a construct. But the geometric space of a real economic system, as I shall argue, is only under highly contrived conditions approximated by this extreme form. Its unreality is simply too much for us to take the model seriously as a representation of reality. Most generally, and for all cases in which time is a non-negligible factor, the correct basis for economic theory is a geometry of economic space that is not a field. The purpose of this chapter, however, is to establish by delimitation the essence of an alternative system of microeconomics and one, furthermore, that I believe can underpin a synthesis of heterodox economics.

So what then, as the final point of introduction, is this essence? Simply, if an economic system can be initially defined as a set of elements—say individuals, agents, commodities and suchlike—between which we can, in principle, draw connections such that we may relate everything to everything else, then the question is whether this complete set of relations does actually exist. And this is an ontological question that overarches both empiricism and theory. If it does, such that the same form of relation defines all interior connections, then we have a suitable basis to proceed making the field the analytical canvas. If not, then such a foundation is fallacious and any theoretical structure that is built upon it will be liable to be precariously wrong for reasons that are effectively untraceable, as has been precisely the experience of much otherwise rigorous economic theory. And what distinguishes this? In essence, it is whether there are elements in the system between which there are no connections. Or from a different perspective but one that will form the key link to many other aspects of heterodox theorizing, it is whether the map of the system shows strong evidence of structural decomposition, such that particular elements are related only to a subset of other elements and not everything else generally. It is the completeness of the set of connections that is the primary criterion, and the neowalrasian theory is the pure expression of economic theory constructed upon the foundation of a complete set of connections, as is the operational meaning of the logical structure of a field as $R^n$.

We proceed as follows. Section 2.2 begins by exhuming, as it were, the theoretical concept of economic space. In Section 2.3, the concept of a field is then defined as a special case. In Section 2.4 this is then related to the annals of heterodox criticism of the orthodox microeconomics, so gathering otherwise separate schools of thought into aspects of a single idea. In Section 2.5, the concept of a connection is thus exposed for its rudimentary analytical significance for an evolutionary microeconomic framework. Section 2.6 concludes.

## 2.2  Exhuming the Concept of Economic Space

The concept of a field is a special case of the geometry of economic space. All conceivable systems of microeconomics must necessarily begin with the existence of a set of elements (agents, commodities, endowments or whatever) placed in some form of relationship to one another. The concept of 'economic space' refers to the nature of these interactions, and the geometry of economic space defines a particular set of interactions.

This is perhaps a rather abstract concept to apprehend, but consider it thus. Means and ends must of course somehow relate, whereby the relations must be defined over some geometric space. If we have an *action* at a specific point and a *reaction* at a different point, then there must exist something everywhere between these two points. In modern physics the 'everywhere between' is the field (see Jammer 1969). In the neowalrasian microtheory (*pari passu* classical physics) the everywhere between is the space $R^n$. The concept involves more than just the notion of continuous space, but of an actuality that carries force (affect) from point to point by a traverse of everywhere between. Yet curiously, the neowalrasian microtheory has remained silent about the nature of this everywhere between.[5] Economic agents and commodities and other such things are, from a scientific perspective, real phenomena and therefore we may presume that they exist in some kind of real space. Whether this space is understood as an aether, field, medium, web or whatever it must nevertheless be acknowledged to exist. If it is our contention that there exist forces in the economic system then it behoves us, ultimately, to speak about the medium (and not just the mechanism) through which these supposed forces act. That is, if our thinking involves both cause and effect then by logical and inescapable necessity it also involves the space between.[6] If our subject is action or interaction then it necessarily invokes a domain and the particular form of this domain is described by the geometry of economic space.

Two sets of concepts can now be disentangled. First, we distinguish between a field of actions from a set of interactions. This leads to the distinction between an integral and a non-integral geometry of economic space. Finally, we link this back to distinguish between orthodox and heterodox microeconomics.

### 2.2.1 Actions and Interactions

In its most rudimentary sense, the economic problem is a choice problem linking given means and given ends. But it is a peculiar type of choice problem, as Loasby (1976: 5) recognizes: 'if knowledge is perfect, and the logic of choice complete and compelling, then choice disappears; nothing is left but stimulus and response'. If we completely define both means and ends, typically technology and utility or preference functions respectively, then their linkage—the *modus operandi* of the economic problem—is rendered a purely technical problem with a general form of solution under certain formally defined circumstances. The economic problem and the neowalrasian statement of that problem in terms of choice has acquired orthodoxy, it would seem, from extraction of the purely logical aspect—given means and given ends—from the mechanisms of the actual medium over which and by which this occurs. As critics have often argued, it remains something of a travesty of investigation to interpret the economic problem as a problem of choice and then to abstract from all the essential features of choice in the human context (Coase 1937, Richardson 1953, Shackle 1972, Simon 1976). Amongst other aspects, for instance, we must recognize that both the end-points and the pathways between means and ends are often prima facie impossible to conceive, let alone incorporate into an optimizing plan so as to collapse all possible states of the future into the present (compare, Debreu 1959). In formulating the economic problem as a problem of simple optimization subject to explicit constraints, the essential context of the problem, the context of procedural rationality, is swept away. Then, as Debreu insists (1984: 267), 'one can describe the action of an economic agent by a vector in commodity space $R^n$.' I will comment in turn on the meanings of 'commodity', 'agent' and 'action', but my immediate concern is Debreu's idea of 'space'. Because it seems that the point Loasby is making is that if we can predefine everything about the space of economic actions, which Debreu presumes, then this is not a space inhabited (or inhabitable, Heiner 1983) by human agents. Loasby is making a statement about knowledge and the nature of the economic behaviour of an agent, Debreu is talking about the actions of an economic agent; we begin by recognizing that these are wholly different concepts.[7]

The difference is that Loasby, by invoking the concept of knowledge, and therein a specific association between things as all knowledge must be, is conceiving of interactions. For Loasby, the conditional 'if knowledge is perfect' is a limiting case, made up of a complete set of theories and intentions connecting the agent epistemically and operationally with every other element. Debreu, however, refers only to actions. He does not build up this set by increment, but conjures it complete, as mandated by the logic of a field. Debreu's agent does not interact with any other element/agent in particular because this agent interacts with every other agent simultaneously. And in this sense, a simultaneous interaction with everything is, as Debreu correctly terms, a singular action. Alan Kirman (1997b: 492) argues that this fundamental distinction then leads analysis to:

> model the economy as if there was only one individual in a sector. Thus, the aggregate behaviour of consumers is modeled as though it were the behaviour of one, maximizing 'representative individual'. This essentially assumes that the direct interaction between individuals has no consequence and that micro- and macrobehaviour are of the same type.

Kirman further notes that the consequence of moving away from the vision of an economy as a collection of individuals reacting in isolation to market signals towards models of a system where there is interaction is that 'the notion of equilibrium may need to be modified'. Debreu's agent is equally all agents, and thus at once a micro-agent and an aggregate phenomenon. Loasby and Kirman, among others, deny such logic on the grounds that Debreu achieves this transmogrification by denying the agent interactions. Kirman, however, then felicitously speaks of a general problem that Debreu presumes solved, namely 'the general problem of establishing the relationship between microeconomic interaction and aggregate phenomena.' One may also interpret this as the 'Richardson problem' (Richardson 1960, Earl 1998). We can make sense of such incongruities by noting that each conception derives from a different assumption of the geometry of economic space. I suggest we unfold this as the distinction between an *integral* and a *non-integral* space.

There is no interaction, knowledge or structure in the neowalrasian microtheory because the nature of economic space is assumed to be integral (see Mirowski 1990: 301). That is, the microtheory harbours no provisions for the existence of cognitive structure (Kelly 1963), heuristic structure (Simon 1959), organizational structure (Chandler 1962, Williamson 1975), spatial or temporal structure (O'Driscoll and Rizzo 1985, Hodgson 1988), market structure (Callon 1997), nor social structure (Burt 1992). The quality of a space being integral derives from the assumption that a single (mathematical) operation links any point in economic space with any other point. Interactions, knowledge and structure are specific connections between points in space and therefore the very existence of these concepts is excluded by the assumption that all points relate, *a priori*, to all other points directly; that is, with a single mathematical operation. In a world of omniscience there can be no such concept as knowledge, as in a world of omnipresence there can be no such concept as organization: both knowledge and organization, along with structure and processes, are meaningful only in the particular. That is, they are phenomena of particular interactions not generalized actions. Particular interactions cannot be defined in an integral space. Interactions exist only in a non-integral space.

The mathematical character of this abstraction (from particular interactions) is the concept of a field. In a field, 'interaction' does not mean anything because there is no example of non-interaction—everything interacts with everything else. A field, then, is the operational expression of an integral space. When this situation is inferred, the analytical system reduces from a non-integral complex of interactions to an integral set of actions (the entire canvas is filled, as it were). The motive for doing so is that this makes an enormous conceptual simplification to the representation of the system of otherwise interacting elements.

This path-breaking mathematical treatment—the assumption of an integral system—was introduced many centuries ago by Isaac Newton and Gottfried Leibniz and then mathematically refined into the concept of a field by Karl Gauss and William Hamilton. The concept of a gravitational field (combining the mathematical concept of a field with the physical concept of an integral system into the physical concept of a field) was then formalised by Leonhard Euler,[8] Joseph Louis Lagrange and Pierre Simon Laplace. This then led to field-based investigation into the phenomena of heat (Joseph Fourier), electricity (Alessandro Volta) and magnetism (Michael Faraday). James Clerk Maxwell, in the famous Maxwell equations, then achieved a remarkable breakthrough by showing that the field concepts can be combined. Maxwell's equations unify the separate field concepts of electricity and magnetism into a single electromagnetic field, which established among other things the electromagnetic nature of light. It was at this point that the field concept most clearly revealed its enormous power as a truly general unifying framework. And so from this point onwards, as the modern developments in quantum field theory, gauge field theory (fields of fields) and so forth all attest, it developed that the essential component of modern physical theory is the concept of a field. But that, we must immediately recognize, is physical theory. It remains to be shown that the very first assumption that set this entire scheme of development in progress (Newton's physical notion of an integral system) actually has any real basis in the ontology of an economic system.

Economic theory has not so much shown this but outrightly assumed it to be the case. Indeed, it is fair to say that we have plagiarized (and not merely paraphrased) the concept by not calling it by its proper name: the technology and preference functions which are otherwise labelled as firms and consumers are, strictly interpreted, technology and preference fields. Samuelson (1948: 153), Clower (1995: 314) and Foster (1993: 977), for instance, are rather uncommon instances of proper recognition of these concepts as fields and not entities. But it is Mirowski (1989) who has most comprehensively described this appropriation. He explicates the concept of the 'utility field' (*ibid.*: 231–9) and the 'technology field' (*ibid.*: 312) as what are otherwise, but incorrectly, referred to by the less incongruous notion of 'functions'. Furthermore, he notes the logical necessity of mathematical equivalence between the two field concepts. For instance, in recognizing that 'the production field must be static and path independent if it is to be consistent with the utility field', Mirowski provides the (perhaps oversimplified) reading that 'the Cambridge capital controversy made clear that the paradigm of the production function was imported into neoclassical theory as the parallel analogue of the utility field'. For our present first principles purposes, the point is that these functions (the utility/preference fields and the technology/production fields) are assertions about the nature of economic space. They are not statements about the nature of the things that populate the space (as the concept of a function seemingly implies); which is to say that they are not statements about consumers or firms, as they are almost exclusively sold.

## 2.2.2 On Economic Space

According to Shackle (1972: 277) 'a space, in the most general and abstract sense of the word, is simply a class or set of items'. As such, for the set of elements constituting an economic system the domain of actions and interactions constitutes the formal meaning I am to attribute to economic space. The geometry of economic space I then define, also formally, as a mapping of these actions and interactions. Yet before we proceed further we ought first to distinguish between concern with the geometry of economic space and the economic subject of spatial geometry (for example, Greenhut 1995).

Spatial geometry[9] has grown out of inquiry into the phenomenon of spatial clustering in the growth patterns of such entities as industrial regions, certain types of markets and cities. The economic subject of spatial geometry overlaps with logistic, geographic and ethnographic investigation so that spatial geometry is clearly an applied subject domain with respect to economic theory. Yet what I infer as the geometry of economic space is a far more abstract and metatheoretical domain. An investigation into the geometry of economic space concerns, as above, the mapping of the actions and interactions between elements of a system yet not with regard to a particular subject domain but, instead, with regard to the type of space (topology or topography) that a theoretical framework infers. As such, an inquiry into the geometry of economic space is an attempt to make explicit the nature of the economic space that is otherwise implicit in a microeconomic framework.

The primary division in the population of geometric forms is between integral and non-integral spaces. If a space is integral then we define a field. If it is non-integral, in the sense that the set of interactions cannot be collapsed to a field of actions, then the geometry of economic space must be mapped by a set of specific connections (on a lattice). If, for example, we are to recognize that uncertainty exists then we must attribute this as a property of the geometry of economic space. Which is to say that from a particular point in space, the agent cannot connect with any point in space which lies beyond the constricted event horizon. Uncertainty is a name we have given to an aspect of a non-integral space.[10] Similarly, if we are to recognize that organization exists, then this too is a property of the geometry of economic space, whereby there exists a knot of complex local interactions. Yet first we must recognize that there exists a space—that is, that there exists a structure of interactions. Once we can exhume this basic notion it becomes apparent that there are many different geometries of space. Transcending field theory, then, is a topographic geometry of states.

### 2.2.3 Integral Orthodoxy and Non-integral Heterodoxy

Thus the domain of actions and interactions interlinking the operations of an economic system is the meaning of economic space. As such, at the basis of all economic theory is the concept of a set of elements and the corresponding notion of a space. Expressed in this barefaced way we may perceive a basic dilemma at the foundations of economic theory: which metatheoretical construct is primary—the elements, or the space of connections between the elements? For instance, underneath the contrast between the orthodox conception of a firm as a production function and the New Institutional conception of a firm as a governance structure (see Williamson 1996) are the two sides of this basic ontological issue: is a firm a set of factors or is it a set of interactions? Similarly, the sometimes subtle difference between the Austrian school of economics and the broad neoclassical school (Endres 1997) turns on this same point: is an agent a set of behaviours or a set of endowments? In other words, is knowledge (including technology) a thing or a relation between things? Do the fundamental units of an economic system exist *in* space, or are they in fact the structure *of* space?

In this format we may see plainly the heritage of the question. It is the conceptual distinction between modern and premodern physics. In modern physics the concept of the space is primary, expressed in terms of a field. In premodern physics, including Newtonian physics, the elements were primary and real. Modern economics has gone the same way as modern physics by emulation of the field logic. In Mirowski's (1989: 198–201) account, there was in the nineteenth-century economics a growing tension between then emergent notions of value in exchange and classical notions of value in use, or some such phenomenal basis linked to theories of production. This was the mirror image of the growing tensions in physics between the emergent field account of physical phenomena over the classical ideas of physical phenomena as conceived in terms of some substance. The outcome, as we know, was the 'the gradual supersession of field theories over substance theories in physics over the course of the nineteenth century'. Mirowski then suggests that it was this external effect that was the key to the so-called marginal revolution. He explains:

> The rise of field theories was the most decisive influence because it finally provided the definitive epistemic break between classical and neoclassical economics, In short, classical economics had become inextricably identified with the paradigm of substance theories in physics, and therefore its days were numbered. As physics progressively moved toward field theories and models of motion, and energetics seemed to hold out the promise of the unification of all the sciences, economists (with some lag) adopted their own field theory of value, which we now call neoclassical theory.

The orthodox research programme has thus, over the course of the twentieth century in the guise of the neowalrasian paradigm, endeavoured to make sense of a field (integral) geometry of economic space. Technically, it has been enormously successful. In contrast, the heterodox schools of thought have been somewhat adrift over this same period: neither inheriting the classical substance-based theories of value, nor developing a clear sense of a competing paradigm to the concept of a field. Physics was absolutely field theory and thus provided no inspiration, but evolutionary biology did, and particularly so for the emergent school of Institutionalism. Yet the basic problem has been that the evolutionary metaphor has no clear sense of a relation to the field concept. These two paradigms are, from the perspective of economics, massively incommensurate. In this way it has been the case that any points of criticism or insight levered from the evolutionary perspective (see Hodgson 1993) have had no significant effect on anything done within the field paradigm. For heterodox economists this has been frustrating, to say the least. Similarly, orthodox economists have been equally bewildered by the rumpus coming from the heterodox tribes.

There is, however, a subtle way through, a way of positioning economic thought in terms of the relationship to the paradigms of natural science and their concepts of space and time. The evolutionary paradigm is based on the ontological and analytical axiom that the geometry of economic space (and time) is non-integral. Heterodox economics is that which endeavours to make sense of a geometry of economic space (and time) that is not a field.

## 2.3 The Nature of a Field

A field is both a mathematical and a physical construct and arguably the most fundamental concept in modern physics. A single instance of testimony will suffice. In describing the path from Newtonian to modern physics, Albert Einstein (1953: xvi) states that 'the victory over the concept of absolute space or over that of the inertial system became possible only because the concept of the material object was gradually replaced by that of the field'. He goes on to assert that 'under the influence of the ideas of Faraday and Maxwell the notion developed that the whole of physical reality could be represented as a field'. And as with most fundamental concepts or abstract universals, its definition is naturally slippery and must be handled with care.

Observe that Einstein is referring to two distinct entities, the concept of a field and the representation of a field. The difficulty, seemingly pervasive for those who have been concerned with the explanation or appropriation of the concept of a field, is that these are distinct notions: the first concerned purely with (algebraic) logic and the second concerned with an explication of a physical phenomenon (generalized interaction). This distinction is vital, as the second necessarily invokes the first but not vice versa. Which is to say that the physical concept of a field derives from the arithmetic concept of a field,[11] which defines a set of elements (real numbers, say) and a set of operations connecting each element to every other (the operations of arithmetic, such as addition). In a physical field, both the elements and the operations of an arithmetic field have, or are assumed to have, real counterparts; the elements are the fundamental quantities of mass, energy, charge or some such, and the operations are the forces described by the field equations. As Einstein indicates above, the march of theoretical physical science has trampled the concept of material existence and smeared it out over the entire space. In this way, the field is more than the space over which interactions occur and are universally defined, but rather makes the complete set of such interactions the ultimate locus of existence for the element in the space. In other words, $R^n \rightarrow R^n$.

The implications of this for economic theory, although to be elaborated as we proceed though this section, can be spelt out immediately. Physics is reductionist, but it does not reduce to elements such as atoms, electrons, quarks or whatever the fundamental particle may be at any particular stage of the investigation; these concepts are (merely) placeholders in the framework. Physics reduces to fields, as phenomena of generalized interaction. And this, I argue, is the basic misunderstanding that plagues modern economic theory. It has appropriated the mathematical logical structure of a field but has ignored its most direct implication: the existence of such things as demand and supply functions must be spread out over the entire domain of economic space, as a perfect integral. In other words, and as the neowalrasian microtheory assumes, everything must be directly connected to everything else. But it also invokes something much stronger: *these connections must then be understood to constitute the essential reality of the system.* Yet this is in direct contradiction with the other pillar of the theory, namely that the economic system is simply the aggregate of free agents who are themselves the basic units of analysis. This is the hypothesis of Methodological Individualism, and is the keystone for all formulations and interpretations of the theory. Thus the fundamental problem of the orthodox microtheory is that the set of operations that connect all elements in the space together, and which by the mandate of field theory must be the ultimate locus of existence, yet has no basis for existence. The fundamental problem is ontological mis-specification, and to paraphrase Frank Hahn (1984: 175), one half of economic theory is missing.

But this is not to say that all economic theory has ignored this problem. Economists of the Austrian school, and especially Mises (1949), Kirzner (1973) and Casson (1982), have been directly concerned with the workings of the market process from an interior perspective that aims to reveal the nature of the particular interactions and connections between agents. In particular, emphasis is drawn to the entrepreneurial function. The Austrian school is critical of the neoclassical framework, which, as Kirzner (1981: 111) argues, is 'seriously deficient in any genuine understanding of the workings of market capitalism' precisely for their presumptions that these connections just happen. The Austrian economists are particularly interesting at this juncture, as their theoretical basis is in many respects concordant with the neoclassical schools of thought. But unlike these schools, and in particular the neowalrasian variant, the Austrian economists have actually interpreted the field model in its proper context by directly examining the space between agents—which is the logic and structure of market interactions. However, and as their point of departure, they find (in the language of the present framework) that the geometry of economic space is non-integral. That is, there are substantial regions over which connections do not exist (both logically and phenomenally), which is precisely the emphasis they draw to the phenomenon of time and the existence of uncertainty and ignorance (Shackle 1972, O'Driscoll and Rizzo 1985).

Still, we must first establish the basic relation. Neowalrasian economics is 'field economics' in the following way. In general equilibrium, all markets are interrelated. But according to Clower and Howitt (1997: 27), this is not an accurate statement.

> In practise, however, virtually everyone (including Hicks in the purportedly 'pure logical analysis' of *Value and Capital* (1939: 7) and Debreu in the even more pretentiously 'formal' *Theory of Value* (1959) talks freely about 'markets' when they are referring (formally) to supply and demand functions because their supposed reliance on formalism is always more or less sham; what they actually talk about is the real world as they conceive it intuitively . . . not the abstract world of sets, elements, axioms and mathematical operations which they pretend to take as their formal, technical universe of discourse.

It is evident, then, that there are no markets in neowalrasian theory, only supply and demand functions and we may explain this as follows. Consider a pure exchange economy, where there are $n$ goods in fixed supply. We may then suppose that $S_i(i = 1,...,n)$ is the total supply of good $i$, and that the price of good $i$ is $P_i(i = 1,...,n)$. Labour and factor inputs are presumed to be part of the 'goods' set. The total demand for good $i$, then, depends upon all the prices $D_i(P_1,..., P_n)$. If we write the vector of all prices as $P$, then general equilibrium pertains to the equilibrium price vector $P^*(P^* \to P)$ such that $D_i(P^*) = S_i$. Whether or not such an equilibrium exists (Arrow and Debreu 1954) is irrelevant to the field context of this formulation. The preference function that contributes the demand function is a field $u:(x)$ in $R^n$. The price vector $P$ is a field vector in $R^n$. So it is not 'markets' that are interrelated, but all supply and demand functions simultaneously through $R^n$.

This context is explicitly noted by most textbooks and is clearly presented in all explicitly 'formal' reputable treatments of the subject. No one is denying that this is the case; but then again, no one is actually admitting it either. The pertinent fact of the matter is that the concept of a field—as the use of the space $R^n$ and the definition of all actions to take place simultaneously within this space—arrived with the 'marginal revolution'. The more difficult idea to admit, as Mirowski (1989) has laboured to do, has been that the nature of this marginal revolution was essentially the arrival of the field concept.

According to Mirowski (1988a), the rise of 'energetics' as mid-nineteenth century physics, is to be understood as the conjunction of two conceptual innovations: (1) the theory of the physical field, and (2) the principle of conservation of energy (see Harman 1982). He then argues that economics fell very strongly 'under the influence' of this paradigm, and that the product was distinctly the 'marginal revolution' as associated with Walras, Edgeworth, Pareto and Fisher (but not Menger). Scholarship internal to economics has sometimes denied that such a revolution occurred (for example, Blaug 1978), but Mirowski's case does not hinge internally. He unequivocally judges that 'the essence of the neoclassical analysis is the appropriation of the physical concept of a field' (Mirowski 1988: 41). His critique, however, focuses mostly upon the second principle, arguing that (*idem*: 17):

> The rise of energetics in physical theory induced the invention of neoclassical economic theory, by providing the metaphor, the mathematical techniques, and the new attitudes toward theory construction. Neoclassical economic theory was appropriated wholesale from mid-nineteenth century physics; utility was redefined so as to be identical with energy.

For Mirowski, the case for the appropriation of the concept of a field is written plainly in the testimonies of the progenitors themselves, as they openly aspired to reproduce the theory of rational mechanics into the economic domain.[12] In this way, Mirowski (1988a) is not explicitly concerned with the logic of the field *per se* (compare, Mirowski 1989) but with the subterfuge concerning the implicit smuggling of a conservation principle into the framework of analysis. It is my own conclusion that this aspect is not so important. It is the field appropriation, and not so much the appropriation of the conservation principle (despite its far richer array of analogues: variational equations, maximization, utility and so forth) that is the absolute and ultimate basis of the neowalrasian paradigm.

Like the physical sciences, neowalrasian economics was to purge the concept of interaction and thus the concept of protean and effectual material reality by instating the mathematical logic of a field.[13] Mathematically, and excepting the higher dimensionality, there is no formal difference between the economic agent and, say, an electric charge or point mass, in that a single time-invariant field vector (preference function) describes the sum of all interactions extending from the agent.[14] The possibility of non-interactions must necessarily be ruled out, and by definition this collapses a complete field of interactions into the concept of generalized actions. And although this is well defined and seemingly *prima facie* acceptable within the theory, the intrusion of time (as another dimension) then requires that this same logic be extended fully through this dimension because it is also in the field. Debreu (1959) 'solved' this problem by assuming the existence of a complete set of forward contingent markets. The dubious nature of this solution has been a persistent theme for critics of the theory,[15] but, it must be acknowledged, the problem does not suddenly appear as the temporal dimension is added, it just becomes more apparent. The nature of the problem is identical: all points in the field must be connected to all other points in the field and through all dimensions of the field.

Whether the concept of a field can be carried over into the economic domain is something that must from a Realist perspective (for example, Lawson 1995, 1997) be decided by appeal to the nature of economic interactions, and whether these are sufficiently integral to suffice the notion of a field. Yet the instrumentalist perspective (*à la* Friedman 1953) has been more pervasive and the appropriation has never been debated in such realist terms. Field theory allows complete off-the-shelf mathematical formalisms and analytical principles, ergo, its appropriation was much influenced by the temptations of mathematical respectability, and, it must be acknowledged, this has in its own right brought enormous successes. But the fact remains that unlike physical space, economic space is not amenable to a field representation because it is not integral in the sense that every element (that is, agent) affects every other element. This is a wholly satisfied empirical condition for physical field theory but for reasons both definitional and observational it is a most audacious step to define an economic system as anything remotely resembling a perfect integral. Such sleight of hand has not passed unnoticed, as Loasby (1976: 44) remarks:

> In practice, economists normally employ a simple and comprehensive theory of non-equilibrium behaviour: an economy out of equilibrium always moves towards equilibrium—except when it doesn't. In the former case one uses microtheory, in the latter, the techniques of macroeconomics. These latter techniques, as is fairly well recognized, imply the abandonment of some of the foundations of general equilibrium theory; what is less well realised is that the use of equilibrium theory to explain behaviour out of equilibrium, though preserving the illusion of full theoretical rigour, is a course of breathtaking audacity.

And it is audacious, because the specific foundation that is abandoned is the assumption that no trade takes place outside of the final equilibrium configuration. (As in Edgeworth's process of recontracting, where no trade takes place until all agents have interacted with every other agent, such that when trade does supposedly occur it is as a set of singular actions.) Disequilibrium trading cannot be logically defined within the context of a field because a disequilibrium trade is by definition in non-integral space: each agent interacts with only some other agents.

The reinterpretations of Keynes's *General Theory* by Clower (1965) and Leijonhufvud (1968) are themselves, I think, well reinterpreted in this manner. Leijonhufvud's argument, for instance, aimed to shift attention away from price rigidities as the orthodox explanation for the Keynesian problem of persistent unemployment, towards the pattern of information flows in the market network of a monetary economy. Essentially, the reason for such coordination failure derives from the fact that the economic system is intrinsically non-integral, and it is the price mechanism itself that disseminates information (as Hayek stressed, see Buchanan and Vanberg 1991, Vriend 1999), tending the system towards the Walrasian integral state, but it can only ever do so imperfectly. As such, Clower, Leijonhufvud and Hayek alike all begin from the opposite end of the geometry of economic space to that presumed by the neowalrasians. They do not presume the connections exist but rather that the function of the market system is to enable these connections to form. Inevitably, they do not form perfectly and much economic activity necessarily takes place out of what is theoretically understood as equilibrium.

In this vein, Clower and Leijonhufvud were perhaps far more radical in their thinking than was even recognized at the time. Their recent absolute rejections of the neowalrasian paradigm (Clower 1995, Leijonhufvud 1993, 1997) indeed attest to this assessment. And what they were rejecting, then, was the concept of a field as the starting point of analysis, because, unlike the physical domain, there is persistent macroeconomic evidence that there are both logical (for example, Clower's Dual Decision Hypothesis) and phenomenal (Leijonhufvud's attention to the mythical Walrasian auctioneer) unconnected regions in the geometry of economic space.

Before continuing with this point we must acknowledge that the ground has already been broken by Georgescu-Roegen (1971); although it would seem that this has not much been widely, or indeed even narrowly, recognized. Georgescu-Roegen's analysis and critique concerns, as titled, *the entropy law and the economic process*, and unfolds the case for the necessary primacy of the dialectic mode of analysis in economics. A most curious concomitant to Georgescu-Roegen's work, given the compass and brilliance of his study, is that the explicit theoretical attention it has drawn from the community of heterodox economists has been, for the greatest part, a deeply respectful deference. It seems that his outlying point has been taken—that the economic process is not that of a closed system[16]—but with respect to the internal theoretical ramifications that form the ultimate substance of his critique Georgescu-Roegen has, I think, been massively misunderstood. For although the implications of his analysis clearly unfold to link with the entropy law and modes of dialectic reasoning, for which he is well cited, the theoretical point of departure that he painstakingly belabours (1971: pp. 39–141, also appendix A) is the logic of an arithmetical continuum. Apart from Foster (1993), there does not seem to be any explicit recognition of this point of analysis, and yet it is the basic platform of his entire edifice. He identifies in the construct of an arithmetical continuum the crux of the reason why the neoclassical theory cannot explain qualitative change; the symptom then is the confusion and neglect of dialectic constructs. From a suitably abstract perspective, the basis of Georgescu-Roegen's theoretical departure to account for the flow processes of an economic system stems from a critique of the (arithmetical) geometry of economic space conceived in space and time as a continuum. Maintaining this level of abstraction and applying formalisms, an arithmetical continuum is equivalently a number field $R^1$, known as the real field.

Georgescu-Roegen recognizes the arithmetical continuum as the aggregate of all discrete points such that it may be conceived in its structure as 'beads on a string, but without the string' (1971: 65). A less metaphorical reference is to be found in Poincaré (1963: 30) who observes that each element, Georgescu-Roegen's 'bead', is 'an individual thing absolutely distinct from the others and, moreover, absolutely indivisible' (see also Whitehead 1929, Bergson 1911). For Georgescu-Roegen, this conflux of ontological and methodological criticism surfaces as neglect of dialectic concepts, and, in particular, his investiture of the entropy law as fundamental to understanding the nature of the economic process. And yet his starting point, the arithmetical continuum, we must recognize, is equivalent in algebra to a one-dimensional field. The subtlety of the matter is that Georgescu-Roegen only required one dimension, as such, to make his points concerning the analytical treatment of time and the logic of dialectics but the essence of his argument carries to higher dimensions where a continuum is more generally a field in $R^n$. It would seem the point has gone unnoticed that when Georgescu-Roegen rigorously set up and vigorously tore down the concept of an arithmetical continuum (so as to define the existence and logic of dialectic principles in the domain of economics) the symmetry of this argument with respect to a field undercuts the entire neowalrasian mode of analysis. It is not my opinion that Georgescu-Roegen overlooked this implication, for he was far too erudite a mathematician in this primary respect, but rather that, wisely perhaps, he chose not to draw attention to the absence of a more general analytical system in his own critique. In Mirowski's opinion (1988b: 825), 'Georgescu-Roegen seems to pull his punches, never extending his critiques to their most devastating conclusion'.

And while such a system is latent it is not altogether obvious, requiring the recognition that a field is a special case of an integral domain, which is a special case of a commutative ring.[17] And this path is only recognizable (as interesting) if we already have a vision in mind of a solution space as a topographical state-space, with graph-theory ordinants, that is essentially non-integral over the same metric space. And further it must be recognized that these arithmetic concepts have direct bearing on the theory of complex systems, and that the theory of complex systems applies directly to the constructs employed to model an economic system. This, in abstract, is the formal path from neowalrasian microeconomics to a more general evolutionary system of microeconomics. Georgescu-Roegen took the shorter path, directly from an arithmetic continuum to the logic of dialectic constructs. But in doing so he skipped over the chain of abstraction that renders the generalized field theory approach a special case of the more general topographical approach which harbours the system of algebraic constructs upon which to rebuild an analytical system of microeconomics incorporating specific interactions.

By the standards of applied mathematics, rings, fields and integral domains are highly abstract concepts, yet they are primitive entities at the foundations of algebra. And usually unnoticed, these systems are the formal laws under which elementary arithmetic and algebra are constrained to operate. For approximately a century now, economists have laboured under the sway of a deep and fundamental algebraic presupposition concerning the geometry of economic space. In essence, we have assumed that the laws of algebra and logic are ubiquitous in the economic domain, in a similar sense to which they are in the physical domain. For it is a curious but profound fact that the principles of natural law are amenable to expression in mathematical form, which is to say, in the form of a ring or field (a classic essay is Wigner 1969). As many scientific luminaries have reflected, it is something of a mystery why principles of natural law can be expressed so succinctly in the language of mathematics. But that this extends to the economic domain, *in situ*, is not implied by the fact. That physical nature is (seemingly) intrinsically mathematical and furthermore of a particular mathematical form does not *ipso facto* imply that all domains of science are ordinantly so and of the same generalized form (Kwasnicki 1996: 6–13). Put bluntly, the fact that the motion of celestial objects is well described by a system of linear equations does not, in itself, imply that all systems of mutually interacting elements will also be well described by the same mathematical system (*pace* Debreu 1991). Yet, notwithstanding occasional explication or acknowledgement, this logical fallacy of generalization has proceeded largely unchecked.

There has of course been direct criticism (for example, Blatt 1983, Quddus and Rashid 1994), and modern investigation into the theory of decision making, rationality, technological change and the theory of the organization have ever weakened and cast doubt upon, albeit indirectly, the universal applicability of inherited mathematical foundations. First, it is being increasingly recognized that the systems under investigation are not only never integral but that they are typically very far from this state. It is because economic systems are so definitively 'non-integral' that concepts such as bounded rationality, pure uncertainty (*à la* Knight 1921) and hierarchic structure (Simon 1962, 1991; Radner 1992) emerge.[18] However the assumption of an integral system is the *sine qua non* for all techniques of dynamical construction (including a field). Second, the laws of summation do not seem to apply generally such that the sum of the parts is not always equal to the whole—for example, synergy (Kay 1982) or competence (Foss and Knudsen 1996). The fact is that the underlying principles of geometry and arithmetic that work (spectacularly) well in the physical domain (I have in mind principles of simple mechanics) simply do not carry over to the economic domain in anything like the degree necessary for them to be cemented unexamined into the foundations of analysis. Yet in the appropriation of the concept of a field, precisely such symmetry has been made an axiom.

Mathematically, then, a field is a system of elements over which basic algebraic operations are universally defined. A field, thus, is defined over a space $R^n$ as the domain of scalar coordinates mapped by $n$ orthogonal axes. The type of field realised depends not upon the definition of the space but on the algebraic operations that are internally and universally defined.[19] A field is an integral space plus the set of operations (usually implicit in the definition of the space). A field may be defined in any number of dimensions—as $R^1$ to $R^n$—but makes a simple and crucial requirement, the integral assumption, that all points in the space $R^n$ are included in the field. This point is, I think, more subtle than has been generally recognized and discussed in the transmutation of the concept between mathematics, physics and economics. First, the context of a field is always a set of interacting elements, say $A$ and $B$. Suppose $A \leftrightarrow B$ (where $\leftrightarrow$ denotes interaction). The field concept breaks this interaction into two action components intermediated by the field. For example, the formation of a demand and a supply curve is a field concept replacing the intrinsic interaction symmetry of market exchange. As such, $A \leftrightarrow field \leftrightarrow B$. In contra example, Clower's (1965) dual-decision hypothesis breaks this field simultaneity back into its interaction components. Households ($A$) demand goods and sell labour, firms ($B$) sell goods and demand labour: thus in $A \leftrightarrow field \leftrightarrow B$ equilibrium will arise in terms of the field variable (prices). But Clower suggests that this situation is in reality composed of two sets of interactions (the dual decision): household demand for goods, A → B; and firm demand for labour, B → A. Whatever effective demand manifests in one market will consequentially manifest in the other. This causal structure was interpreted in the macroeconomic literature as a disequilibrium phenomenon, because trade takes place out of equilibrium. Yet the fact is that it has nothing to do with equilibrium because this is classically a non-integral situation (where the non-integral aspect is manifest mostly in the temporal dimension, and thus suggests the nature of the service performed by money as liquidity). But when the field context of an interaction ($A \leftrightarrow B$) is broken into two action components, each with the field ($A \leftrightarrow field \leftrightarrow B$) all such reasoning is confounded.[20]

The critical point is that because interaction occurs by definition between all points we do not then require a specific representation of interaction such as $A \leftrightarrow B$: this abstraction *is* the field. However, the mathematician Henri Poincaré proved a profound result pertaining to the generality of such instances early this century. Poincaré was able to show that, in general, dynamical systems are non-integrable. As Prigogine (1993: 8) remarks,

> this is a very important result, because if in contrast Poincaré had shown that all dynamical systems are integrable, that would mean that interactions could always be eliminated; that we would essentially live in a noninteracting world, a world that would be isomorphic to a world of free particles floating independently of each other.

The assumptions of the neowalrasian framework are precisely those that generate the necessary specification of a field, and thereby circumvent the otherwise logical requirement of formulating agent interaction. The central assumption that carries the logic of the field is the axiom of completeness. It is not, primarily, as many critics have suggested, the rationality postulate, the homogeneity assumption or the maximization hypothesis that is the core of the neowalrasian framework, but it is the axiom of completeness that is primary and these other postulates, as such, are secondary in their analytical bearing.

It is this field accession, then, and its correspondence with the theoretical core of the physical sciences that is principally responsible for the mathematical verisimilitude of the neowalrasian model. Mirowski and Georgescu-Roegen attack this pretension directly: Mirowski for uncritical appropriation of the mathematical logic and Georgescu-Roegen for the uncritical adoption of the logic of the mathematics. Although these critiques are but two amongst very many others, by my reckoning they have struck the core of the neowalrasian model, which is the mathematical logic and concept of a field.[21]

## 2.4  Convergence of Criticism

The neowalrasian microeconomics certainly has its critics. The Austrian school, for instance, contends that the orthodox model does not illuminate the actual machinations of the market process. They say it lacks organization. The Schumpeterian school, among other things, argues that the orthodox model neglects the importance of novelty and the creative function of the entrepreneur. They say it lacks imagination. The Post-Keynesian economists have slated the standard closed-form conception of uncertainty, probability and money. They say it lacks emotion. The Institutional school criticizes the absence of habits and routines in the orthodox model. They say it lacks structure. The Behavioural economists argue that *homo economicus* has few recognizably human qualities. They say it lacks passion. And so on. But in Frank Hahn's opinion (1981: 129) 'the ease with which so much current critique of General Equilibrium analysis can be countered is potentially dangerous. For the citadel is not at all secure and the fact that it is safe from a bombardment of soap bubbles does not mean that it is safe'.

These separate lines of critique, Hahn's 'soap bubbles', have indeed been relatively easy to ignore and in the final resort, it would seem, are perhaps best understood not as dedicated critique, but as markers indicating by stylized account some failing in the orthodox model, and thereby the point of departure for the corresponding heterodox school. In this way each heterodox school is known, and indeed knows itself, by its angles of incidence and refraction from the orthodox microtheory.

So the situation is this. There exists a much criticized but nevertheless predominant intellectual orthodoxy. The orthodoxy consists of a metatheoretical core (Weintraub 1979: 73) in the neowalrasian general equilibrium theory, which is then used to construct economic theories. Hausman (1992: 55), however, argues that it is the other way around, such that 'equilibrium theory is the fundamental theory. General equilibrium theory is a particular application of the fundamental theory'. I am inclined to agree with Hausman. The field construct builds the set of axioms, the axioms build the hard core, the hard core builds equilibrium theory and general equilibrium theory is then instated by extending the full logic of the axioms of completeness and continuity (which are themselves the essential logic of the field). General equilibrium theory, then, is dependent upon the field construct much more so than partial equilibrium theory.

However in criticism of neoclassical economics, equilibrium theory or general equilibrium theory, the heterodoxy has often been confused about what it is actually criticizing. This is not to say that the defenders of orthodoxy are significantly more enlightened; there has been much confusion all round. The general presumption is that the core logic of neoclassical economics is conditional upon a series of axioms—continuity, completeness, transitivity, reflexivity, monotonicity, regularity, convexity—which the heterodox schools have variously taken issue with (usually in terms of their hard-core translations, that is, perfect information, rationality, equilibrium, constant returns, equimarginal equivalence and so forth) to distinguish new theoretical positions by some form of rejection of one or other of these axioms. For example, such negations imply: uncertainty, bounded rationality, disequilibrium, increasing returns and hysteresis. But the mistake has been to presuppose that these axioms are in fact 'axiomatic', which is to say that they are not derivatives of some more fundamental aspect. Yet this is precisely the case. Beneath the metatheoretical framework (equilibrium theory) is the hard core, beneath this are the axioms, but beneath these is the construct of a field. What I now endeavour to show is that the heterodox criticisms of both the mathematical axioms and the analytical assumptions have targeted the wrong point. Neowalrasian theory is field theory, and the axiom assumptions are simply the workable expressions of the field concept. Below I set out how this single target can be read in the various thematic criticisms of orthodox microtheory.

The enormity of this topic confines a brief treatment to proceed in a highly stylized manner, concentrating mostly on delineating different types of criticisms and to touch upon consideration of a representative critique. The point I make is that extending from many different heterodox schools of thought is a mass of criticism of the neowalrasian paradigm, seemingly diverse and *prima facie* independent, but which ultimately reduces to a single criticism of the abstract analytical leap from a space into a field. A space is a well-defined theoretical construct, as is a field, but I argue that it is the set of primary logical conditions defining the special case of a field from a space that is the seat of all fundamental heterodox criticism.

The first task is the organization of criticisms into a series of stylized modalities as below. There is no strict correspondence between these classifications and the different heterodox schools, although an approximate alignment may be discerned as (1) Evolutionary; (2) Realist; (3) Behavioural; (4) Institutional; (5) Austrian and Post-Keynesian. However, given the complex hybridisation of any particular heterodox economist with respect to such rubric conceptions, any such attempt at saddling is unlikely to improve the clarity of the argument. The modalities I distinguish are thematic convergences, and it is these leitmotif across the many individual instances of departure that afford the most striking and simple characterization of the congruence of fundamental criticism. They are critiques of: (1) optimization and maximization; (2) positivism; (3) *homo economicus*; (4) the treatment of dynamic structure; (5) closure and determinism.

It should be inferred then, that I do not regard the separate schools of economic thought as contributing separate criticisms of the orthodox model, and therefore justifying separate departures. Instead, I observe that the same criticism has made, over and over again, but that this has not been apparent because it has been directed at many different points of the orthodox model and without clearly recognizing that the whole edifice rests on a single point.

### 2.4.1 Critique of Optimization and Maximization

According to Hahn (1981: 128): 'The fundamental element of neoclassical theory [is] that agents will, if open to them, take actions they consider advantageous'. This is an entirely reasonable presumption about the deep nature of human economic behaviour. What is in dispute is whether 'advantageous' can then be interpreted as 'optimal' in the individual instance, and then whether the forces at work in an economic system suitably conspire to generalize this result. There are thus two components to such criticism: first, whether it makes sense to speak of optimization or maximization in respect of the individual; and second, whether there exist forces that generalize the sum of individual optimization. The first point relates to the axiomatics of the neowalrasian theory, the second to the nature of a selection process. It is the latter that has received the most critical and in-depth treatment, and will be the main subject of this section.

Essentially, it is the axiom of completeness (or connectedness or connexity) that is the most troubling, and for several reasons. Completeness states that all commodity bundles can be compared, such that the agent can say either bundle $A$ is as good as, better than or worse than bundle $B$ or vice versa. Completeness orders all bundles in accordance with the agent's preference map. In simple, low-dimensional 'apples and oranges' type situations this is perfectly reasonable. The trouble arises in higher dimensions (that is, general equilibrium) and for less stylized goods. Bundle $A$, as above, is a particular set of commodities. So is bundle $B$. Each bundle is drawn from the set of all commodities, $X = (1, ..., n)$. The underlying problem is that this $n$ is not in practice a small number; it is not the amount of fruit in a basket but more akin to the number of stars in a galaxy. The number of comparable bundles is exponentially greater still. Indeed, it was precisely this problem that the inventors of gravitational field theory simplified with the integral concept: every point mass affects every other point mass such that the entire system may be written as a single field equation, a perfect integral. But this logic does not carry over to economics in the same plausible manner. The agent's preference map is only realistically conceivable as a field when $n$ is a very small number, and certainly this will be very much less than the number of goods in an economy, or even a supermarket for that matter.

The second point is a more introspective critique, challenging the concept of comparability in specific situations (for example, Hausman 1992: 15). The underlying problem is that the act of choice, say between bundles $A$ and $B$, may often proceed without the agents yet knowing whether they prefer $A$ to $B$ due to the nature of these goods as experience goods (such as a pre-booked holiday or even an apple, if one has never tasted an apple before) or due to the fact that quality may only become apparent in the course of consuming the good (such as a meal in a restaurant, or any consumer durable). There is a phenomenal mass of social and legal conventions and institutions associated precisely with this problem (for example, consumer guarantees, or the social institution that enables one to send a meal back if dissatisfied). However the logic of the theory does not make sense of such things, but rather asserts that the act of choice reveals preference (Samuelson 1938). And although seemingly a tidy rebuttal it does not actually deal with the problem at all but shifts it onto the axiom of transitivity. Other problems with the concept of completeness and preference, such as discussed in Sen (1973) need not concern us further. It is sufficient to note that the axiomatic logic of individual rational choice as maximizing behaviour stumbles on the axiom of completeness for the simple reason that the connections that are presumed to exist mostly do not.

The second part of the critique of maximization concerns the workings of the market process as a selection process. In the above line of criticism the argument was conducted first-hand, as it were, but in this second aspect the essence of the argument stems from the findings of an external science, namely evolutionary biology. In short, the concept of a competitive selection process effecting optimal outcomes was once the paradigm of orthodox evolutionary biological theory and economics leant heavily upon this argument to buttress the analogue of a competitive market process. Biology, however, has now collected far too many exceptions to sustain this belief, and has reworked its underlying theory of the selection mechanism to reject the concept of global maximization applied to the concept of fitness (see Salthe 1985). The theoretical reason for this rejection amounts to the fact that 'biological space' is not integral.

There are many specific and dedicated criticisms of the strong assumption of maximization as the outcome of a selection process. Rather than dealing with these separately I wish to proceed with reference to Hodgson's (1993: 186–207) most comprehensive survey and synthesis of all such lines of critique. Hodgson challenges the axiomatic conflation of a force of selection (a competitive force) with an optimal outcome on a number of fronts. In all cases it is argued that there is no strong reason to presuppose that a force of selection necessarily or even generally produces an outcome that can be universally regarded as efficient or the product of single-valued maximization. I shall not dwell on the individual points of the argument, but proceed directly to his conclusion: 'It has been demonstrated . . . that the nineteenth-century idea of unhampered evolution necessarily leading to optimal outcomes is misconceived' (*ibid.*: 212). The idea that a force of selection leads to optimal outcomes is pure Darwinism (Sober 1993), and was appropriated by economic theorists to justify the logic of competitive optimization (Alchian 1950, Enke 1951, Friedman 1953; see Vromen 1995: 101–4). The point that Hodgson correctly makes is that modern theories of evolutionary processes no longer regard this to be generally true, and, indeed, in many cases it is phenomenally misleading (see Depew and Weber 1985, Vromen 1995). If Darwinism once gave credence to the assumption of maximization by appeal to a 'survival of the maximizers' type argument then this Darwinism is no longer regarded seriously by the successors of Darwin.[22] The selection argument in evolutionary biology is now a far more complicated story than it was in the 1950s, when economics last appealed to biology for support of its assumptions (notwithstanding Becker 1976). Hodgson (1999) and

Vromen (1995) have communicated this clearly to the heterodox economists, but it would seem that this news has not affected the orthodox paradigm.

We must be careful not to misunderstand the critical context of this argument, as it seems that many hasty dismissals of the issue tend to perceive only a debate about metaphor (and therefore sterile) or pertaining to the subject domains of biology or economics (in a respective and therefore closed context) or that such things are consequential only to the meaning of 'in the long run' (semantic, and therefore academic). Yet the issue is fundamental and concerns the logical conditions pertaining to the existence of a force that acts continuously and ultimately upon all elements in a space. It seems that while such a force can be conceived in the physical domain, such a singular force does not act in the biological domain. The force of selection, as it were, is only partially a field force in the parameters set up by the environment, and for the greatest part these are mostly stable over long periods. The major component of a force of selection, however, consists of the specific interactions that construct niches, where a certain species interacts with a set of others in the context of a web. The concept of fitness then arises within this localized context. Changes in this web structure are the far more routine cause of extinction and macroevolutionary dynamics (Eldredge and Gould 1977, Gowdy 1994). It seems that this same mode of dynamics applies to economic change as well (Gowdy 1992, Andersen 1994).

Yet this concept is still to be clearly expressed in economic theory as statements about the nature of a selection mechanism as a process occurring in historical time. In the neowalrasian system, selection is equated with perfect competition such that it is a selection mechanism that produces the perfectly competitive outcome. But as Leijonhufvud (1968: 102) long ago pointed out (in the context of the micro–macro riddle of unemployment existing in competitive markets), this association is a riddle only when competition is presumed to mean perfect information. In the neowalrasian system the selection mechanism is not perfect competition, it is perfect information, and this does not logically exist in any reasonable meaning of historical time. The point then develops, and this is the part yet to be fully comprehended, that processes in historical time may not ever correct the departure from a theoretical optimum either. (Convergence to a theoretical optimum is only a theoretical idea.) This being the case, selection does not optimize but is irreducibly a historically contingent process.

That a force of selection is not a ubiquitously optimizing force and does not lend support to the strong notion of maximization is a fundamental result, but even Hodgson who amasses the elements of this argument still remains somewhat vague about the precise nature of its conclusion. Ultimately, at the level of basic logical conditions, the substance of such critique is to be most effectively read as a rebuttal to the field theory method in biology, such as espoused by orthodox Darwinians such as Dawkins (1976). Ultimately, then, the analytical constructs of maximization and optimization (and therein efficiency) are hinged from the logic of a field. If the concept of a field is weakened then so too are the efficiency concepts that are predicated upon it.

A specific instance is the phenomenon of hyperselection or chreodic development or, most generally, lock-in by increasing returns affecting path dependency. This phenomenon occurs when the forward development of a system occurs in a space that is not represented by a flat equipotential surface but by a number of distinct channels—*chreods*, as Waddington (1972) calls them. Historical contingency (a bifurcation point) alone may account for the determination of which channel a system enters, but once in a channel, so to speak, the system will tend to continue down that channel. In economics we know this as increasing returns, as the supposed enemy of the optimality conditions afforded by perfect competition (Young 1928, Loasby 1991, Arthur 1994). This generalized phenomenon Waddington coins *homeorhesis*, and although omnipresent in an economic system, from institutional development to technological standards and growth patterns, its basic logic is denied by field-theory models. Those who have studied such phenomenon in an economic system have therefore tended to be critical of the orthodox microeconomic framework. Such topographical complexity (or feedback) is denied in field theory because the logic of a field framework precludes the possibility that complex local interactions can systematically affect the path of the system in a way that is not (ultimately) corrected by wider interactions. Complex local interactions cannot exert systematic effects because complex local interactions decoupled from other elements in the space cannot be defined in the first place.

To be sure, such critique does not suggest an alternative hypothesis that selection is ultimately random or that there is no statistical evolutionary advantage in selective fitness. What is argued, however, is that there is no systematic relationship that may be ultimately expressed as a dynamical law. In other words, the phenomenon known as natural selection, which is really just a set of mass interactions between individual organisms, or genes, according to Dawkins (1976), is irreducibly complex. The mass interactions cannot be abstracted to a field of actions, which would be required to secure the link between a mechanism—natural selection—and an outcome—Panglossian optimality (Hodgson 1993: 197). The other lines of reasoning that Hodgson gathers to refute the strong relationship between a force of selection and an optimal outcome all concur in this fundamental way. In the neowalrasian paradigm the concept of a force of selection is translated to mean perfect competition, which is manifestly defined as a large number of firms but operationally means simply that no single interaction matters (Hicks 1948: 6). Perfect competition is presumed to mean perfect information (connectedness), which is the assumption of a field.[23] The strong linkage between selection and maximization, such that competition can be said under certain conditions to produce optimal outcomes, is an internal consequence of the axiomatic derivation of a field from a space. If in that space complex local interactions matter, then a strong relationship between a general causal force of competition or natural selection and a generalized outcome of optimality is decoupled.

Critique of the assumptions of maximization or optimization, from the perspective of a selection argument, have pointed out that these assumptions rest upon a particular type of selection process, namely one that is continuous over a field.[24] If this field concept is weakened, then the mechanism of selection is decoupled from a globally optimal outcome. The introduction of path dependency, historical contingency and other such processes all occur, then, in a non-integral space.

## 2.4.2 Critique of Positivism

This is the line of critique that focuses upon the methodological underpinnings of the neoclassical and neowalrasian economics, and specifically its claims to scientific legitimacy.[25] For this reason, it is also the line of critique that has most drawn response (D'Autume and Cartelier 1997).

Charles Sanders Peirce, Thorstein Veblen and Henri Bergson, alongside the German Historical school of Schmoller and the Hegelian doctrines of Karl Marx, can be considered the founders of critique of positivism and deductivism. (Although strictly interpreted, this pedigree traces back to Aristotle's conception of organicism (Whitehead 1929).) This core critique of epistemology, and in a nascent way of method, was further developed by Nicholas Georgescu-Roegen (1971) on irreversibility, George Shackle (1972) on probability (see Potts 2000) and in certain respects by Hayek (for example, 1991) on self-organization. So there has been no lack of concern with such matters, with critique of the method of deductivism and the ontological tenets of positivism well established, both in general philosophic terms and in its underpinning of economic theory and econometrics. Indeed, it can be argued that a certain consensus has arrived, as summarized by Tony Lawson's (1997) critique of deductivist method and Francesco Louçã's (1997) critique of the misconceptions of positivism. If it is possible to conceive of the post-war period, or more specifically the period following what Shackle (1967) called 'the years of high theory', as fraught with undercurrents of epistemological dichotomy (as opposed to plurality) then it would seem that these years of seismological activity are now over. Clower and Howitt (1997: 31) offer a more caustic portrayal: 'were we seriously, by a single phrase, to attempt to characterize the modern age—the age of Keynes, Samuelson, Hicks, Arrow, Debreu and so on—we would call it the age of delusion'. Whatever we call it, Lawson and Louçã have clearly announced that it must now be disbanded if economics is to advance as a science.

Lawson (1997) and Louçã (1997) both furnish comprehensive and deeply constructed critiques that will surely stand as landmark monographs in the evolutionary reformation of economic theory. Lawson and Louçã both resolutely and fundamentally reject the orthodox research programme and its underlying paradigm. Lawson rejects the deductivist mode of explanation, instating Critical Realism instead. Louçã rejects Frisch's impulse-propagation metaphor, which has since established itself as the dynamic expression of the Cartesian model. Instead Louçã offers 'turbulence' as an alternative metaphor. Both establish *ontological* solutions to chronic methodological problems. That is, they both ultimately turn criticism of the deductivist/Cartesian paradigm back towards reconstruction of a new paradigm by first principles appeal to the nature of the existence of the elements of an economic system. In Lawson's case, it is appeal to the structure of interactions between agents (the theory of the social ontology). In Louçã's case, it is appeal to the underlying dynamic structure of more generally conceived interactions (as the metaphor of turbulence in historical processes).

The final breakthrough achieved in this reduction to ontological essence is absolutely consonant with the critique of field-theory appropriation when it is recognized that the distinction between an integral and a non-integral geometry is both logical *and* ontological. The latter sense is manifest in the focus upon specific interactions and connections as concern with existence; that is, with the ontology of the economic system revealed as the geometry of economic space. What Lawson establishes is a redirection towards a critical realist ontology and, as I shall show, this can be formally[26] locked into place by recognizing that this ontology describes a non-integral geometry of economic space. A reinvestigation of ontology was the solution drawn from extensive critique of the hypothetico-deductive methods and the framework of positivism. I argue that this ontological solution is more generally and usefully stated as a non-integral geometry of economic space.

Lawson (1997: 282) concludes his comprehensive study with the assertion that

> the most fundamental feature [of contemporary mainstream economics] is a generalized insistence on the deductivist mode of explanation, including the unsustainable commitment to the 'whenever this then that' structure of 'laws'. And it is in this very essence that the perpetual disarray of the subject is rooted. . . . The ultimate source of all problems is the epistemic fallacy, the belief that questions of ontology can be reduced to questions of methodology.

If we may glean the substance of criticism from the form of solution suggested, then what Lawson contends is necessary, as a fusion of Austrian, Institutional and Evolutionary constructs, is a reinvestment in ontology and an explicit abandonment of the methodological thesis of social atomism.

In Lawson's ontological conception 'society is constituted in large part by a set of positions, each associated with numerous obligations, rights and duties, and into which agents, as it were, slot' (Lawson 1997: 164–5), such that 'on this conception the basic building blocks of society are positions'. Lawson conceives the elements of a social ontology to be decoupled from agency, thus retaining an autonomy for deliberate action by an agent, who may variously occupy one or many such positions. Agents are free to move within this giving up certain positions, taking on others, merging positions or creating new ones. The social ontology is to be identified with agency but is not to be reduced to it. In this way Lawson (*ibid.*: 159) dispenses with methodological individualism and the associated epistemological positivism—social atomism—to define the social reality as

> conceived as intrinsically dynamic and complexly structured, consisting in human agency, structures and contexts of action, none of which are given or fixed, and where each presupposes the other without being reducible to, identifiable with, or explicable in terms of, any other.

The elements, as positions, have properties of existence independent of the agent, but are able to be transformed by the agent. These elements are construed with respect to other elements by relationships. It is the existence of internal relationships between positions (not agents) that rejects social atomism and allows a picture 'of a set, or network, of positions characterized by the rules and the practices associated with them' (*ibid.*: 164). The rules describe how the relationships are structured. The existence of rules, internal relations and positions becomes a recursive explanation for the largely routine nature of social life. But more than that, it is the process of acting out such rules and relations (praxis) that perpetually reproduces, or in other circumstances transforms, this ontological structure.

In the final abstraction Lawson extrudes the key point (*ibid.*: 170–1), change and existence are the same thing. Or in other words, the reality of existence and the reality of change are on the same ontological level.[27] In offering this framework Lawson (*ibid.*: 283) is unequivocal in

> arguing for nothing less than orthodox economics' effective demise (as a general approach and mainstream position). This orientation follows inescapably once it is recognized that the source of all the project's problems and difficulties (in dealing with an open system) stem from that project's very essence.

Such strong concatenation marks fundamental criticism, and the essence of this is unmistakably, again, the field conception of economic space. This is apparent in the solution he proffers, as an ontological system making explicit the existence of connections between elements. Lawson's terminology is positions and relationships, but this may then be regarded as a particular assignment of a general logic of elements and connections. And the key point is that relationships—connections, as it were—exist by the symmetry of a relationship not existing. In this respect, Lawson unfolds a critical difference between internal and external relationships and draws attention to the structure afforded by rules (structural relationship), which in full logical abstraction is an ontological attack on the field theory of economic space.

While much methodological critique may seem far removed from speculations regarding a complex systems theory approach to microeconomics, as the full circle of Lawson's argument demonstrates, it is in fact upon precisely such issues that the criticism turns. The long-standing critique of deductivism and of positivism in economics ultimately finds recourse in a fundamental ontological reconception. This is what Lawson has made clear. But what he did not furnish was a description of the ontology in a format amenable to general microeconomic basis. This requires only one more step past his conceptual conclusion, namely that the Realist ontology (as a general epistemological framework) amounts to the argument that the geometry of economic space is non-integral. In the limit of an integral space, as a field, the Realist ontology collapses to the Cartesian ontology.

### 2.4.3 Critique of Agent Models

There are two main aspects to critique of the mainstream treatment of economic agency. First, there is critique of the information and rationality assumptions attributed to agency (and specifically to *homo economicus*). Second, there is the question of just how many agents are sufficient to model an economy, and whether agent variation is to be an important part of modelling and analysis. This can be viewed as critique of the definition of the agent in microeconomics (for example, Simon 1959, Vriend 1996) and in macroeconomics (Kirman 1992, Hartley 1997). However, the study of heterogeneous populations of locally interacting agents has shown that this is really two aspects of the same critique The microeconomic critique has been mostly led by the Behavioural economists (and more recently by those gathering under the rubric of *agent-based computational economics*). The macroeconomic critique has come from the Post-Keynesian and Austrian schools, as well as others who have set themselves in opposition to the New Classical school of macroeconomics.

The microeconomic line of critique is easily stated (in three parts): (1) it is not the case that economic agents have access to all the information necessary for them to make the sorts of decisions attributed to them; (2) even if they did, it is not the case that economic agents possess the computational faculties to process the information required of them by the theoretical formulation; and (3), it is not the case that the single valued and hedonic behavioural premises are universally applicable to economic agents.

Veblen (1919: 73) started it, of course, criticizing a single valued hedonic conception of a perfectly rational, fully informed and infinitely able calculating automaton, the 'isolated, definitive human datum', the 'homogeneous globule of desire' and 'lightning calculator'. Yet his critique was not that this image was too far removed from reality. No, that would be too easy, and Veblen clearly appreciated the role of abstraction in logical analysis. Veblen's critique was of the compass points of agency, and whether these could be meaningfully set in a static context. For Veblen, emulation and creativity were for the prime movers.[28] But nevertheless, the preposterously overblown portrait that Veblen painted clearly highlighted the need for empirical investigation of the nature of cognition and interaction in the market context. Just how much do people know? What are their reference points? What is the geometry of interaction? How independent are their choices? How pliable are their preferences? What sort of computations are they really capable of? What sort of computations do they actually perform? That sort of thing.[29]

The information available to an agent—irrespective of its content, meaning and all such aspects corresponding to the signal—can be conceptualized as the extent of the connections extending from the locus of the agent. Suppose we imagine a set of elements $x = (x_1, x_2, x_3,...)$ distributed over some space $X$, in which each $x_i (x_i \in X)$ emits a continuous signal that extends over the domain of $X$. If we are to say that $x_1$ and $x_2$ interact, then it is evident that a signal must somehow pass between $x_1$ and $x_2$. This requirement is true for all investigations of physical phenomena in a real space. It is not a unique problem for economics. We usually suppose these signals to be prices, but they may be other things as well (for example, Richardson 1960, Hirschman 1970). If this signal does not exist, then we cannot speak of $x_1$ and $x_2$ interacting or being causally related. In this situation whatever changes may be occurring at $x_1$ these will have no effect on $x_2$ because the information of these changes does not reach $x_2$. Rationality is in some senses (as in game theory) directly interpreted as the inverse of this, corresponding to the connections incident to the locus of the element.

More generally, though, the definition of rationality requires to be understood in procedural rather than substantive terms (Simon 1976). The orthodox meaning of rationality, which pivots about consistent and transitive rankings in the instance of choice, presupposes the concept of an integral space over which choice occurs. Indeed, the two concepts of rationality that Simon calls substantive and procedural are in the present context integral and non-integral referents. For Simon (1959: 272), the context of bounded and procedural rationality is not that of 'choosing among fixed and known alternatives, to each of which is attached known consequences' but with respect to the intervention of 'perception and cognition which recognizes that alternatives are not given but must be sought'. Which is to say that connections must be actively made, which implies a non-integral space.

For the Behavioural school of economics (for example see Earl 1988) the issue revolves not so much about the various manipulations of a given field of information (the total concern of neowalrasian axiomatics) but about the acquisition and interpretation of the information in the first place (also Kelly 1963, Loasby 1991, Leijonhufvud 1997: 333–4). The informational nature of rationality is neither integral nor a partial integral, but very much less; indeed, reference to the integral as a benchmark is taking the wrong end of the scale.

> The decision-maker's information about his environment is much less than an approximation to the real environment. . . . In actual fact the perceived world is fantastically different from the 'real' world. The differences involve both omissions and distortions, and arise in both perception and inference. The sins of omission in perception are more important than the sins of commission. The decision-maker's model of the world encompasses only a minute fraction of all the relevant characteristics of the real environment, and his inferences extract only a minute fraction of all the information that is present even in his model. (Simon 1959: 272)

Third, the behavioural premises attributed to agency relate to the uniformity of the map of connections with respect to the purpose of the connection. Multiple and/or conflicting objectives introduce the idea that an agent may be pursuing more than one objective simultaneously, such that different connections may be for different purposes. Etzioni (1986), for instance, conceives of the concept of multiple utility in this manner. In essence, the criticism from this geometric point of view is that the map of connections in economic space is not described by the geometry of a field but by the geometry of a web.

This general line of critique, however, need not proceed in such terms as relating to the geometry of the space in which the agent rests, but may proceed directly from the 'faulty conception of human nature' (Veblen 1919: 7) built by the axioms of the hard core. Georgescu-Roegen (1971: 1) continues in this vein:

> The motives of dissatisfaction [with neoclassical economic science] are many, but the most important pertains to *homo oeconomicus*. The complaint is that this fiction strips man's behaviour of every cultural propensity, which is tantamount to saying that in his economic life man acts mechanically.

But, as so often, Shackle (1972: 3) said it best:

> [Neoclassical] economic theory took on a character belonging to the manipulable, calculable, external world of things, not the world of conscious mind whose being consists precisely in the endless gaining of knowledge. Knowledge and novelty, the essential counter-point of conscious being, was given only a causal and subsidiary

role. . . . The question of knowledge, of what is and what can be known, the governing circumstance and condition of all deliberative action, was assumed away in the very theories of deliberative action. Or rather, the natural, inevitable and irremediable insufficiency of what is at any moment known was assumed away and largely neglected.

He continues, pivoting his critique about the 'logical non-existence of complete knowledge' upon which the neoclassical theory depends. It is evident, then, that the most ubiquitous point of heterodox critique concerning the conception of agency is that of necessary incompleteness. In their sensory, cognitive, inferential, and in sum, rational bearing, agents are not completely integrated in to their environment. Hayek (1969) referred to this as 'the primacy of the abstract'. The reach of each agent across the economic system is only ever partial and quasi-local. And for all its subtlety and complexity, this amounts to just a single point: a field does not describe the geometry of economic space.

A second line of heterodox critique of agency focuses upon the almost exclusive use of representative agent models that supposedly furnish microfoundations to macroeconomics. Such critique has largely arisen in response to the ascendancy of the New Classical school to a dominant position in macroeconomic theory. The New Classical school is field theory applied to macroeconomics (including the field theory expression of expectations, as I examine in Chapter 7). Critics, such as Kirman (1992) and Hartley (1997) and indeed the entire Austrian school,[30] have mustered many specific concerns on the validity or otherwise of treating the aggregate economy as a scaled-up version of an individual decision problem. I shall consider just two criticisms. The first, which is the most well-developed line of critique, concerns the logic of aggregation and the abstraction from heterogeneity. The second, and more speculative, concerns the use of multiagent models as an alternative to representative agent models.

The Austrian and Post-Keynesian schools, for somewhat different reasons, argue that the mapping of microeconomics into macroeconomics, *à la* representative agent models, stumbles badly upon the fallacy of composition problem (see Dow 1985). A fallacy of composition is the attribution of properties of the parts to properties of the whole. For instance, bricks are small and red, therefore brick walls are small and red. Neurons cannot think, therefore brains cannot think. Or, beehives are composed of bees, therefore we can study a beehive as if it were one giant bee. Macro-bee may be quite a useful approach for the study of, say, giant bees, but it is clearly a fallacy to suppose that macro-bee is equivalent to beehive. The same invocation of the fallacy of composition applies to the equivalence of macroagent to macroeconomy. The reason for this is obvious, although a curious blind-spot in the orthodox syllabus. A beehive is more than just lots of bees; it is bees as well as the interactions between bees and, furthermore, the coordination and structure that arises from these interactions (institutions, in a word). The point is that it is the interactions, not the just the bees, that aggregate. For instance, bees have wings but beehives do not. Macro-bee theory would predict otherwise. Similarly, there is no trickery involved in the idea that individuals may be rational but the aggregate is not (for example, herding), or that a collective may exhibit properties beyond the sum of the individual elements (for example, consciousness).

But a theory of how interactions aggregate cannot logically proceed from the study of a single element, irrespective of how representative it may be. Even two elements do not often interact in ways sufficient to engender the properties of self-organization characteristic of complex systems such as beehives and macroeconomies. As Poincaré established so long ago, complex systems theory begins with the three-body problem (more generally, see Agliardi 1998). The field construct abstracts from interactions and therefore cannot by definition make sense of the aggregate consequences of interactions. The most promising method of studying agents *and* interactions is to employ multi-agent models, which have the further advantage that they allow the use of heterogeneous agents. (Game theory also claims this advance.) Multiagent models allow a way of studying the aggregation of interactions and, because they are defined over a lattice, are analysis of a non-integral geometry of economic space.

### 2.4.4 Critique of the Treatment of Dynamic Structure

This line of critique is arguably the heart of the evolutionary economics proper. It has two faces: critique of the treatment of dynamic structure (institutions), and critique of analysis of structural dynamics (evolutionary economics). What is meant by dynamic structure? I shall suggest the scheme of an answer to this in the subsequent chapters, but for now I shall offer that institutions are an example of dynamic structure in the sense that they are constructs that primarily involve (analytical) expression in terms of structure and order. All such constructs are analytically excluded by the logic of a field.

Veblen (1919: 239) defined institutions as 'settled habits and thoughts common to the generality of men', a basis that has been since refined to distinguish between habits, rules, routines, paradigms and conventions (see Hodgson 1988, Choi 1993, Rutherford 1994). Institutions conceived as stable patterns of behaviour in time (Katona 1951) exist then as stable relationships between basic components of behaviour (Hodgson 1996). According to Mirowski (1988a: 132), 'Institutions can be understood as socially constructed invariants that provide the actors who participate in them with the means and resources to cope with change and diversity; this is the non-mechanistic definition of individual rationality'.

These components of behaviour themselves may be conceived in elementary terms, as basic abilities or skills (organic, cognitive or social reflex), but that it is a stable combination as an emergent complex form that is the nature of an institution. The essential point is that institutions are not fundamental elements. Their existence is composite and made of specific interactions, forming a structure in time. In other words, dynamic structure.

It is this composite structural quality of existence that excludes institutions from a field-theory-based framework, and equally so other entities which are necessarily described in this emergent structural form. The domain of exclusion is more than just denial of institutions, but all such structure, including the structure of decisions or strategies and, most significantly, the internal structure of firms. Langlois and Robertson (1995: 1) make this conjunction explicit, focusing their analysis upon the idea of a business institution:

> By using the term business institutions, we intend to stress that our concern extends beyond business organizations—which connotes the idea of the business firm—to encompass a wide variety of structures, including those institutions generally described as markets. . . . In the broader theory of social institutions, the fundamental concept of an institution ultimately boils down to the idea of recurrent patterns of behaviour-habits, conventions and routines.

Langlois and Robertson recognize an essential commonality across institutions and organizations pertaining to both being instances of structures. This seems to me an absolutely fundamental point that, moreover, extends across theoretical concerns with structure in consumer decision heuristics (Earl 1986), organizational decision processes (Cyert and March 1963, Baumol and Quandt 1964), modes of integration in organization (Williamson 1996, Kay 1997), industrial networks (Best 1990, Powell 1991, Heertje and Perlman 1990), competence-based theories of the firm (Prahlad and Hamel 1990, Montgomery 1995, Foss and Knudsen 1996) and broad principles of industrial organization (Richardson 1972). All such phenomena—institutions, firms, decision heuristics, networks, competence and industrial organization—are instances of structure, and more abstractly of an association between elements that may be regarded as having a particular geometric form. For instance, Chandler's (1962) notion of M-form and U-form organizational structure is a distinct imputation of geometric structure in the interactions between elements. Sah and Stiglitz (1986) employ the term 'architecture', as does John Kay (1993), in discussion of the structure of economic systems.

All of these instances depart from neoclassical microeconomic logic. In part, such departure is the simple consequence of enquiry outside the realm of orthodox theory, something particularly true of network-based theories, or resource- and competence-based theories of the firm, where there is no such corresponding entity represented in the orthodox theoretical framework. But in other instances the complexity and order revealed in structural investigation has direct bearing upon the relevance of an orthodox explanation in which such aspects of determination are excluded by definition.

In terms of the geometry of a space, the concept of structure derives from particular connections between elements. To define structure (with respect to a set of elements in a space) we must be able to define the existence of a connection between any two elements, which, symmetrically, requires that we must be able to define the absence of a corresponding connection. That is, we can theorise about structure only if we can proceed to define the uniqueness of a particular structure (encompassing both discrete states and typologies or classes of structure). Therefore, if we can define specific components of interaction or connection we can proceed from microfoundations to theorise about the dynamics of structure. However this approach is specifically excluded by the logic of a field. A field, by defining all connections as complete, excludes the explanatory context of structure. All of the above mentioned domains—spanning Institutional, Behavioural and organizational theoretic schools—are notable for their absence of neowalrasian microeconomic foundations, and the reason, it seems, is that all involve the theoretical construction of structure, which is precluded from the neowalrasian field theory system of microeconomics. The implicit criticism by theoretical departure is all driven by the same fundamental reason—economic space is not described by the algebraic geometry of a field.

The second line of heterodox critique of this type concerns analysis of structural change. This is foremost an econometric concern, and specifically with identification and measurement of parameter shifts in time-series data (see Baranzini and Scazzieri 1990, Hackl and Westlund 1991). And while such discontinuities, non-stationarities and structural breaks plague most time series, and thereby provide for a veritable industry of econometric white-washing and other such manipulations, theoretical understanding of these strange trajectories remains weak. Yet it is not especially difficult to construct non-linear dynamical systems models that display bifurcations and phase transitions and other such complex movements that may then have some similarity to the observed data structures (see, for example, Rosser 1991, Day and Chen 1993). The problem is that in order to tell stories over such domains requires an inescapable injection of historical circumstance. In short, when the data is not smooth, it begs models capable of generating complex paths, but the theoretical content of this becomes severely strained and ultimately must fall back upon a specific account of the historical events and conditions (Hodgson forthcoming). One wonders, then, why the formal models are necessary at all.

But new theoretical ideas have arisen, and many models of structural change now feature technological regimes or trajectories that are stable for a time before abruptly giving way to new trajectories in a manner somewhat similar to punctuated equilibria models of palaeontology (see Dosi et al. 1988, Gowdy

1992). Dopfer (2000) has extended this notion towards a general 'histonomic' framework of institutional change. Yet one of the most well-founded lines of investigation to integrate both econometric evidence and theoretical explanation is the use of the logistic diffusion equation as a model of large-scale economic dynamics as a process of self-organization. This has been most clearly enunciated by Foster (1993, 1997), who, following the entropy law foundations of economics suggested by Georgescu-Roegen (1971), the open system thermodynamic framework of Prigogine and Stengers (1984) and the entropic resetting of biology by Brooks and Wiley (1986), pieces together a coherent vision of evolutionary economics based not on biological analogy but on principles of self-organization. From this basis, Foster (1997: 444) indicates four fundamental characteristics of economic evolution:

> Firstly, self-organizational development is a process of cumulative, non-linear structural change. Secondly, as such, it is a process which contains a degree of irreversibility. Thirdly, this implies that systems will experience discontinuous nonlinear structural change in its history; therefore, fundamental uncertainty is present. Fourthly, economic self-organization involves acquired energy and acquired knowledge which, in combination, yield creativity in economic evolution.

The point then is clear. Rather than being a theoretically troublesome aberration to be washed out of the analysis, structural change is instead viewed as a functionally normal part of the dynamics of open systems.

Now how does all of this relate to the geometry of economic space? The crucial point as stressed by Foster and Georgescu-Roegen alike, is that self-organization is a *process*. It takes place in time, and in so far as time is simply a device to prevent everything from happening at once, processes are not defined over fields. Processes are local and cumulative. As such, self-organizational processes are only meaningfully defined over a non-integral space.

## 2.4.5 Critique of All Things Linear, Closed and Determinant

This line of critique is arguably the most straightforward. An analytical description of a system is 'closed' when we can exhaustively define everything in the set of things that exist, and then permit nothing else to enter.[31] For instance, 'there are $l$ goods and $n$ agents'. Implicit in such formulations is that there is also a complete set of connections between the $l$ goods and the $n$ agents. It follows then that all reference to technological change, entrepreneurial processes, imagination, creativity, uncertainty and suchlike is excluded from the domain of analysis. Such phenomena exist only with respect to an open system, and in so far as they are regarded as important explanatory factors, the closed system format becomes the subject of critique. We broadly associate this with Schumpeter and the Post-Schumpeterians, Shackle (1979) and Georgescu-

Roegen (1971). It is evident that one cannot theorise about endogenously driven technological change, for instance, if 'technological space' is *a priori* defined complete (see in overview Dosi et al. 1988, von Tunzelmann 1995, Saviotti 1996).

It seems to me that there are two ways of interpreting this matter. The first extends from the logic of a field, wherein all connections are defined complete. For if it is significantly the case that new technologies, skills, organizational forms, strategies and other such 'building blocks' of the economic process are correctly inferred as simply rearrangements of extant building blocks (see Koestler 1969, Shackle 1979), then the element that has newly come into existence is, at base, the new set of connections. A new food technology, as a new recipe, rarely calls for fully novel ingredients (for example, the use of, say, aardvark) but typically advances new ways of combining commonly known elements. The same is essentially true of industrial and service technologies (as discussed in Romer 1990, or Saviotti 1996). And this is of course plainly recognized in the logic of a production function, but it supposes that it is only the change in the quantities of these ingredients (following from the assumption of universal substitution) that constitutes the underlying dynamic. It is this presumption that constricts change to be modelled within a closed system. In an open system it is not the relative quantities of ingredients that is the underlying dynamic, but the way in which the ingredients are put together. And if this is to be sensibly interpreted, then the complete set of connections cannot be meaningfully defined *a priori*.

The second interpretation in many respects follows from the first. In essence, if the connections are part of what is the technology or suchlike, then it is the case that the whole is greater than the sum of the parts. The Cartesian paradigm and the concomitant logic of a mathematical field is explicitly and absolutely based upon the principle that the whole is the exact sum of the parts. The context of such rejection of the Cartesian principle of summation is highly interdisciplinary and pivotal to all understanding of emergent structure and systems. I shall have much more to say on this matter in Chapter 3.

## 2.5  The Point of Departure

In sum, while neowalrasian microeconomic theory still retains a great many sagacious and faithful adherents there is also much dissent. Dissent from within is notable; for instance Kenneth Arrow (1986: 388) has remarked that 'in the aggregate, the hypothesis of rational behaviour has in general no implications And, indeed, there have been several such critical reflections from deep within (for example see Leontief 1982, Leamer 1983, Hicks 1986, Hahn 1991). However more direct assessments have come from without (see Georgescu-

Roegen 1971, Shackle 1972, Nelson and Winter 1982, Kirman 1989, Loasby 1991, Hodgson 1993, Lawson 1997, Louçã 1997). Coricelli and Dosi (1988: 126) summarize this sharply: 'The project of building dynamic models with economic content and descriptive power by relying solely on the basic principles of rationality and perfect competition through the market process has generally failed'. And it seems to me that we may trace these lines of dissent to a single point, arguing that the many criticisms of the neowalrasian system of microeconomics, spurring the various points of departure for the many heterodox schools of economics, can be generally and ultimately recognized to be the same criticism. It is a criticism of the 'sleight of hand' in the algebraic logic that conjures a set of elements in a space to then appear as a set of elements in a field.

On the other hand, critique from outsiders—the heterodoxy—must be set against a context of nebulosity. For instance, Simon (1979: 499) writes of the Institutionalists:

> It is not clear that all of the writings, European and American, usually lumped together under this rubric have much in common, or that their authors would agree with each others views. At best they share a conviction that economic theory must be reformulated to take account of the social and legal structures amidst which market transactions are carried out.

Much the same thing can be said about the explicitly evolutionary economists[32] and the Post-Keynesians and Neo-Ricardians. In important respects, those gathered under the separate rubrics of Austrian and Behavioural economics share a definite measure of accord, which, it would seem, can be attributed to the relatively singular nature of their epistemic and methodological origins. In contra-position the eclecticism within the Evolutionary and Post-Keynesian encampments is in certain measure to be associated with the ambiguities of founding documents and central notions.

Still, the overarching point I have endeavoured to make in this chapter is that the basis of commonality is something deeper. It is ontological. All heterodox schools of economic thought share the analytical presupposition that connections meaningfully exist within the economic system. It is this point that ultimately distinguishes heterodox from orthodox microtheory, in which no such concept is admissible. Notwithstanding this, there need be no definitive link between description and prescription and so we need not be concerned that the validity of the argument may fall on prescriptive differences of opinion.

I am not aware of any previous general critique of this singular nature (although compare Kornai 1971, Georgescu-Roegen 1971), but that ought not to be surprising, given that in itself it is essentially nihilistic and rebutted with (rightful) appeal to assumptions of sufficient abstraction and the requirements of analytical tractability. Yet I make this singular point of critique with a view to offering a general alternative formulation that incorporates what has been thus far excluded from first principles consideration. It is the deep consistency stemming from a singular form of critique that suggests that a general microeconomic system that incorporates the geometry prior to (and including) a field will be a microeconomics that can potentially sustain a unified heterodox paradigm.

## 2.6  Conclusion

The neowalrasian theoretical edifice might be imagined to look something like Figure 2.1. At the deepest level are a set of subterranean pillars (or axioms, as they are known) which are presumed to be the foundations. Resting upon these is the basement of the house containing the hard-core propositions, which are the translation of these axioms into statements about the economic object. Although the basement is open for public viewing, the economists who live in the house of the Econ[33] do not venture there. There is something of a superstition that it is haunted by the ghost of careers failed.

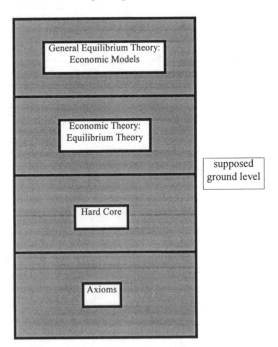

*Figure 2.1*  The house of the Econ

The first level above ground is equilibrium theory, which consists of a sparsely decorated foyer adjoined by a number of elevators. It is evident that the young recruits must pass through this foyer if they are ever to reach the upper levels. Whichever elevator you take, and they are helpfully marked by subject denomination, you end up in the same place—the great hall of general equilibrium theory. Here, craft stations scattered about the hall are devoted to the industry of building models.

The reports of those who have visited the house of the Econ vary. Some have been critical of the neoclassical architecture, but they are reassured that this is a style that never goes out of fashion. Many have been disturbed by what they saw in the basement, marvelling at how such a large house can be held together by such seemingly flimsy underpinnings. Others (for example, Leontief 1971, Leamer 1983) were concerned by its recycling policy, observing that the same trucks seem to deliver the same supplies of crude data every day. But on these and other such matters the visitors may well be mistaken. For despite such design and practices, the house still seems to hold together.

However notwithstanding these concerns, some visitors have reported a most curious and striking observation: the whole house seems to be floating in the air. The occupants insist that this is a delusional mirage, and impatiently point out that from the foyer one can clearly see the concrete steps that lead to the basement and in that basement is a series of vaults (unhelpfully labelled with hieroglyphics: continuity, transitivity, reflexivity, completeness, convexity, monotonicity, regularity) that are, it is assured, very secure. This last observation, that the house is indeed floating in the air, has been the subject of this chapter. I have further suggested that many of the critics' concerns about the inside of the house can all be made sense of in terms of this feat of levitation, which is achieved by the conjuring up of a very powerful economic field, $R^n$.

In conclusion, the foundations of an evolutionary microeconomics will not be manifest from an aggregation of the various negations of the axioms or hard-core propositions that so define the orthodox microtheory, and as such have *prima facie* appeared to be the obvious points of departure. This allows us to see the problem, but not the solution. For us to forge a path forward and to set a new system of economic microtheory it must further be seen that all such criticisms amount to the same criticism, which amounts to the simple statement that the geometry of economic space is not integral. Ergo, the basis for an evolutionary microeconomics must be one that derives from a non-integral geometry of economic space in which connections are afforded existence as a rudimentary building block of the economic system.

## Notes

[1] Following Clower (1995: 307), I shall use the term 'neowalrasian' (compare, Neo-Walrasian) throughout.

[2] Formally, $R$ is the set of real numbers. 0 is the origin of $R^n$ where $n$ is the number of dimensions. $R^n_+$ is a nonnegative orthant in $R^n$. So, for example, if $l$ is the number of commodities, then $R^l$ is 'commodity space'. Few textbooks that treat general equilibrium theory plainly express the foundational importance of this space. Ross Starr's (1997: 46–53) *General Equilibrium Theory* is a notable (and excellent) exception.

[3] Clower (1995: 316) playfully enters his conclusion thus: 'When straight talk comes from a child, it is called 'telling it like it is'. When it comes from an aging academic, it is more likely to be called 'sardonic', 'iconoclastic', or 'curmudgeonly'. Be that as it may, it is time someone 'told it like it is' for Arrow–Debreu general equilibrium analysis'.

[4] In the *Handbook of Mathematical Economics*, Frank Hahn (1982: 747) concludes: 'a great deal of skilled and sophisticated work has gone into the study of processes by which an economy could attain equilibrium. Some of the (mainly) technical work will surely remain valuable in the future. But the whole subject has a distressing *ad hoc* aspect. There is at present no satisfactory axiomatic foundation on which to build a theory of learning, of adjusting to errors and of delay times in each of these. It may be that in some intrinsic sense such a theory is impossible. But without it this branch of the subject can aspire to no more than the study of a series of suggestive examples'.

[5] Walras, however, did not neglect consideration of this, even if it was ultimately unnecessary for this mathematical framework. 'What must we do in order to prove that the theoretical solution is identically the solution worked out by the market? Our task is very simple: we need only show that the upward and downward movement of prices solve the system of equations of offer and demand by a process of groping [par tâtonnement]' (*Eléments*, 1874, section 125. Cited in Van Daal and Jolink 1993: 9). Yet as Van Daal and Jolink (1993: 10) maintain, the tâtonnement is a disequilibrium phenomenon and 'falls outside the scope of interest [as merely a] hypothetical scheme of what might have happened when the general bidding rules are applied to a pre-equilibrium situation.'

[6] See, furthermore, Bourbaki (1968: 312) on the concept of 'between' in Euclid.

[7] See Finch (1995) on the distinction between *action* and *behaviour* in Ludwig Wittgenstein's writings in the *Philosophical Investigations*.

[8] It was Euler who developed the first comprehensive mathematical theory of a continuous material media, applying it to fluids. Here the techniques of Newtonian point-particle mechanics were extended to deal with variables (density, velocity, pressure) as continuous functions of position and time. In this context, a field is a region of space in which each point is characterized by some quantity or quantities that are functions of the space coordinates and time. It is significant that the difficult problems of generalizing Newtonian mechanics to deal with continuous media were solved only by a deliberate neglect of the specific character of the material medium involved. This treatment ushered in the 'potential' theories of gravitation, electricity and magnetism associated with the above mentioned physicists and mathematicians.

[9] The recent work of Paul Krugman (1994, 1997) on the 'New Economic Geography' is more in the vein of the non-integral geometry of economic space that I am advancing. Krugman's approach draws upon Kauffman's (1993) model of 'complex landscapes' (non-integral space) to investigate the self-organization patterns of spatial agglomeration as the formation of particular linkages and self-sustaining webs. That is, emphasis is drawn to the existence of specific connections in economic space.

[10] The implication this has for a theory of liquidity and money will be obvious to Post-Keynesian scholars.

[11] By an arithmetic field we mean a number field. Examples are the set of all rational, real or complex numbers. In contrast, the set of all integers is not a number field because it does not exist over an arithmetic continuum.

[12] See also Thoben (1982), Norgaard (1987), Hamilton (1991), Rothschild (1992), Hodgson (1993), Louçã (1997).

[13] It is worth noting that in the 1940s, psychology flirted with formalistic notions of field theory to represent, with what was called topological and vector psychology, the idea of 'psychological space' (see Lewin 1952). Fortunately for psychology, the main import of the concept, the idea that behaviour is a function of environment, was able to be freighted through without sterilization or contamination of the rich empirical basis of the subject.

[14] Consider the logical equivalence between, say, an electrical field and the economic field construct of a pure exchange economy. An electrical field $E$ is defined over a space $R^k$ (constrained to $R^3$). We suppose that a set of charged particles $q = \{q_1,..., q_n\}$ is arbitrarily distributed over this space. Each $q_i$ is a $k$-vector. In corollary, the market is defined over a space $R^k$ (k unconstrained but finite). We then suppose that there exists a set of agents defining an allocation $x = \{x_1,..., x_n\}$ arbitrarily distributed over space. Each $x_i$ is a $k$-vector. The amount of good $j$ that agent $i$ consumes is denoted by the scalar $x_j^i$. If $R^3$ is represented by the dimensions $x$, $y$ and $z$ then at each point in the space a force vector can be defined $F(x, y, z)$ decomposed into $\mathbf{F} = F_x\mathbf{i} + F_y\mathbf{j} + F_z\mathbf{k}$. The strength of the electrical field at each point in $R^3$ is given by the vectors $(F_x, F_y, F_z)$ each parallel to the unit vectors (i, j, k). In corollary, if $R^k$ defines the space of $k$ goods (which for the purposes of congruence we define to be three: $x$, $y$ and $z$) then each point in the space defines a possible allocation $\mathbf{W} = W_x\mathbf{i} + W_y\mathbf{j} + W_z\mathbf{k}$, where $W_x$ is an $n$ vector and $i$ is the unit vector of good $x$. $W_x\mathbf{i}$, then, is an $n$ vector, as the sum of quantities of good $x$ held by $n$ agents. As the analogue of the force vector, we introduce the price vector $p = (p_1,..., p_k)$. The standard assumption is to regard the scalars $p_i$ as fixed, such that given $p$ then at each point in the space the equation $p.\mathbf{W} = p_xW_x\mathbf{i} + p_yW_y\mathbf{j} + p_zW_z\mathbf{k}$ describes the allocation scaled by $p$. As such, because $\mathbf{W}$ is an identity in $R^k$ then so too is $p.\mathbf{W}$. In sum, although in its dimensional and vectorial specification a market field in $p.\mathbf{W}$ is a far more involved construct than an electrical field in $E$ (as our representative physical field), the underlying logic of interaction is conceptually identical.

[15] As the impossibility of specifying contingent contracts for commodities that do not yet exist (for example, ruling out the possibility of innovation) or simply as the problem of missing markets.

[16] However, this point is usually associated with Iyla Prigogine's (1976) work on the thermodynamics of open systems, (for example, Allen 1988, Radzicki 1990, Buchanan and Vanberg 1991, Foster 1994, Schweitzer 1997).

[17] To define the mathematical concept of a field, first requires that we define the concept of a ring. A ring is an algebraic system defined as a set $R$ with a selected element $1 \in R$ and two binary operations $(a, b) \rightarrow a + b$ and $(a, b) \rightarrow ab$ which are both associative and commutative. An integral domain is a non-trivial commutative ring with no zero divisors. Two elements $a$, $b$ are zero divisors if $a \neq 0$, $b \neq 0$ and $ab = 0$. All finite integral domains are fields. A ring is an algebraic system defining the arithmetical processes or rules of combination (addition and multiplication) that can be defined over a space and the integral domain defines this as a continuous space. A field, then, is a non-trivial commutative ring in which every non-zero element $a$ has a multiplicative inverse $a^{-1}$. For example, the set of real numbers $R$ is a field, and in particular the real field has the special property of completeness (defined as every Cauchy sequence has a limit).

[18] And what of Adam Smith's division of labour and Allyn Young's (1928) dynamic reading of it into the evolving structure of economic growth? Why is the division of labour so absent from economic theory (excepting the introduction of most textbooks on microeconomics)? Because, in an integral space, the 'division' has already proceeded to its limit. It is quite insensible to refer to the division of labour from within an integral space. And so it is not done, and, in consequence, orthodox growth theory has been largely theoretical nonsense ever since.

[19] Given, say, three coordinate axes $x$, $y$, $z$ mapping a space $R^3$ then a scalar field exists when each and every point $P(x, y, z)$ in $R^3$ has associated with it a scalar quantity $\phi(x, y, z)$. A vector field exists when we define a vector function $F(x, y, z)$ for each point in $R^3$. For each point, the sum of forces can be defined as the sum of component parts parallel to the coordinate axes such that $F(x, y, z) = F_x\mathbf{i} + F_y\mathbf{j} + F_z\mathbf{k}$. A tensor field exists when we define the product, rather than the summation, of the forces.

[20] As Lucas (1972) succeeded in perverting Clower's formulation by placing it back into a field context with rational expectations. This re-established the field in the temporal dimension.

[21] Consider Keynes (vol. X: 262) in the context of a critique of Edgeworth: 'The atomic hypothesis which works so splendidly in physics breaks down in psychics. We are faced at every turn with the problem of organic unity, of discreteness, of discontinuity—the whole is not equal to the sum of the parts, comparisons of quantity fail us, small changes produce large effects, the assumptions of a uniform and homogeneous continuum are not satisfied'. Precisely.

[22] In Alchian's (1950) classic paper he correctly interprets that the Darwinian argument does not imply 'survival of the fittest', in Herbert Spencer's misleading phrase, but survival of the fit, as in those that fit with their environment. The concept of 'fitness' has nothing to do with health or innate quality, as is commonly misinterpreted, but refers to the sense of appropriateness in the context of a situation. Those that 'fit' survive, 'misfits' do not, wherein this 'not fitting' *is* what we refer to as the selection process.

[23] As Scitovsky (1993: 16) points out: 'It is not enough, however, that the number of competing sellers should be sufficiently large to enable the customers of one seller to shift their custom away from him. It is also necessary that all the buyers should know about the existence of alternative offers and that *all* of them should be prepared to shift *all* their custom in response to even the *smallest* change in price. This second condition is fulfilled only if the buyers are experts in the appraisal of the goods they buy, and only if they are experts in the strictest sense of the term' (emphasis in original).

[24] The literature on contestable markets (Demsetz 1968, Baumol 1982) can I think be well interpreted as a revival of field theory in which the word 'contestable' otherwise means 'potential'.

[25] See, for instance, Caldwell (1990: 64), Hausman (1992: 262) or Lawson (1997: 12–13), who are all critics of the hypothetico-deductive method and positivism.

[26] It should be noted that the Critical Realist school is by its very nature, inherently sceptical of formalistic methods of analytical capture.

[27] This is of course not a novel concept, and was pivotal to the theorising of both Hayek and Schumpeter. Stiglitz (1994: 204) writes: 'Perhaps the most important characteristic of an economy is its ability to adapt to changing circumstances'.

[28] The portrait of the agent that I shall develop in Chapter 5 is premised precisely upon an algorithmic expression of creativity.

[29] And indeed, precisely the sorts of questions that the nascent applied science of propaganda, which developed in the early part of the twentieth century (and thus paving the way for marketing, its mercantile offshoot), came to ask.

[30] Kirzner (1997: 64) writes: 'At the individual level Austrians have taken sharp exception to the manner in which neoclassical theory has portrayed the individual decision as a mechanical exercise in constrained maximization. Such a portrayal robs human choice of its essentially open ended character, in which imagination and boldness must inevitably play central roles'.

[31] The distinction between an open and a closed system is not the same as the distinction between a finite and an infinite number of agents (an infinite set of agents or commodities occurs when defined on a continuum, which is then sampled from). The finite/infinite distinction refers to properties of the limit of an equilibrium. The open/closed distinction refers to the nature of boundary conditions in process dynamics.

[32] See, for example, the introductory essays in Witt (1993a), Magnusson (1994) and Foster and Metcalfe (2000).

[33] Apologies to Axel Leijonhufvud (1981: ch. 12, 'Life among the Econ.') at this point. . . .

# 3. Economic Systems

*The whole is more than the sum of the parts.*
(Aristotle, *Metaphysica* 1045a, 10f.)

## 3.1 Introduction

There is no such thing as description without language. But different languages recognize the existence of different things. That was the point of the previous chapter. The use of the real field as a generalized analytical space (a paradigm, a language) did not enable expression of the concept of connection in much the same way that some natural languages have no verb tense; they function without them, but are expressively and conceptually limited because of that fact. To express the idea of a connection we need a language that has this concept as part of its structure. That language is graph theory.

A number of prominent theoretical biologists and systems ecologists have recognized that graph theory is a universal framework for the study of complex systems (for example, Green 1996, Kauffman 1993). An economist, Alan Kirman (1983, 1987b) has too. Graph theory is a powerful and obvious foundation for an evolutionary microeconomics. It enables the representation of a complex object as composed of two primitives: elements and connections. It enables us to track changes in this object as the discrete dynamics in either elements or connections. It enables representation of elements embedded within systems, which are themselves elements in higher-level systems (I refer to this as a hyperstructure). As such, it provides a foundation for the study of the dynamics of networks, hierarchy and, most significantly, of emergence. Finally, graph theory provides the geometric foundation for models constructed in terms of algorithms. I shall also show, as something of an aside, how a graph-theoretic framework can make sense of Aristotle's proposition about summation (at the head of this chapter).

When you learn a new natural language the objective is usually explicit and functional; you struggle for months with French, say, so you can communicate with the French. Graph theory, understood as a language, does not have such a purpose (and nor will it take so long to grasp the basics). Graph theory is a way of thinking, and it is a way of thinking, as I argued in the previous chapter, that most heterodox economists already do. Its rationale, rather, is to sharpen that

55

thinking, to provide a way of saying exactly what you mean, and, as a secondary objective, to *enhance* communication both within the heterodox communities and between heterodox and orthodox economists. It is a way of saying—this is what I mean, here is my model. And I would emphasize that this is precisely the same reason that powered the accession of field theory in the first place.

A graph-theory model looks like this: $S = (V, E)$. The crux of this logic for the evolutionary microeconomics is that connections $(E)$ are afforded the same ontological and analytical status as elements $(V)$. This concept can only be defined over a non-integral space, thus suggesting an important relationship: connections are the building blocks of systems, and these systems then become elements in higher-level systems. Once clear of the erstwhile field framework, we do not plunge headlong into some ill-defined analytical oblivion but emerge into a topographic framework ordered according to the logic of local structure, nested hierarchy and emergence. The purpose of this chapter, then, is to set these principles into the foundations of an evolutionary microeconomics.

First, we discuss the concept of connections afforded ontological existence. Second, the basic graph theory model is introduced and employed to define the analytical concept of a system. Section 3.4 then extends this framework to define a hyperstructure, which is a system of systems. The concept of system-element duality is defined in Section 3.5, and a discussion of the arithmetic of evolutionary systems is provided in Section 3.6. Section 3.7 concludes.

## 3.2 On Connections in an Economic System

Following from Chapter 2, the second of the 'first principles' of an evolutionary microeconomics is that connections exist. In the evolutionary economics research programme this ontological assertion is in the hard core. There are two hard-core propositions, both of ontological bearing.

Evolutionary-HC1: There exists a set of elements.
Evolutionary-HC2: There exists a set of connections.

E-HC1 does not differ fundamentally from the first proposition in the neowalrasian hard core, in that both essentially acknowledge that there exists a set of things that we may infer as agents, goods or some such. E-HC2, however, is fundamentally different from the neowalrasian hard core and is in contrast with the concept of a field. The concept of a field, as I have shown, is set up by the axioms of continuity, transitivity, reflexivity and completeness, plus the hard core propositions (Hausman 1992: chs 1–3). According to Weintraub (1985: 109), the hard-core propositions of the neowalrasian framework are:

HC1: There exist economic agents.
HC2: Agents have preferences over outcomes.
HC3: Agents independently optimize subject to constraints.
HC4: Choices are made in interrelated markets.
HC5: Agents have full relevant knowledge.
HC6: Observable economic outcomes are coordinated, so they must be discussed with reference to equilibrium states.

It is apparent, I trust, that the reader will now perceive that propositions HC2–HC6 are simply the dimensioning of the underlying field axiom into its intuitively relevant economic aspects.[1] They are all statements to the effect that there exists a set of connections and that this set is complete in all dimensions. Ergo, and this is the sleight of hand, it is as if, for all analytical purposes, there does not actually exist a set of connections. At the risk of labouring this point, it is not the case that the neowalrasian framework denies the existence of connections, clearly it does not, but in axiomatically treating them as complete it *effectively* denies that they exist in that they have no explanatory content. Instead, it is broadly within the heterodox schools of thought and in particular within the more explicitly evolutionary approaches that connections have re-emerged as central to analytical representation and explanation. Admittedly, a reading of this level of generality is not explicit in any particular heterodox treatment, but, rather, is the point of synthesis that I am advancing. As such, it will be worth briefly reconsidering the treatment of connections in heterodox theorizing.

Following the seminal work of Nelson and Winter (1982), which re-established the agenda of an evolutionary economics, theoretical approaches to evolutionary model building have proceeded in an explicitly microeconomic manner.[2] A microeconomic model is a type of story that is centred about what agents do and why they do it. And in the context of an evolutionary framework, and thus a process dynamic, a microeconomic model must further find some measure or identification of what is actually changing in the dynamic process of change. If we are to theorize about evolution then we must be clear about what it is that is actually evolving, which is to say that we must be able to distinguish the dynamic null state of 'no evolution' because a certain phenomenon has not changed (compare, Bedau et al. 1998). This is perhaps an obvious or trivial statement but it is absolutely fundamental and, it seems, it has been precisely the lack of explicit formulation of this basic prerequisite that has thus far impeded the development of a general theoretical framework of evolutionary microeconomics. The answer is simple: it is connections that change.

It was not until the 1980s that an evolutionary economics was reformulated to a sufficient degree to present itself as a definite theoretical possibility. Prior to then, Kenneth Boulding (1966) had performed a critical service in gathering the momentum of the evolutionary idea by making this point of critique the necessary basis of such a framework. For Boulding, the answer to 'what is actually changing?' is knowledge; a fundamental point also stressed by Loasby (1976, 1991) and Hayek (1945, 1974) and both in a similar metatheoretical context. Romer (1994, 1996) has also argued this point in terms of theoretical treatment of the growth of an economic system. Yet in pushing forth a highly eclectic fusion that lent heavily upon analogy with evolutionary biology, Boulding (1978) then made what I believe was a wrong-turning, emphasizing a genotype/phenotype distinction analogous to that pertaining in biology (also Alchian 1953, Gowdy 1985, Boulding 1989, Faber et al. 1996). The wrong-turning, however, was not obviously wrong, for the metaphorical concept of a genotype and a phenotype is clearly illustrative of the distinction between knowledge of how-to (genotype) and the resultant product (phenotype), and, moreover, the logic of evolutionary biology places the moment of evolution expressly in the genotype, which is also clearly applicable to the locus of economic evolution (Vromen 1995: 92).

In this respect it was an obvious yet difficult path to follow, a thick tangle of metaphor, metaphysics and metamathematics with only the foggiest sight of reference points. Yet it is Loasby (1976, 1986, 1991, 2000) who has most clearly seen through the haze, fixing 'the growth of knowledge' as the fundamental of economic change and evolution (see Harper 1994). My point of criticism does not pertain to this essential insight, but with the difficulties of analytical formulation it then requires. Identifying that knowledge is 'what is changing' centres the paradigm, but exposes a wide ontological and analytical flank. It begs the question 'What, then, is knowledge?'.

I suggest a more abstract approach. Admitting that what is changing is indeed knowledge, we may yet invest a conception of knowledge with a far wider meaning than either Boulding or Loasby, amongst others, attribute. Knowledge, in the abstract, is a specific instance of association. Technological knowledge, of the blueprint kind realized by moving discretely through production possibility space, is a set of combinations between factors (elements), and can be represented in geometric form as the specific connections between the specified elements in a space. This corresponds with the genetic meaning (and metaphor) that inspired Boulding, which is a DNA sequence as a set of elements (bases) in particular association (strings of base-pairs). Information is, in part, structure. Knowledge is a structure that can interpret structure.

Yet this knowledge does not map the integral of a production function, but rather consists of independent points each realizing a geometry of connections that we may classify as an instance of knowledge, or, as I shall propose in Chapter 6, a potential competence. A firm, in this sense, is both a set of resources (factors, in the orthodox model) and the connections between them. And this is the crucial distinction, for in the evolutionary microeconomics these connections are also to be regarded as resources of the firm. Structure has value, and can be thought of as an asset. The value of connections derives from the fact that they too are building blocks of such assets.

It is in this sense that we shall regard a firm as a system which is a more encompassing object than a simple factor endowment. The connections also form an endowment of the system, such that different connections would form a different system. In the neoclassical and neowalrasian models the firm is in a technology field so that the particular point it occupies on the production possibility map includes all other points (from a single point it 'knows' all other technologies and can implement them at will and without cost). Retreating from field theory, a firm is not effectively at all points in the space and therefore the particular connections it makes must be recognized to be inclusive in the resources of a firm as a system. Competence, then, is a (knowledge) resource. Foss (1996) and Loasby (1996) have both suggested that a competence-based theory of the firm will most likely be furnished with theoretical underpinnings from an evolutionary perspective (see also Hodgson 1999).

Technology is a particular set of connections, as is competence. Skills, habits and routines, in the context of a firm, can also be directly interpreted in this manner (Nelson and Winter 1982). But how far can we actually extend this conception? Is it the case, for instance, that all is knowledge, and that in the final analysis firms are to be understood as knowledge structures for creating further knowledge? If we follow this line of abstraction it becomes apparent that commodities, capital and labour must also then be knowledge. But this is not what we mean. Consider the concept of knowledge as constructed from a reduction to physical essentials. This would refer broadly to a stable relationship between a set of neuron connections which then form a cognitive interpretation system which then orders signals from the environment into a meaningful structure that can then be epistemologically codified and tested (Simon 1957). Knowledge is not a simple quantitative concept in this respect (and unlike mass or charge, for instance), and very much a subjective and constructed human phenomenon. But this is not to say that the concept of knowledge is hollow, totally without material basis. For when we generalize the concept of knowledge, as above, we take purchase upon what is surely its most objective aspect, namely the concept of specific connections. When we argue that technology, competence, skills, habits and suchlike are instances of knowledge, we mean by this metaphor that they are structurally similar to the epistemic phenomenon of knowledge in that they are instances of specific connections that seem to work in a particular environment.

The key transfer is the concept of a connection. Neurologists can point to synapses, identifying specific connections. Cognitive psychologists can map associations, as mental connections. Behavioural psychologists can identify constructs, as sets of connected associations. And Loasby speaks of knowledge precisely in this sense; not as an epistemic phenomenon, not an encyclopaedia of unrefuted facts, but as a structure of connections. The growth of knowledge, then, is the accumulation and flux of connections, wherever these may occur. The growth of knowledge is a metaphor, but its analytical bearing into objectivity fixes on connections.

In this respect the significance of an economic agent's assembly and use of knowledge is far wider than the theory of production and also encompass the skills, decision heuristics and habits of an agent, be they in the consumer, input factor or entrepreneurial context (see Boisot 1995). For example, Earl (1986) conducts an extensive critique and reconstruction of the theory of consumer choice, drawing crucial attention to the structure of decision heuristics and issues of information sufficiency and complexity. Extending the seminal work of Simon (1959) and Kelly (1963), Earl implicitly but outrightly rejects the field model of consumer theory so that the economic agent is functionally charged with the information tasks of gathering, filtering, organizing, processing, acting and reviewing as an interplay of imagination and habituation. The rejection of the field construct is achieved by incorporating specific connections pertaining to the agent's sources of information, the connections forming the agents information processing (decision heuristics), and the set of constructs (mental connections) with which the agent acts. The economic agent is completely reconstructed so that all internal and external connections are explicit. The framework is a synthesis of psychological foundations (Scitovsky 1976, Leibenstein 1976) and epistemic considerations (Shackle 1972), and also lends synthesis to newly emergent approaches to algorithmic modelling (Dosi et al. 1999) and consumer innovation and learning (Swann 1999). Like both Lawson's (1997) and Langlois and Robertson's (1995) fusions of Institutional, Austrian and Post-Keynesian foundations, Earl's eclectic framework is fundamentally singular and coherent, but not with respect to a field-theory framework. From a neoclassical perspective such instances appear rather *ad hoc*, but the point is that they are wrongly conceived from such a perspective. These three instances— Earl, Lawson, and Langlois and Robertson, among others—are concordant with respect to a framework of knowledge as connections, and structure as connections, and dynamics as change in the connections. Ultimately it is an ontology of connections that underpins the theoretical substance of these heterodox advances.

If an evolutionary microeconomics is to encompass the full domain of heterodox concern with the nature and dynamics of information, knowledge and structure then it will be based upon an ontology of connections. That is, a theoretical system in which connections between elements have the same ontological bearing as the elements themselves.[3] From the perspective of first principles, then, we define two components to existence in the specification of an economic system: the elements and the connections (E-HC1 and E-HC2) and it is the conjunction that forms the system, and the dynamics of the system are to be represented in terms of changes in the set of connections.

## 3.3   The Definition of an Economic System

> What is curious nevertheless is that in a world where the importance of the organisational structure of an economy is being more and more explicitly recognized, where external effects and who causes what to whom are more frequently discussed, where the question of the search for opportunities in a world of uncertainty receives considerable attention, and the question as to who learns what from whom is increasingly posed, in such a world a mathematical tool, graph theory, particularly apt to handle such problems remains largely unused.
>
> (Alan Kirman 1987b: 559)

If we want to think in abstractions about interaction then we should use the mathematics of specific connections says Kirman. But we do not. Why not? From the perspective of the previous chapter, it can now be seen that the reason graph theory remains unused is simply that its proper place is fully at the level of microeconomic foundations.[4] Attempts to fit it anywhere else will inevitably result in confusion unless it is plainly understood that the concept is incommensurable with all field-based theory.

A graph, $G$, is a mathematical object composed of two classes of sets— vertices $V$, and edges $E$—such that $G = (V, E)$. I shall modify the terminology immediately to reflect the specific ontological purposes required of it for economic analysis, the reasons for which will become apparent soon. A graph I will call a *system*, and denote it $S$. The other symbols I leave untouched, but will refer to the vertex set as *elements*, and the edge set as *connections*.[5] A system, then, is an object made of elements and connections:

$$S = (V, E) \tag{3.1}$$

The evolutionary microeconomics is a study of systems, and in that way it is a study of a set of things (elements) and the relations (the connections) between them. Let there be $n$ elements in a system, which defines the *order* of the system. The set of elements is denoted $V(S)$, but I shall refer to it simply as $V$, such that:

$$V = (v_1, \ldots, v_i, \ldots, v_n) \tag{3.2}$$

Let each element $i$ be connected to $k_i$ others, defining the *degree* of the element. The set of connections in the system $E(S)$ is then a set of binary elements, such as $v_1 v_2$, $v_a v_b$, indicating a connection between elements 1 and 2, or $a$ and $b$, and so forth. When a connection exists between, say $a$ and $b$, $a$ and $b$ are said to be *adjacent*. If two elements are not connected they are *non-adjacent*. We denote these individual connections $e_{ij}$:

$$E = (e_{ij}, \ldots) \tag{3.3}$$

When all elements are of the same degree $k$, the system is a *k-regular* system. It follows that the relation between $n$ and $k$ determines the total number of connections in the system, termed the *size* of the system, and denoted $M$.

$$M = {nk}/{2} \tag{3.4}$$

A standard way to represent the connective structure of a system is with an n×n matrix of 1s and 0s termed an adjacency matrix, $S(A)$. Suppose the set of elements and connections are as such (which may be represented as in Figure 3.1):

$$V = (a, b, c, d, e)$$
$$E = (ab, ac, cd, ae)$$

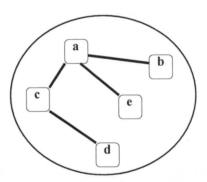

*Figure 3.1* A system

$S(A)$ is then a 5×5 triangular matrix with rows and columns corresponding to the elements of $V$, and 1s as described by the set $E$, else 0s. By definition the main diagonal consists of 0s (an element is not connected to itself).

$$S(A) = \begin{bmatrix} 0 & 1 & 1 & 0 & 1 \\ 1 & 0 & 0 & 0 & 0 \\ 1 & 0 & 0 & 1 & 0 \\ 0 & 0 & 1 & 0 & 0 \\ 1 & 0 & 0 & 0 & 0 \end{bmatrix}$$

The set of elements that are adjacent to any given element $i$ defines the *neighbourhood* of $i$, denoted $\Gamma_i$. We can now define two limiting case systems— a *null* system and a *complete* system—which serve to bound the *state-space* of a system, which is the set of all possible systems (connective structures) with $n$ elements. The number of possible states (particular connective configurations) that a system can occupy is in most cases large. There are $s$ distinct $n$-systems (Kauffman 1993).

$$s = 2^n \tag{3.5}$$

We may order the set of states of a system between two extreme states, a null system and a complete system. A null system is defined as the situation where for a set of elements $V$ there are no connections between any of the elements. If connections are interpreted to mean interactions, then in the null state no interactions occur, which is to say that no element is able to affect any other element. The null state is causally inert. For a null system then, the set $E$ is the empty set and thus the adjacency matrix $S(A)$ consists entirely of zeros. This is represented by Figure 3.2.

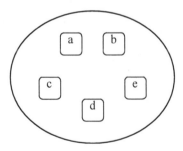

*Figure 3.2* A null system (no connections)

A complete system is where every element is adjacent to every other element and is a special case on the spectrum of state-space, otherwise known as a field. Every element is adjacent to every other element because of the complete set of connections. In terms of causal structure, a change in any element affects every other element. This can be described, for instance, by a system of simultaneous equations. A complete system might look like Figure 3.3, and is topographically equivalent to the topological construct of a field.

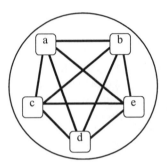

*Figure 3.3* A complete system

State-space includes these extrema along with all other possible systems for a given number of elements. For the case above where $n = 5$ it follows that $s = 32$. This is to say that there are 32 possible systems, including the null system and the complete system, that may be constructed with five elements. The range between the null and complete systems we shall term the range of incomplete systems, and this is associated with the concept of a non-integral geometry of economic space. An incomplete system is defined when $k < n$, mapping the domain of a non-integral space between the null system and the complete system. In this sense a non-integral space is associated with the domain of an incomplete system, and is the general case. The null system and the complete system (a field) make the special case. Figure 3.4 illustrates some of the states near the null state.

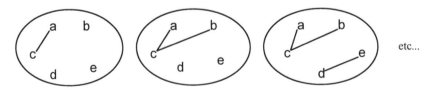

*Figure 3.4* Some states in state-space

It is to be noted that of the three systems sketched above, the middle one is adjacent in state-space to the other two because it differs only by one connection. It is evident, then, that each system will be adjacent to $n-1$ other systems, so defining the neighbourhood $\Gamma_i$. This relation is crucial to the nature of dynamics in state-space. For although it is the case that for a set of five elements in $V$ there are 32 possible systems $S$ that we may represent, from any particular state of a system there are only nine states that are adjacent and can be reached by a single change in the connective structure of the system. The significance of this relation becomes more apparent, I think, if we use a larger set $V$, say 20. For this there will be 1,048,896 states, but from any particular state only 189 will be adjacent (that is, approximately 0.02 per cent of all states!). The logic of a field, however, hides this problem by collapsing state-space such that all possible states are simultaneously potential. That is, there is no such concept of adjacency and every point in the field can be reached by a single change (as the logic of a technology or utility field). Further, if there is no such concept of adjacency (or neighbourhood) then there can be no concept of search strategies or of adaptation. The basic question is how does a system which exists at a point in state-space come to know whether or not it is at an optimum point, and when it does believe it is not at an optimum, how does it go about tracking it? We do not yet have an answer to the question of how an economic system moves through state-space because we have hardly acknowledged that a system actually exists at a point in state-space rather than as a 'potential' across the field of all possible states. The field assumption is far more analytically tractable, but it is an entirely misleading description of the nature of existence and dynamics of the systems that are the building blocks of the economic process. We return to this matter in the following chapter in the context of the work of Stuart Kauffman on adaptation in complex systems.

To see how this relates to the neowalrasian framework, it must be recognized that in that framework, the constructs $S$ and $V$ are identical (the set of elements *is* the system), such that $S \leftrightarrow field$, in $R^n$. Yet it remains the case that while these two frameworks are radically distinct in their ultimate analytical bearing, both begin with the same logical foundation of a set of elements in a space $R^n$. The evolutionary and neowalrasian microeconomic frameworks diverge, however, with the next step when we specify the form of interaction between the elements in the space. The essential theoretical difference between these two microeconomic frameworks is, then, that in place of a field the evolutionary framework constructs a set $(E)$. The set $E$ is the set of connections in the system, and each possible configuration then defines a state of the system which is a particular topographic geometry of economic space. The domain of possible geometric forms ranges between the null system in $S$, which occurs when there are no connections in the system ($E$ is the empty set), and the complete system in $S$, which is when every element in $V$ is connected to every other element. So constructed, a complete system in S is axiomatically equivalent to a field. The evolutionary microeconomic framework, then, encompasses the neowalrasian framework as a special case.

### 3.3.1 Example: A Firm as a System in State-Space

Consider, by way of example, a firm as a system in state-space. Suppose this firm consists of five agents (*a*, *b*, *c*, *d*, *e*) with a structure of connection as according to the example in Figure 3.1 above. By inspection it can be seen that element *a* is at the centre of this firm and element *d* the furthest removed. Consulting the adjacency matrix it can be seen that element *a* is of degree three (*c* is degree two and *b*, *d* and *e* are degree one) and has the largest neighbourhood of all elements in the system.

Other static properties include a relative measure of the centralization of the system. This can be calculated by taking what is termed the moment of an element (Robinson 1966).[6] The method is, for each element sum the number of connections between it and every other element as individual paths. This will calculate *n* moments, which we shall denote $M(V_i)$ as the moment of the *i*-th element in *V*.

$$M(a) = 5, \; M(b) = 8, \; M(c) = 6, \; M(d) = 9, \; M(e) = 8$$

We then take the minimum and maximum moment (*min* = 5, *max* = 9) and calculate the value of *m*,

$$m = \frac{\max - \min}{\min} \qquad 0 \le m < 1 \qquad (3.6)$$

We note that as *m* varies between 0 and 1, the system ranges from extreme decentralized to extreme centralized. In the above instance *m* = 0.8, which is tending towards centralization. Such a statistic is not so valuable in itself, but serves as a metric for comparison between different systems. It is to be noted that the moment *m* of a field is 0, (because all elements are adjacent to each other thus $M(i) = n$ for all *i*). That is, a field is by definition a model of extreme decentralization (compare, Stiglitz 1994: ch. 1).

The ratio of the number of connections over the number of elements, which we shall term λ, is also an important measure for the analysis of emergent properties in sets of connected elements. If there are *k* connections incident to each element, and *n* elements in *V*, then:

$$\lambda = \frac{k}{n} \qquad (3.7)$$

It is a well established result pertaining to random graphs[7] that for λ < 0.5 most elements in a system are isolated, but beyond 0.5 a phase transition contains most of the points within a single connected component (Erdos and Renyi 1959, 1960). State-cycles and closed loops, emergent complex behaviour, are not expected to occur until $\lambda > 1.0$ (Cohen 1988). In the above case, $\lambda = 0.8$ (coincidentally the same as $m$) and we therefore have a system that is entirely connected, but well short of a phase transition into emergent dynamic behaviour (Kauffman 1993: 307–12).

But most interesting, I think, is the application of graph theory to the study of adjacent states. Once past the initial identification problem of defining the sets $V$ and $E$, thus analytically constructing a single state, we can systematically map all states that are adjacent. This is done by simply flipping, one at a time, each entry in the upper triangle in $S(A)$, from $0 \rightarrow 1$, or $1 \rightarrow 0$. A complete system of order $n$ has $M$ connections; that is, there are $M$ places we can place a connection in a system of $n$ elements. By definition (from (3.4) and (3.5)),

$$\text{Number of adjacent states} = \binom{n}{2} - 1 \qquad (3.8)$$
$$\text{Number of total states} = 2^n$$

Thus for $n = 5$, there are nine adjacent states (corresponding to the number of elements in the upper triangle of $S(A)$ minus one; we do not count the present state). Thus from the present structure there are nine other states that can be reached by a single change in the connective structure of the system. As we seek to model the dynamics of structure, the first thing we need to define is the set of adjacent possibilities from each point, and, if we assume incremental change, then one will eventuate and also have nine adjacent states. In this way we can start to build up maps of the pathways taken by firms as they explore the state-space (of 32 possible forms between the null system and the complete system).

Of further interest, then, is how the number of adjacent states and the size of the state-space changes with a change in the number of elements. A number of points are immediately apparent. First, growth in the number of adjacent states and the total size of state-space increases in non-linear proportion with respect to growth in the size of $V$. If we add to this a bounded rationality constraint, such that an element can connect to no more than, say, seven other elements (see Miller 1956) then beyond $n = 7$ we expect structural decomposition to occur. That is, the ability of the firm to grow in the standard sense of adding more elements to $V$, is in fact conditional upon the position of the system in state-space. Which is to say that from certain positions the firm will not be able to grow, because all elements will already be of degree 7 (which is the constraint). However, from other regions of state-space the system may be able to grow in many directions. In this sense, the economic problem for the firm is not only the search of state-space by incrementally moving through adjacent states (see Allen 1988, 1993; Leydesdorff 1994) for global optima, but also avoiding becoming trapped on local optima (see Arthur 1989, 1994) and retaining enough flexibility such that the number of adjacent states is maximized. This problem will be discussed in a more general context in Chapter 4.

It may be objected that the above conception is no more representatively a firm than the standard model, but I would suggest that two major new dimensions have been added. First, a formal way of conceiving the space between extreme centralization and decentralization has been furnished. We may now begin to study the populations that live between these states, including Chandler's (1962) notion of U-form and M-form structures, Kay's (1997) maps of corporate synergy, and in particular the creation or emergence of networks as a major new form of business organization (see Teece 1992). This framework provides us with a way of ordering the relationships internal to a firm, and thus providing a structural metric that has been so conspicuously absent from theoretical work. Second, and more importantly, marginal difference is given a structural meaning with the concept of adjacency defining a neighbourhood. And, moreover, this adapts easily to consideration of non-marginal change, where many connections may be changed simultaneously so that a system may make a 'long-jump' in state-space (Kauffman 1993: 69–76).

## 3.4  System-Element Duality and Hyperstructure

A third foundational component of the evolutionary microeconomics is system-element duality, which expresses the concept that once a system emerges as an entity, although itself a complex entity, it can serve as a singular building block for a higher-level system. A system can itself be an element for a higher-level system and symmetrically, an element may itself be a system at a lower level. In this way routines build skills, skills build competence, competence builds firms, firms build industries, industries build economies and so on. There are many levels of systems in an economic system and the elements of each system $S$— that is, the elements of the set $V$—will themselves be entire systems at a lower level. It would be highly convenient from a mathematical and logical perspective to abstract from this complex stratified reality, which is what a field-theory-based approach does, but the cost of doing so is that we forgo all insight into the nature of emergence and hierarchy.[8] These are the twin principles by which systems are constructed into higher-level systems (emergence) and the resultant structure (hierarchy). More than anyone else, Herbert Simon has endeavoured to introduce these principles to economists (see Loasby 1989). This conception is wholly distinct from the paradigm either of atomism or of a field. Following Baas (1994, 1997), I propose to call this geometric conception 'hyperstructure', which he explains as 'higher order or cumulative structure'. A hyperstructure is a power set: that is, a set of sets, or, as in this case, a system of systems. The geometry of economic space is defined not as an integral field but as a topographical hyperstructure.

The evolutionary microeconomics combines the notions of emergence and hierarchy into a single construct: hyperstructure. A hyperstructure is a system of systems, or a system of systems of systems, and so forth where we may then speak of an *x*-level hyperstructure as the number of layers of emergence within. I shall deal only with 3-level hyperstructure as this allows us to conceptualize a primary system (a human agent) which is both made of systems (routines and skills, for example) and also an element in higher-level systems (such as a firm or institution). Thus, hyperstructure is the geometry created by synthesizing the concept of emergence and hierarchy, and system-element duality is recognition that the definition of an element or a system depends entirely upon the level at which it is viewed. The concept of an element or a system depends upon our frame of reference.

The following definitions apply:

1) Superscripts denote emergent levels of hyperstructure. We define a three level hyperstructure with integer superscripts 0, 1, 2. Thus $S^0$, $S^1$ and $S^2$ are respectively the zero-th, first and second level systems. So if $S^1$ is an agent, then $S^0$ would be systems interior to the agent, such as decision heuristics, and $S^2$ would be systems exterior to the agent in which the agent is an element, such as a firm.
2) Subscripts denote coordinate enumeration at a given level of hyperstructure. For example, $V_1^1$ is element 1 in system level 1. $V_2^1$ is element 2 in the same system. For the sets of connections, $E_{1,2}^1$ denotes the connection, if it exists, between $V_1^1$ and $V_2^1$. Symmetrically, $E_{1,2}^1 = E_{2,1}^1$.

A three-level hyperstructure equates the following nest of equations.

$$S^2 = (V^2, E^2) \qquad S^1 = (V^1, E^1) \qquad S^0 = (V^0, E^0)$$
$$S^2 = [(V^1, E^1), E^2] \qquad S^1 = [(V^0, E^0), E^1]$$
$$S^2 = \{[(V^0, E^0), E^1], E^2\}$$

Thus it follows that if $S^1 = (V^1, E^1)$ then, $S^2 = (S^1, E^2)$. Similarly, if $S^0 = (V^0, E^0)$, then $S^1 = (S^0, E^1)$. The duality condition (system-element duality) then is:

$$V^2 = S^1$$
$$V^1 = S^0$$

In general, system-element duality is defined by the identity:

$$V^n = S^{n-1} \tag{3.9}$$

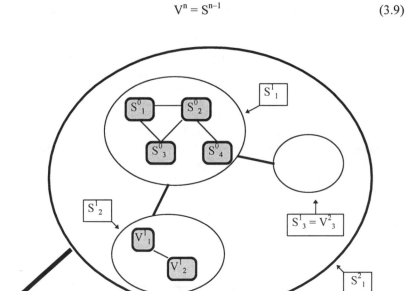

*Figure 3.5*   A three-level hyperstructure

*Figure 3.5 represents a system ($S^0$) embedded in a system ($S^1$) embedded in a system ($S^2$). It is a three-level hyperstructure, as might be agents ($S^0 \equiv V^1$) in a firm ($S^1 \equiv V^2$) in an industry ($S^2 \equiv V^3$).*

To summarize, the concept of hyperstructure is simply the concept of a system extended heirarchically. In this respect it is not a new idea, and has been fully presaged by early systems theorists (for example, Bertalanffy 1962, Koestler 1969). Herbert Simon (1962, 1981) has also presaged the scheme of this concept in his discussions of modular decomposable systems. The point I emphasize, however, is not so much the mathematical form (which has been suitably defined by others, Baas 1997) but its ontological aspect, namely system-element duality. The conceptual and mathematical framework of hyperstructure will certainly have analytical applications (see, for example, Kirman 1997b, Padgett 1997) but our present concern extends only so far as first principles. In short, system-element duality makes the identity of an element or of a system arbitrary. In the realm of the economic, there are neither absolute systems nor absolute elements. Whether something is inferred as a system or an element depends entirely upon one's level of analysis. This problem does not occur in the context of a field. To begin to make sense of this analytical paradigm we now turn to discuss the concept of building blocks of economic systems.

## 3.5 The Building Blocks of Economic Systems

Markets, hierarchies and networks are pieces of a larger puzzle that is the economy. The properties of the parts of this system are defined by the kinds of interactions that take place among them.

(Walter Powell 1991: 270)

### 3.5.1 On the Representation of Existence

In introducing and defining the framework of graph theory I have employed the terms element, set and system as if such terms were *prima facie* self-evident and unproblematic. Yet on closer inspection these concepts prove to be somewhat slippery. As it transpires, however, these concepts have always been vague of meaning, fudged by the concept of a field. Because an evolutionary microeconomics rests squarely upon such concepts, rather than obliquely, the measure of abstraction which proves acceptable for the orthodox analysis is wholly unacceptable for the heterodox framework. We shall thus unpack the concept of categorical existence in an attempt to make clear the nature of the building blocks of the economic process.

A system is made of elements and an element is defined as a member of a set, such that $v_i \in V$ *iff* $v_i$ is a member of (belongs to) the set $V$. By the term 'set' I mean a collection of objects, in which given any object it can be determined whether or not it is in the collection. Epistemically, either $v_i \in V$ or $v_i \notin V$ must be true for any $v_i$ if it is the case that we can define $v_i$ as an element and $V$ as a set. Mathematically, these definitions are simple and self-evident.

Yet mathematical definitions are only logical and not ontological: they describe relationship but not existence. Still, a purely concrete definition does not necessarily fare better. For instance, as the first Polish encyclopaedia (of 1834) insists: 'What a horse is, is evident to everyone'. This may well be, yet economic abstractions regarding elements and sets are not generally in the same league of self-evidence as Polish horses. The problem, however, is that they are typically treated as such, but without nearly as much candour.

In its atomistic mode, the neowalrasian microtheory defines the rudimentary units of an economic system—as factor inputs, commodity outputs and agents—in a way that is credited with being self-evident according to the form of the set definitions above. A commodity, for instance, is abstracted to an element in the context of a set, both as an individual entity $c^i_j$ (a particular banana in the set of all bananas) or as an entire class $c^i$ (the element bananas in the set of all commodities $c$). The typical textbook treatment of commodities is no more insightful than the encyclopaedic treatment of Polish horses, in that it acknowledges existence but provides no indication of the nature of that existence. Similarly, a firm is conceived as an element in the set context of an industry (or supply function), as is a consumer in the set context of a market (or demand function). Consumer and firm endowments are sets, as described by the term 'bundle'. These are presumed to be the building blocks of an economic system, in the sense of being the basic elements of the categorical sets.

The notion of categorical sets derives from the heritage of political economy, where factor based theories of value explained the emergence of value in terms of the mixing of basic elements. John Stuart Mill, characteristic of the Classical theorists, makes 'labour and natural agents the primary and universal requisites of production' (*Political Economy*, Book 1, ch. 4 § 1). Similarly, Böhm-Bawerk argues 'all production is the result of two and only two elementary agents of production, nature and labour' (*Kapital and Kapitalzins*, 1884 pt. ii, p. 83). This doctrine accounted for both the emergence of value and surplus, and was (and remains) in tidy accord with the tripartite of economic returns: wages, interest and rent. These notionally different income streams were and are thus associated with notionally different productive wellsprings. Thus the construct of categorical sets was well entrenched prior to the emergence of the neowalrasian microtheory and the associated shift of analytical emphasis from production to exchange.

The mathematical requirements of the nascent microtheory pivoted about the methods of the differential calculus, engendering, as Kirman (1987a: 493) notes, 'an implicit acceptance of the perfect divisibility of goods'. Kirman continues with this ontological point, observing that 'if we consider the most elaborate extension of the basic Arrow–Debreu model it is one in which there is a continuum of agents and a continuum of goods' (*idem*). In this context, it makes no sense whatsoever to conceive of the economic elements as anything other than abstract points in the context of a one-dimensional field (a continuum, $R^n$). The concept of a categorical set ($v_i \in V$) has been collapsed to a representative element ($v_i^*$) which has been interpreted as a point on a continuum ($v_i^* \in R^n$). In this way, the atomistic mode ($v_i \in V$) has transmogrified into the field mode ($v_i^* \in R^n$).

What has occurred, gradually and seemingly imperceptibly, is that as the spotlight of analytical focus has swung from production to exchange, switching attention from the study of the emergence of value to the distribution of value, and therefore from combinatorial methods to differential methods of analysis, the necessary requirement of integrability has taken root largely unnoticed and unquestioned (see further, Mirowski 1991a, Carlson 1997). Integrability, as the assumption of a continuously differentiable function, carries the implication that commodities, and indeed all other elements, are credited with possessing elementary point-like existence. As such, if a more general mathematical foundation will allow non-integrability then it remains for us yet to explore the sense in which economic elements are elementary.

Empirically considered, almost all formally conceived elements of an economic system are complex entities or structures. If we consider the class of consumer goods it is obvious that such things as cars, computers or clothing are complex entities, each a specific combination of many and perhaps thousands of component parts (and therefore technologies, Ziman 1998). We also recognize that 'negative combinations' belong equally to the same abstract category. In this way standard commodities such as sugar may also be regarded as complex entities, in that a specific set of negative combinations (refining, milling, and so on) were required to manifest the product. In other words, all economic elements, metaphorically speaking, are molecules. They are composite systems of particular combinations. From this perspective commodities are systems. In the orthodox microtheory, however, such concern is entirely irrelevant because a single parameter (price) suffices to locate the commodity in the market field (commodity space), thus collapsing the subject entity back from a system to a point on a continuum. All further information relating to the state of existence of the commodity is extraneous because in the context of a field, by definition, an entity cannot exist other than as a point. Elementary complexity, heterogeneity, modularity, decomposability and other such aspects of composite structural existence are logically excluded from a field-theory framework.

A small number of economists have advanced the (critical) observation of intrinsic commodity complexity towards theory—Houthakker (1952), Lancaster (1966) and Earl (1986) in the context of demand; Sraffa (1960), Robinson (1962) and Langlois and Robertson (1995) in the context of supply. Lancaster argues that it is not commodities *per se* that consumers value, but the characteristics they embody. Therein, a commodity is to be understood as a set of characteristics. Earl integrates this notion with the algorithmic form of the consumer decision process, recognizing that if there are manifold points of contact with each commodity (rather than only price) then the way these points relate to one another can systematically affect the outcome of the decision process. Drawing attention to the work of Simon (1959) and Kelly (1963), Brian Loasby (1991) has emphasized that the way agents mentally construct the world about them is of crucial significance to understanding the behaviour of the agents. For Loasby to make this bridge into the growth of knowledge as the ultimate basis of the economic process, it is implicit in his schema that the basic elements (of the economic process) are irreducibly complex. When theorizing about the behaviour of economic agents, we must recognize that this behaviour is with respect to something. The something will be variously other agents, commodities or, generally speaking, other building blocks. If these building blocks are complex, then our microtheory cannot logically be defined in an integral space, but requires a domain in which we can conceivably map the structure of interactions or relations between elementary units. Yet we have practically no systematic understanding of the multifarious relations internal to the set of all commodities in terms of object properties. Nor, in the same sense, do we have a map, as it were, of the typical patterns of interactions between agents constituting an economic system (although see Kay 1997). As has been sometimes lamented, the economic science contains a conspicuous gap in its empirical knowledge of the characteristic structural forms of the various subsystems of the economy.

Along these lines Leibenstein (1979) long ago proposed that 'a branch of economics is missing: micro–micro theory'. What Leibenstein means by micro–micro theory—as the study of what goes on inside the black box', and as associated also with the works of Scitovsky, Baumol, Marris, Williamson, Simon, Cyert, March and Day, among others—is essentially concerned with the study of individuals as complex entities. He observes that 'microeconomics has avoided the study of individuals but that is no reason why we should continue to do so' (Leibenstein 1979: 497), and moreover he suggests that the study of micro–micro theory may constitute the first clear sense of a research frontier in economics since the macroeconomic revolution instigated by Keynes. That was in 1979 and prior to the Nelson and Winter (1982) spurred re-emergence of evolutionary economics. I venture to suggest that Leibenstein's proposal equates now not as micro–micro-theory but as evolutionary microtheory.

Leibenstein, however, remained somewhat unclear about the ultimate nature of the micro–micro theory, and in particular, I think, failed to distinguish carefully between a theory of elementary units and the units of elementary theory. The distinction is crucial and revealed by the construct of a complex system as a theory of elementary units in which the elementary units are themselves lower-level systems. Once this principle is recognized, it becomes clear that the micro–micro theory in fact transcends the microtheory in generality. It is significant that every subject that the domain of Leibenstein's micro–micro theory addresses is of the abstract form of a complex system. The micro–micro theory is the study of a complex of elements and thus fits within the rubric of an evolutionary microeconomics. Evolutionary microeconomics, then, constructs in part the microtheory of microeconomics, addressing itself to the logic by which elements interact to form systems. But this, we may now recognize, overlaps with macroeconomics when the elements we identify are, say, entire production sectors or aggregate market demand (Leijonhufvud 1993). And herein arises the difference between Leibenstein's conception of micro-micro theory and the definition of evolutionary microeconomics that I propose. Essentially, what is meant by an element in the evolutionary microeconomics is entirely arbitrary with respect to the level at which this is identified. Yet we must simultaneously recognize that if both the part and the whole are both in the same sense an element then there must also be a referent system of taxonomy descriptive of the nested hierarchy of sets of elements forming higher-level elements.

### 3.5.2 Species of System

A taxonomy of sorts can be outlined in terms of five distinct species of system that seem central to the study of economic evolution. These are: (1) organizations as systems; (2) commodities and capital as systems; (3) cognitive and skilled agents as systems; (4) technology as systems; and (5) institutions (including markets) as systems.

It is not difficult to conceive of a firm as a system, in the sense that it is a set of component parts interacting in specific ways. Within any firm, individual actions are guided by the systematic specification of subordinate and superordinate relations, as pertaining to departments, teams, divisions and so forth, and by other forms of relation external to the firm, such as interactions with customers, suppliers or contractors. A firm, as a species of organization, is obviously a species of system. To be clear, the nest of definitions from a firm to an organization to a system is one of increasing abstraction along the line of structural form, such that the epistemic classification 'all firms are systems' recognizes that all firms are organic composites of separable parts.

In recognizing that a firm is a form of organization and therefore a species of system it follows that all instances of organization are systems. Evidently, then, we may regard commodities and capital, as well as durable goods and services as systems in the sense that they are all specific combinations of elements. It is easy to conceive of such goods as computers or automotive machinery as systems, in that they are complexes of engineered componentry, but it is perhaps more of a stretch to conceive of such primitive household items as toothpaste and paperclips, for instance, as systems. Yet all stocks and services are systems in that they are complex wholes. A paperclip is a definite refinement of wire into a particular form that exhibits a set of engineered qualities. That the virus is a more primitive organic system than the elephant does not diminish its status as an organic system, so too this principle extends to the set of systems traded and procured within an economic system.

The human agent, as a cognitive and skilled being, is also to be understood as a system in the economic context. The agent is a decision-making system in the sense of being a complex of rules for filtering and evaluating information. In a wider sense the agent is a system of constructs, and organic and social reflex (skills and routines) forming a behavioural complex that we may regard as a system. This perspective is well founded in the Behavioural school of economics, and, increasingly, in the algorithmic and computational approaches to rationality being developed within the Santa Fe school (see Morowitz and Singer 1995).

Technologies are systems by definition. A technology is the know-how of combination to form a complex outcome, with the elements of technologies themselves being other technologies. When we understand institutions as system we are recognizing that they are complexes composed of elements of social behaviour. The abstract concept of a system applies widely over the phenomenal domain of an economic system, such that we may identify the components of an economic system as systems in their own right forming populations of different species of system.

The simple point I make is that a single abstract concept—system—can represent a very wide domain of subject phenomena. By centring upon the concept of a system we bring institutions, technology and cognitive processes all under the same analytical rubric and therefore place them on the same conceptual basis as the more orthodox material components. By making our basic analytic object-abstraction a complex system we attain a great generality of analytical scope and clear identity of subject. This is essential if we are to hope to understand the phenomenon of economic evolution, which presents itself incessantly in qualitative form with the flux of technologies, institutions, skills and organizational dynamics in a penumbra about the more quantitative dynamics of linear growth. By defining a wide domain of systems we may effectively place the analysis of otherwise highly qualitative dynamics on a basis which is, in principle, well defined in respect of what is changing in an evolutionary process.

## 3.6   The Arithmetic of Evolutionary Systems

> One of the great opportunities . . . for the next few decades is the development of a mathematics which is suitable to social systems, which the sort of 18th-century mathematics which we mostly use is not. The world is topological rather than numerical. We need a non-Cartesian algebra as we need a non-Euclidean geometry, where minus minus is not always plus, and where the bottom line is often an illusion. So there is a great deal to be done.
>
> (Kenneth Boulding 1991: 3)

The scheme of the argument thus far has been essentially geometrical (specifically combinatorial). But a geometry also implies an arithmetic. In the spirit of first principles completeness, I now submit some remarks on the relationship between arithmetic and geometry in the context of an evolutionary framework. In the quotation above, which is from Boulding's introductory remarks to launch the *Journal of Evolutionary Economics*, he suggests that 'we need a non-Cartesian algebra'. But what is such a thing, and what is meant by the suggestion that we need one?

What Boulding is saying, it would seem, is that we need a way of making sense of the observation that the whole is not necessarily equal to the sum of the parts. This is an observation that many heterodox economists have, directly or indirectly, struggled to make analytical sense of. A system $S = (V, E)$ is a geometric object in which the parts are the elements ($V$) but the system itself ($S$) is more than the aggregate of these elements. The set of connections also makes up the totality of the system. But this concept cannot be expressed in arithmetic, at least not in arithmetic as we know it.

Nevertheless, here is a way of thinking about it. Consider the algebraic equation $1x + 1x = 2x$, and the underlying arithmetic equality $1 + 1 = 2$. We note that the cardinality of the operations (the '+') does not systematically affect the logic of the equality. For instance, in the equality $1 + 1 + 1 = 2 + 1 = 3$ the fact that there are two explicit operations of addition in the first part, one in the second and none in the third has absolutely no bearing on the status of the equality. But what if these operations were not neutral? That is, what if we could fold arithmetic back upon itself. This would be an algorithm that after completing the set of operations tallies the number of distinct operations involved, say, as an integer variable $\lambda$, and then multiplies this by a scalar $k$. The product $\lambda k$ would then correct the first-order sum (itself by an arithmetical process involving a further operator) to obtain a second-order sum, representing the equality. In this framework an epistemic equality can be drawn between, say, $1 + 1$ and any real number we choose as proportional to the parameter $k$. Note that when $k = 0$ the correction $\lambda k = 0$ and the second component of the algorithm makes zero contribution such that the system is effectively 'ordinary'. (This conception is not the same as a finite arithmetic, where a counting system periodically cycles back upon itself.) When $\lambda k > 0$ we have an arithmetical phenomenon of superadditivity. When $\lambda k < 0$ we have the phenomenon of subadditivity, where the whole adds up to less than the sum of the parts. This is not an argument that arithmetic is in a general sense arbitrary, such that the sum of any two numbers can be anything at all (I am not plotting to unhinge arithmetic!) but rather an exploration of the effect of treating the arithmetic operators as part of the same. This is, analogously, what is meant by considering connections (as explicit operators) as distinct from the concept of a field (which embeds operators).

Boulding has not been the only one to notice that arithmetic fails to account for basic features of social and organizational processes. This was a persistent leitmotif for the early systems theorists (for example, Bertalanffy 1962; Simon 1965, Koestler 1978; Koestler and Smythies 1969, Doyle 1976, Boulding 1978). Ansoff (1968) associated such non-summation with the concept of synergy, or economies derivable from shared resources. Kay (1982, 1984) further identified synergy with activities undertaken by firms, and in particular with firms that are involved in multiple activities. Synergy then becomes a story of why firms engage in multiple activities, form strategic alliances, and other such agglomerate behaviours. It is sometimes known as economies of scope (see Baumol et al. 1982, Langlois 1999). The primary observation, though, is that certain complex wholes, such as the collective activities of a firm, the behaviour of teams or the phenomenon of consciousness for example, are not easily reduced to the sum of the component parts. The parts seem to be only part of the story. The concept of synergy has arisen, as such, to express this seeming observation. But it does not in itself make sense of it, which was precisely Boulding's point. According to the extant mathematical logic, we should not witness this phenomenon. But to the extent that we do observe 'arithmetic violations', we may explain these in one of two ways: either (1) that we have failed to account for some part; or (2) that the underlying mathematical logic is inapplicable to the circumstance (and therefore not of universal application). The Cartesian paradigm always responds in the first way. The second way suggests, in effect, that there may be other forces at work rather than unaccounted elements. Synergy, then, is not an explanation of a phenomenon (it is not a theory) but a recognition that a phenomenon has occurred which lies beyond the theory. Synergy is to the theory of the firm what, for instance, phyletic punctuations in the fossil record were to palaeobiology: it is a recognition that the theory is, in a fundamental way, incomplete.

It is my argument that the framework of an evolutionary microeconomics can furnish the scheme of a theoretical explanation. To do so, however, we must translate this arithmetic problem into a geometric equivalent. Algebra is the branch of mathematics in which the procedures of arithmetic are generalized and applied to variable quantities, as well as numbers. In the abstract sense, algebra is the study of mathematical structures in which there are operations that have the properties of addition and multiplication (that is, groups, rings, integral domains and fields). Algebra also refers to the study of algebraic geometry, which interlinks the study of geometric objects, such as a conic section, with an algebraic description, such as a polynomial equation. In this way, arithmetic is the base of mathematics which consists of numbers and relations among numbers and algebra, then, is the generalization of arithmetic such that numbers are generalized to include variables, and relations are generalized to universal operations, as transformations and mappings.[9]

It is evident that the arithmetic operations that relate variables to one another have no systematic affect on the variables or numbers themselves. This is a rudiment of algebra and carries through to algebraic geometry with the concept of a field in $R^n$. However, we may interpret the argument of the previous chapter, in which a non-integral framework was a statement about the geometry of the space, in terms of arithmetic by noting that the same non-integral conception can be arrived at if the arithmetic operations themselves are not complete. In this case, synergy, or suchlike, can be given a geometric interpretation to the effect that the connection between the elements combined exists. The simple message is that in so far as our representation of an evolutionary system requires a new framework of geometry, then, by association, arithmetic will also be affected. But our recourse to explain perceived arithmetic incongruities must come from geometric argument. The arithmetic of an evolutionary system is simply an expression of the geometry of an evolutionary system.

## 3.7 Conclusion

> In economics, we have gotten the relationship between the system and its elements—
> that is, between the economy and its individual agents—backwards.
>
> (Axel Leijonhufvud 1993: 3)

At this point we now have before us the foundations of an evolutionary microeconomics set in the ontological dimension. Which is to say that we have now given analytical form to the way in which the economic process exists as elements which are variously connected such that they form systems that then become elements for higher-level systems, and so on. In this analytical framework, the concept of a set of connections replaces the concept of a field. In the neowalrasian framework there was only one component of existence—the set of elements—plus the construct of a field, which stood in for all issues of information, knowledge and structure. An evolutionary system of microeconomics reinstates these aspects with two components to existence—the set of elements and the set of connections—that then gives rise to a third mode of existence with the concept of a system. We may define this as a third entry in the hard core:

E-HC3: There exist systems. Systems are the basic objects of theory and
units of analysis.

The most significant aspect of this conception, from the perspective of heterodox theorizing at least, is that (like Einstein's reinterpretation of Newtonian space-time) space and time are interior constructs of the framework, and, moreover, they are non-integral. Evolutionary microeconomics rests squarely on the idea of essential incompleteness over the 'space–time' of connections. In this way, it is the existence or not of these connections that effectively defines the spatial and temporal dimension of an economic system. These dimensions do not exist *a priori*, but are created in the processes of economic coordination. By looking forward into the future, economic agents thereby create that future.

Many connections in the economic system are predominantly temporal, in that they extend most manifestly in the temporal dimension. Contracts are an obvious example, but so too are implicit contracts, goodwill, tacit understanding, repeated trading relationships, trust, familiarity, brand names, marketing mechanisms and other such phenomena. Skills, competence, strategies, habits and institutions are irrepressibly temporal in their mode of existence. When we speak of knowledge, uncertainty, expectations and suchlike we are projecting the domain of what we perceive to be the economic system forward into the future. Yet the framework of orthodoxy does not allow us to go there, rather it requires that the future be collapsed back into the present. Despite its temporal dimension, all neowalrasian theory denies time its primary reality: time is change. But where does such change have its effect? Certainly it moves and displaces the elements within the system, and the neowalrasian theory describes this well. But change also occurs within the connections between the elements, and as such upon the nature of the systems such connections then build. This is the phenomenon of economic evolution, and it is human behaviour that causes this phenomenon to occur. In many respects we are free to choose connections, in other respects many are chosen for us; there is also the phenomenon of self-organization, whereby systems of interacting elements tend to be connected in characteristic ways. This will be the subject of the next chapter. The point is that economic behaviour fully extends over the realm of connections and systems and there is a primary economic problem associated with this phenomenon: how do we, both as individuals and as collectives, make good choices of the connections that build systems?

There are many symptoms of this overly narrow circumscription of the economic problem to exclude the choice of connections, and thereby denying the existence of systems, and as such of higher-level structure. Broadly these come under the rubric of the so-called crisis in economic theory that has surfaced sporadically over the past few decades, but for any particular economist it is perhaps the sometimes suspicion that there is something fundamental missing from the picture. Whatever these may be in the particular, they can be gathered under a common theoretical form: connections, and therefore systems. And as such, the first principles of a new departure in microeconomic theory proceed from this ontological reassessment of the status of connections.

# Notes

[1] As such, a more compact description might be: HC1: There exist economic agents. HC2: There exists a field. The following concepts are embedded within the field: (i) preferences, (ii) optimization, (iii) markets, (iv) knowledge, (v) coordination. (Also technology.)
[2] For surveys, see Hodgson (1993), Witt (1993a), Dosi and Nelson (1994), Andersen (1994), Nelson (1995), Saviotti (1996), Foster and Metcalfe (2000).
[3] Although it does not follow that connections necessarily exhibit the same epistemic or material bearing. Navigation of this aspect is the task of the particular model, or, moreover, the particular assumptions which render the model tractable and epistemically valid. The ontological assertion

does nothing more than instate the logic into the theory (a model of course being a particular interpretation of a theory).

[4] It should be noted that graph theory is not entirely unknown in economic theory (see Kirman 1983, 1987b). For instance, Mirowski (1991a) employs this mathematical form to describe the structure of a closed loop of bilateral exchange and Kirman (1997b: 496) has described the Walrasian system of exchange as a complete graph.

[5] As Wilson (1985: 10) remarks, 'the language of graph theory is decidedly non-standard—every author has his own terminology'. What I call an element, graph theorists have variously termed a vertex, point, node, dot, cell, 0-simplex or junction. It seems to me that graph theorists use the terms 'system' and 'connection' when they want to be understood, and other terms (such as arc, join, locus, and so on) when they want to be precise.

[6] This involves the concept of the *centre* of a graph, which is a vertex $v$ with the property that the maximum of the distances between $v$ and other vertices of $S$ is as small as possible. It is a theorem that every connected graph has either one centre or two adjacent centres. The lowest moment occurs at the centre of a graph, the highest moment at a terminal vertex.

[7] A *random graph* is a graph where the vertices (connections) are assigned in some random way (Kauffman 1993: 205, 307). The main question of interest in the study of random graphs is when *percolation thresholds*, as large connected webs of elements, will form. These have been investigated as corresponding to emergence behaviour (for example, crystallization or superfluidity).

[8] Holland (1998) has recently advanced the proposition that emergence is a separate study in itself, distinct, for instance, from dynamics.

[9] See, for instance, Sklar (1974: 42–54) for discussion of the relation between geometry, algebra and space.

# 4. Systems theory and complexity

## 4.1 Introduction

The economic system is not a system, it is a system of systems. This is the essential point to grasp for analysis of the phenomenon of economic evolution. The building block of this nested framework is thus a system; but a system— defined as a state in state-space, such that the prime variable is connectivity— can be almost anything, from a set of unconnected elements ($E = \varnothing$) to a set of totally connected elements ($E = \Omega$). It is evident that there is a vast range of possibilities between these extrema, which is to say that the same set of elements can be connected in many different ways each defining a different system. There exists an entire spectrum of such systems. The first question that arises is whether these different systems exhibit different characteristic properties that we may associate generally with their location in state-space. In other words, is there anything general we can say about the nature of a system, such that it applies irrespective of what that system specifically is or the level of analysis at which the system is abstracted, in terms of the connective structure of the system? A second question then follows. Can any such statements about characteristic behaviour be linked to general principles of microeconomics? Can we reason from structure, through dynamics, to microeconomics in such a way that we may then turn the argument around to find the outlines of a microeconomics of dynamic structure, of connections? These are the themes this chapter will explore.

We proceed as follows. In Section 4.2, the concept of complexity is defined as a regime of coordination along an axial geometry of state-space. The geometry of economic space is argued to consist of a series of macrostates, which are the regimes of order, complexity and chaos. In Section 4.3, it is suggested that adaptive systems will converge near the regime of complexity. This is the hypothesis of evolution towards complexity and the crux of an evolutionary microeconomics. Section 4.4 then locates this approach to economics within a broader scientific paradigm on the nature of complex self-

83

organizing systems. In Section 4.5, discusses the relation between equilibrium, coordination and complexity, and in Section 4.6 the concept of dynamic efficiency is read in terms of complexity. Section 4.7 concludes with an outline of the positive heuristic of the evolutionary microeconomics research programme.

## 4.2 Coordination in State-Space

What is the complexity of a complex system? There is in fact no definitive answer to this question, but rather a multitude of answers, picking off different aspects of the phenomenon of complexity.[1] However, there are some useful higher-level distinctions.

An intuitive interpretation of complexity is to set it against simplicity or difficulty, and thus to locate its meaning in our understanding of, or rather our ability to understand, the external world. It seems that perhaps a majority of the complexity measures are actually of this form, consisting of measures of minimum description or of the describability of an object. In this way, the more difficult something is to parse and describe, the more complex it is. Complexity, then, is ultimately viewed as a property of understanding, and exists not in the mind, or in the external object, but in the relationship between the two. The problem, however, is that this is an all too subjective measure.

The complexity meaning favoured by Rosser (1999), which derives from Day (1994), is to define a complex system as a dynamical system that does not tend asymptotically to a fixed point, a limit cycle, or an explosion. Complexity, therefore, is located in the behaviour of a mathematical model of a system. Another general approach is to link complexity to information or entropy measures, and therefore to the definition of order, disorder and self-organization (see, for example, Wicken 1986, Shiner 1997, Foster 1997, Collier and Hooker 1999).

The meaning of complexity that is developed here is essentially the latter, in that complexity is located in relation to order and disorder (or randomness, defined entropically[2]) and strongly associated with self-organization. (Although my purpose here is to explain the micro-structural processes of self-organization, rather than simply assuming it.) As such, I mean something quite specific by reference to a complex system. The complexity of the system is located in its structural composition, and abstractly by the measure of connections over elements for some system. If we represent a system with graphical structure, so that $S = (V, E)$ defines a particular topographic state, then it is apparent that there is a vast number of ways in which a non-trivial system can be disordered, many of which can be found simply by assigning the set of connections ($E$) randomly. Similarly, there will be a number of states that display order, many of which would follow from regular structure in the set $E$. By implication, then, there will be a number of different ways in which a system can be complex. In this way, the construct of a complex system, then, refers to a particular set of topographic states. What we shall be interested in, in this chapter, is where such states are likely to occur, the properties they exhibit, and the implications this will have for microeconomic theory.

Consider a set of elements as components entering into a system. The specific state of the system will be determined by the connections that thread these elements together. Now consider the set of all such states (potential systems) arranged so that they can be placed along an axis. This axis defines state-space. State-space is the set of all possible systems that can be constructed from a given set of elements.

State-space spans two extremes: the null set (no connections), which we shall now denote $S = (V, \varnothing)$; and the complete set (complete connections), which we denote $S = (V, \Omega)$.[3] The axis of state-space, thus, is bound by the extreme values of the set $E$ ($\varnothing$ and $\Omega$). The adjacency structure of state-space then distinguishes all $s$ possible $n$-systems. Each system is adjacent to $k$ others, which is to say that from a single point in state-space then by changing a single element in $E$ (adding or removing a single connection) a system may move to an adjacent state in state-space. A path, as a sequence of states, through the adjacency structure of state-space may visit up to $s$ states in a traverse between $\varnothing$ and $\Omega$. However the shortest path between $\varnothing$ and $\Omega$ consists of only $k$ states.

Imagine, if you will, a chess board and a set of 64 pawns. The empty chess board corresponds to the null state ($\varnothing$). When we place all pawns on the board, each occupying a square, we have the analogue of the complete set ($\Omega$). It is evident that between these two extremes there is something of the order of $3 \times 10^{19}$ possible states, however it is also evident that the shortest path between them consists of only 64 steps, sequentially adding piece by piece. This path is independent of the order in which the connections (the pawns, in this instance) are added, which implies that there are $k{-}1$ paths of this minimum length (63, in this instance). Therefore we may construct an ordering of state-space by grouping all states that have the same number of connections (the same number of pawns on the board) as a homeomorphic group. There will be $k$ such groups, and this ordering defines what we shall term, following Kauffman (1993), the axis of coordination (see Figure 4.1).

$S = (V, \varnothing)$ |...............|.........|........................................| $S = (V, \Omega)$

*States of order   States of complexity           States of chaos*

*Figure 4.1* The axis of coordination (the state-space of the set E)

An alternative way of conceptualizing this is to make the axis of coordination the vertical scale and the connectivity ($\lambda$: $\varnothing < \lambda < \Omega$) on the horizontal axis. This plots the phase transition between order and chaos as a function of the number of connections in the system. Typically, this looks something like Figure 4.2, which displays obvious similarities to the logistic-diffusion curve (see Foster 1997).

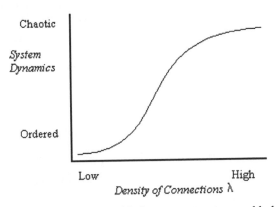

*Figure 4.2* The relationship between structure and behaviour

We shall consider first the nature of the extreme states. The null system consists of a set of elements, none of which are connected. A connection is a causal operator, such that if two elements $A$ and $B$ are connected then a change in the state of $A$ will affect $B$ in some specified way. So if $A$ and $B$ are binary variables connected by the rule $< A = 2B >$ then if $A$ changes, $B$ will be affected according to this rule connecting them. If there are no connections then a change at any point in the state of any one of the elements in $V$ cannot affect any other element, and thus we define the null system as dynamically stable. No element in the system is affected by the state of any other elements in the system. This temporal stability we identify as a state of extreme order.

A physical example of this state would be a block of inert matter. Consider it as a system of $n$ elements, but because no element affects any other in a dynamic way we conceive of this as an extremely ordered system. For instance, if we were to pluck out a single element from the surface of the block, nothing else would change; it would remain the same in all respects except for precisely the gap departed. An ordered system in the extreme is one that is entirely stable with respect to point changes in the elements of the system. This stability derives precisely from there being no elements coupled together, such that the state of any one part of the system is not dependent upon the state of any other part of the system. It is effectively frozen and as such the system of elements will exhibit orderly dynamic behaviour: aggregate change in the system of elements is exactly proportional to change in the sum of the changes in the parts of the system.

At the other extreme is the complete set in $E$, where every element is connected to every other element. Because every element is connected to every other, a change in any element in $V$ anywhere in the system will propagate to all other elements, which will then change each of them according to the scheme of the rule connecting them, which will then propagate back unleashing further escalations of change, and so on. A complete system is massively dynamically unstable because a change at a single point induces waves of change throughout the entire system. This state of temporal instability we shall identify as a state of extreme chaos.

Examples of extreme chaos in this connective sense can be imagined in terms of an electrical circuit consisting of say $n$ light bulbs, each wired to every other, and the switch determining whether any single bulb is 'on' or 'off' being a function of the state (on or off) of every other bulb. Such a model can be represented by cellular automata (CA) or random boolean networks (RBN), and the simulation results from such models are what intuition would expect: pure chaos. Although the state of each element is, strictly speaking, determined by the state of all other elements, the total result is massive (albeit completely determined) instability. A single change in the state of one element (as a bulb switches 'on' to 'off') then propagates to every other element, others of which will then switch states, setting in motion an escalation of feedback that we characterize as deterministic chaos (or white-noise). Natural systems which may provide examples are somewhat rare, because natural selection does not tend to favour such extreme states of chaos. Nor are extreme states of chaos to be found in economic systems, although computerized trading systems developed to their theoretical limit and operating with continuous data structures would certainly tend in that direction.

The extremes of a null system and a complete system are dynamically the extremes of order and chaos. This refers essentially to the structure of feedback and feed-forward where given a change in one part of the system, we are interested in what will happen to the rest of the system. If the system is the null system, such that there are no connections anywhere, then a change at one point will have no effect on any other element and the system can therefore be considered dynamically stable. We term this the state regime of order. Such is, for example, a situation of extreme autarky, each nation completely decoupled from every other. A situation of total self-sufficiency by each household within a nation would similarly constitute an instance of extreme order in the coordination structure of an economic system. If the system is the complete system then a change at one point will impact on all other points, setting off a chain reaction that will escalate into unbridled chaos. Imagine a stock exchange with six billion traders each responding to the signals of all others simultaneously. Also imagine that we start from the unique Arrow–Debreu equilibrium vector. Then imagine that someone sneezes, so to speak. At first everyone adjusts their holdings with respect to the single change, but then it becomes apparent that everything else has changed, and so on. As long as everyone stays connected the system will remain chaotic. However, the fact is that such extremes are for the greatest part theoretical extremes. Real systems are always intermediate.

A system moves through state-space by changing the connections within the system. When a connection is added or deleted the system moves to a different point in state-space. We can represent this analytically in the form of a discrete 'marginal' process. But what is the geometric nature of a dynamic path traced out by a series of such marginal changes? There are two primary hypotheses at this juncture. One, a system will move through state-space according to a continuous and linear function. Two, it will move sometimes continuously, sometimes discontinuously (see Rosser 1991). The Cartesian paradigm suggests the former but despite the pedigree of this logic (for instance, the legend *natura non facit saltum* is afforded unmistakable prominence on the title page of Marshall's *Principles*) it is wrong. It was the process of entrenchment of the marginal analysis towards abstract generality that demanded a denial of discontinuities in economic space (see Mirowski 1989, Louçã 1997). Nature does in fact make jumps, leaps and abrupt transitions (think of the changes of state undergone by water at critical temperature values, variously solid, liquid and gas), and biological and social processes make no exception to this natural logic.

A framework of state transitions can be conceptualized in a number of ways. Perhaps the best known is catastrophe theory, developed by the mathematician René Thom (1975). Catastrophe theory is geometry on a smooth surface in $n$ dimensions which is folded upon itself, such that a trajectory along a surface will at certain points in the space (cusp points) jump from one region to another. If we define the dimensions of a surface as spectral typologies or dialectical concepts, for instance communism and capitalism, then the surface itself will map out all possible combinations of each. That there are certain combinations that are impossible corresponds to 'folds' in the surface mapping. A trajectory that approaches one of these folds must, if it continues with the trajectory, jump across the impossibility region and this jump, this discontinuity, Thom mathematically identifies as a catastrophe. For instance, the recent transition from communism to market capitalism in Eastern Europe was not a continuous transformation crossing all intermediate economic modalities, but jumped from one state to another (see, for example, Kornai 2000). In the language of the theory, it crossed the fold of a catastrophe taking the elements of the system abruptly from one regime to another. Catastrophe theory, as such, constructs discontinuities by folding impossibility regions into the structure of space.

Another general approach is to construct bifurcation points in the state dynamics of a system (see Agliardi 1998, Rosser 1999). A bifurcation is a critical point whereby a deterministic trajectory is split into two or more possible paths, and which path eventuates is decided, as it were, by factors external to the factors descriptive of the trajectory. Which is to say that a critical decision is made in the path of the system, and this decision is determined by local and historically contingent circumstances. This phenomenon has captivated and spurred much recent work in technological and institutional dynamics. The concept of system bifurcations constructs discontinuity in space by setting up multiple future paths in which it is impossible to know which path will be selected prior to the selection actually occurring. The course of the future, thus, is fundamentally unknowable in this framework and cannot be reduced to probabilistic estimates. In this respect, this mathematical approach is closely related to the managerial concept of scenario planning.

In both such frameworks, a smooth geometry of space is overlaid with regimes separated by abrupt transitions (a catastrophe or a bifurcation). Within these regimes, the geometry of space can be considered smooth, or correlated (Kauffman 1993: 45), but between regimes are sharp transitions in the underlying parameter values. And it seems that, in general, the dynamical behaviour of complex systems is often to be associated with trajectories that involve several such regimes and thus transitions between regimes. The reason, simply, is that different regimes have different characteristic properties. For instance, deep in the ordered regime the information that can be said to exist (the structural coordination, the competence, the institutions and so forth) is locked securely into the system and cannot be easily changed by external forces. Deep in the chaotic regime the search of information in state-space is proceeding at its maximal rate (new organizational forms are being tried rapidly and at random, teams are being mixed up, institutions are in a massive state of flux, and so on). The problem is that in themselves these extremes are of relatively low quality; the ordered structure cannot adapt and if the environment changes it will be left behind. The chaotic structure cannot make use of the information it captures, because, like dreams, it is too transient to be useful (a good combination might be happened upon, then lost immediately). High-quality structure requires both at once, stability and flexibility, and this coexistence is precisely the nature of the regime of complexity. A complex system is one poised to switch most easily between regimes (or classes) of dynamical behaviour. That this regime switching is in fact typical of complex systems, rather than a special case (*natura non facit saltum*), has, as I later argue, the makings of a revolution in our theoretical approach to the study of the dynamics of social and biological systems.

If we arrange the sequence of states between the null system and the complete system, then, as discovered by the simulation of Boolean networks (see Waldrop 1992: 12; Kauffman 1993: ch. 5), the structure of this space demarcates three distinct macrostates: order, complexity and chaos. Order is associated with low connectivity, chaos with high connectivity and complexity forms a narrow window of low-to-intermediate connectivity between order and chaos. Each regime may be characterized by a dominant mode of dynamical behaviour. In the ordered regime most of the elements fall into fixed states of coupling with immediate neighbours. As such, a 'frozen' web of connections spans the system leaving behind small islands of unfrozen elements free to interact with one another in complex ways. The system's dominant behaviour is the continuation of the pattern that is frozen into the system, and thus the system is stable and dynamically unsurprising. This 'pattern' we may conceptualize as institutions, preferences and technologies as such, all frozen beneath the surface of economic activity. In the chaotic regime unfrozen elements span the system, leaving behind frozen islands. The system's dominant behaviour is a constant changing of the pattern displayed by the elements, whereby relatively few elements are able to fall into stable relations with other elements decoupled from the driving flux of the system. Most of the system remains in a state of boiling turbulence, as consequences wash back and forth across the system. Between order and chaos is the regime of complexity, a narrow band of state whereby the frozen web is just percolating and the chaotic regime is just beginning to decouple into islands of stability: no one state dominates.

The fact that no one state dominates means that the properties of both states of order and chaos can be simultaneously present, they can coexist. The ordered state maximizes the coherence and stability of information (structure or organization, as it manifests) but minimizes the experimental rearrangements of that structure. In the chaotic state the opposite applies, such that it effects a massive search of the possibilities within state-space, but is unable to lock onto any that are 'good' (as defined by some internal criterion). In the ordered regime the particular configuration of connections locked into (descriptive of preference, technology, institutions) may or may not be optimal in the sense that other combinations may be better, but the system has no internal mechanism to change to these states. As such, other structures cannot enter the web or are confined to the narrow islands that may not effect the rest of the system. In contrast, in the chaotic regime a new pattern may quickly span the entire system, but may then be just as effectively erased by a further transmission. In this way the regime of complexity, which is neither ordered nor chaotic but both, is a balance between information, pattern and coordination being usefully locked into a system (as preferences, technology, institutions) and the continued experimentation and search for new patterns and the maintenance of flexibility within the system so that these may then be adapted.

It is apparent, then, that the growth of knowledge is most likely to occur within and about the regime of complexity. Economic evolution can only occur within and about the regime of complexity. We would expect, then, to observe that economic systems will typically exhibit complex structure.

## 4.3 Evolution Towards Complexity

The hypothesis of evolution towards complexity is a conjecture to the effect that a balance between order and chaos, between stasis and change, is the ultimate principle underlying all evolutionary processes. Where equilibrium is the expression of 'balance' in an inert, mechanical world of point-like existence, complexity is the expression, the structural signature, of balance in a world of interacting dynamical systems. The hypothesis of evolution towards complexity is the logical principle that interlinks the geometry of all economic systems.

An equilibrium, in the sense of a mechanical balance, allows a change in one part of the system to be balanced by a corresponding equal but opposite change in another part, thus restoring equilibrium. A market equilibrium displaced by the exit of a buyer may be restored by the entry of another. A level of consumer utility disturbed by a price rise can be restored by corresponding substitution. Change in one part of the system, so disturbing equilibrium, can be restored to balance by reciprocal action elsewhere in the system. In its most encompassing sense, this is expressed as a hypothesis of general equilibrium. The hypothesis of evolution towards complexity is a connecting principle in the same general sense. Which is to say that it is a conjectural statement about the nature of the total interlinkages within and across an economic system.

To be clear about this point, general equilibrium is not a theory but a hypothesis. As I argued in Chapter 2, the theory part of general equilibrium theory is the substrate of field theory. 'General equilibrium' is the necessary hypothesis consistent with the application of field theory to the study of the economic process in an axiomatic framework (and hence requiring some existence proof as a foundation). The hypothesis of evolution towards complexity is implied in exactly this same sense, in that we may term it general complexity theory, but the theory aspect would derive from the study of non-integral spaces not from ihe epithet 'general complexity'. Equilibrium theory is set up such that the theorist or analyst must make careful distinctions between states that are in equilibrium and those that are not. Similarly, complexity theorists and analysts must first learn to distinguish between states that are complex, and those that are not. (In neither case is this presumed to be a trivial or straightforward exercise, but rather their primary endeavour.) Complexity, then, serves as the connecting principle linking together the components of investigation in the non-integral space.

If we assume complexity, in the same way that we may assume equilibrium, then we can invoke further hypotheses about the dynamic nature of the system. For instance, suppose one part of the system were to become more ordered, as may occur for example in the case of the vertical integration of a supply chain securing a single connection between a primary resource and several stages of transformation. The system has become more ordered in the sense that connections that were once in principle multiple and variable (a market supply of numerous possible connections) are locked into a single connection (the internalization of a previous market dealing). A complex balance is maintained, then, by another part of the system consequently free to behave more chaotically, which is to say experimentally. We suppose, by the hypothesis of general complexity, that a change in one part of a system to be either more or less ordered will either release or constrain another related system. When one part of a system becomes more chaotic, balance is achieved by another part becoming more ordered. The security gained by increased confidence in supply channels may unleash experimentation in the use of these materials. More generally, if this hypothesis is true then it suggests that all institutions— including markets, firms, decision heuristics and so on—are fundamentally interconnected through the geometry of economic space.

The hypothesis of evolution towards complexity arose in the context of investigation into the self-organization principles of genomic regulatory networks simulated with Boolean networks. The regime of complexity was discovered soon after the 'edge of chaos' was revealed (see Gleick 1987, Waldrop 1992). It soon became apparent that it was perhaps far more general than its initial application and true of an evolutionary process in general, in whatever substrate an evolutionary process happened to work through. It was recognised as a candidate 'general law' (Kauffman 1988, 1993; Bak 1996).[4] Kauffman centred upon the logic of an autocatalytic set, arguing, in essence, that there is no strong reason to associate a mechanism of selection with the emergence of order in biological systems. He contends (1993: 6):

> It is not that Darwin is wrong, but that the only got hold of part of the truth. For Darwin's answer to the sources of order we see all about us is overwhelmingly an appeal to a single, singular force: natural selection. It is this single force view which I believe to be inadequate, for it fails to notice, fails to stress, fails to incorporate the possibility that simple and complex systems exhibit order spontaneously.

Order and coordination arise in an economic system both by processes of selection and by processes of self-organization. The upshot is a free lunch; self-organization occurs spontaneously in the complex regime and, if the hypothesis of evolution towards complexity is correct, the process of evolution tends systems towards this state. Free lunches, in this sense, are the spontaneous emergence of order (for free), manifest as a situation where the whole is greater than the sum of the parts. This, as argued in the previous chapter, corresponds to the emergence of a complex system from otherwise free interactions. The emergence of systems, which are then able to act as elements for higher-level systems and so on, is what is meant by the emergence of order.

Kauffman shows very generally that the fundamental principle descriptive of the emergence of order in a complex system relates to the position of the system along the axis of coordination. This principle is remarkably simple: a low ratio of connections to elements produces order, a high ratio of connections to elements produces chaos. As indicated above, when each element is connected to only a low number of other elements, the system exhibits orderly dynamics. As the number of connections in the system is gradually increased the system passes through several phase-transitions to become, ultimately, chaotic in the limit of a complete system. Order is a product of low connective structure. Chaos is a product of high connective structure. For a system, economic or otherwise, to retain coherence and stability in the face of continual environmental change but still to adapt to this change, it will necessarily have low connective structure. With a bow to Simon (1962), it seems appropriate to think of this general principle as the keystone in the architecture of complex systems.

This keystone has two aspects. First, complexity is a macrostate and not a single state. Second, order arises in systems by the limitation of interaction to a low number of connections. Both of these points have previously been recognised in economics.

## 4.4   Economic Systems and Complexity

> The highest ambition of any science is to discover the laws of whatever Change is manifest in its phenomenal domain.
>
> (Nicolas Georgescu-Roegen 1971: 62)

### 4.4.1 The Smudge of Efficiency

The complexity of an economic system is the basis of its dynamic efficiency. The economic process functions not in spite of its complexity, but precisely because of it. Complexity is a dynamic optimum in the sense that departures from complexity, towards either the extremes of order or chaos, are in general to be associated with a loss of dynamic efficiency. A system that becomes too ordered loses the ability to change and incorporate improvements, it cannot coevolve with other systems in a harmonious way. A system that becomes too chaotic loses the ability to retain core structure and is catastrophically affected by every shock that touches its boundaries. Complexity, in this sense, is a balance between these states; a balance between rigidity and fluidity.

The association of complexity and dynamic efficiency is not new to economic theory.[5] George Richardson (1960, 1972) made a seemingly little known, but profound critique of the neoclassical microtheory in terms of the investment coordination problem endemic in a world of imperfect information. Essentially, Richardson argues that it is the frictions, imperfections, and collusive and information-sharing institutions that act to 'solve' the coordination problem, and enable the system to function without chaos. For Richardson, dynamic efficiency has little to do with the concept of static efficiency, such that were the theoretical conditions that define static efficiency to be fully enacted in a real economic system the result would inevitably be utter chaos and very inefficient use of investment resources. That is, there exist institutions, frictions and behaviours that enable the economic system to function as a non-chaotic process, and none of these are recognised in the neowalrasian microtheory.[6] Although Richardson makes his argument in terms of forward investment coordination, it is in fact far more general and resonant with Schumpeter, who also clearly understood the dynamic aspect of efficiency. Although Schumpeter rejected explicit appeal to biological analogy, his reasoning is prescient of the emerging paradigm of complex systems-based theoretical biology, and so too an evolutionary microeconomics. He writes (1954: 83),

> A system—any system, economic or other—that at every point of time utilises its possibilities to the best advantage may yet in the long run be inferior to a system that does so at no given point of time, because the latter's failure to do so may be a condition for the level and speed of long run performance.

So it is argued that the efficiency of an economic system is of two aspects, static and dynamic. Static efficiency is described by the neowalrasian model, and over an integral domain (the field $R^n$). Dynamic efficiency is associated with a non-integral domain, and specifically with the region of state-space near the transition from order to chaos.

The notion of a state of complexity being a macrostate was argued by Leijonhufvud (1973), where he theorized that macroeconomic systems tend to move within a 'corridor' of stability. Leijonhufvud argued that this conception was implicit in Keynes's *General Theory*, and that the formulations of the neoclassical synthesis severely misrepresent this implication. Leijonhufvud has since turned his attention to microbehavioural issues, but this notion remains in his thinking. He speaks, for instance, of agents possessing 'bounded homeostatic capabilities' (Leijonhufvud 1993: 8). Few others, however, have either advanced or afforded such a notion central place in their thinking about the nature of order, stability or efficiency in the dynamics of an economic system.

But then, strictly speaking, relatively few economists have actually given this particular matter serious consideration.[7] The mathematics of an integral or continuous space may define either multiple or single equilibria but always these derive as precise points (or, in the case of the core, a set of points). There is no sense of approximation, and the method does not generally aim to extract a solution region in which anywhere within may be considered an equilibrium. The mathematics is always precise. Indeed, the crest of scientific economics proudly displays the exacting nature of solution space, implicitly regarding it as a supreme virtue. But complex systems theory strongly suggests that this rudimentary and almost entirely unquestioned principle of method and analysis is, for the greater part, a wholly mistaken presumption.

When located in the context of time and ignorance, efficiency is not a precise point in space, as it is deduced in the context of a field, but is irreducibly a region of state-space. Dynamic efficiency is a smudge, a region of potentia, none of which can be separated prior to the unfolding of actual events. So although there exists a set of potential efficient points, and although retrospectively we may establish that of that set only one was in fact efficient, it is nevertheless impossible to establish this any faster than the actual flow of events allows. This is the consummate effect that pure uncertainty brings to the nature of economic action: it smudges quality over a region. As Shackle (1972: 416–7) explains, '[o]f its essential nature, uncertainty involves and veritably consists in the entertainment of rival, mutually exclusive hypotheses'. Uncertainty is multiplicity, variety, and projects its bandwidth onto efficiency as a direct mapping. This comes about simply because time and ignorance add a further aspect to the dimension of efficiency. For an entity to be dynamically efficient it must not only incorporate an immediate functional quality, it must also incorporate contingency. This contingency (with respect to the uncertainty born multiplicity) we may infer as flexibility, or the ability to adapt to changed circumstance (see Potts 2000). Simply put, quality has two aspects: quality of the known moment, and quality with respect to the unknown future. The orthodox understanding of economic quality, termed efficiency, is utterly of the first kind, and deals with the second by collapsing it into the first. Yet we may conceive of these two aspects of quality not as being neatly summed into each other, but, rather, directly trading off against each other. Dynamic efficiency, which is efficiency in the context of time, is a balance of these mutually opposing aspects of quality. This is captured by Leijonhufvud's metaphor of a corridor (also Heiner 1983: 578–9), yet not merely for macroeconomic systems but as a basic concept extended to all economic systems. Efficiency is a smudge, and all endeavours to bring this into point-like focus do so by pushing the dynamic aspect of quality further out of balance (Loasby 1996).

Moreover, we need not be scientifically unsettled by this weakening of a hallowed concept, for the smudge squares well with observation. Selection is a regime, selecting not the most fit or profitable or in some way optimal entity, but selecting a range of tolerably well fit. Selection as a filtering mechanism favours not the fastest, but the sufficiently fast, not the most profitable, but the sufficiently profitable. This is readily observable in nature and economy, whereby even the harshest selection environment yet still contains some measure of variety. But this observation did not accord with the mathematics, which, by the construct of a field and the operation of a limit, deduced a point not a smudge. Ergo, the observation of a smudge must therefore be of inefficiency, of imperfections in the selection mechanism, of weaknesses in the competitive process.

Robinson and Chamberlin drew attention to the persistence of imperfect competition, but generally speaking there has been little theoretical concern with the existence of variety. Notable exceptions are Steindl (1952) and Downie (1958), and more recently Eliasson (1991), Chiaromonte and Dosi (1992), R. Nelson (1994), Saviotti (1996), Metcalfe (1998), Tisdell (1998) and, broadly speaking, those developing the school of the competence- or capability-based theory of the firm and organization (see Foss and Knudsen 1996). However, the full implications have not yet been spelt out. The above, it must be recognized, delves only into the nature and consequence of variety in firms or production techniques as instances of particular systems. There has not yet unfolded a general account recognizing essential heterogeneity in all systems. This would be an impossible step from within the orthodox framework because it would require that the concept of efficiency itself be reinterpreted. There can be no such thing. And as such, investigation into the dynamics of variety has been very much fenced out of the orthodoxy.

Complex systems theory establishes that this trade-off between the demands of the present and the demands of the future—which is, we must acknowledge, precisely the nature of all economic actions—is bought into accord by the regime of complexity. In critical terms, this reconceptualization of the relation between statics and dynamics suggests strongly that the neowalrasian concept of an optimization and efficiency as a single unique state or point is a fallacy of theoretical application when applied to entities that are systems. The neowalrasian conception of efficiency applies only to things that have, or can be conceived of having, point-like existence. When our conceptual focus is upon the economics of systems and our analytical dimension incorporates 'time and ignorance' we can no longer sustain the abstract association of quality with singularity. Instead, we must conceive of a bounded regime, a macrostate, or simply a 'smudge' as the irreducible nature of dynamic efficiency.

### 4.4.2 In Praise of Incompleteness

The second point relates to the principle of order in a complex system, and, as Kauffman argues, a system achieves spontaneous order from a process of localization of interactions about a low number of inputs. Each element's behaviour becomes conditional upon a low number of other elements. There is no necessary specification of which other elements this may be: that is, the general result holds for sets of random interactions provided only that the input parameter is suitably low (Kauffman, 1993: 205). Thus the mystery of a spontaneous order in a completely decentralized market system, for instance, hangs only upon the behaviour of each element (agent) being conditional not upon everything, but only upon a few things. It is to be noted that from Adam Smith to Hayek and to Hahn (1970: 1), this basic question on the workings of a market system has remained unsolved in terms of the extraction of the underlying principle that leads to the emergence of the spontaneous order. And it is simple: incompleteness.

The general equilibrium model consists of a situation where, ultimately, everything is connected to everything else. However the reality of the functional order that emerges spontaneously in a market system is a consequence of precisely the opposite of that which is assumed to explain the logical workings of the market process. That the market system is, through extended chains of affect, totally connected only realizes consistency; the stability of the spontaneous order derives precisely from the sequential and mediated nature of total system interaction. As such, we may delimit the claim of general equilibrium theory to pose as an explanation for how market systems work. The fact is that the basic principle by which order arises in market systems occurs by a mechanism that the neowalrasian theoretical framework does not and logically cannot incorporate. The market works *because* it is imperfect and not in spite of it. These imperfections, and let us call them institutions in the widest sense of the word (Langlois and Robertson, 1995: 2), are not imperfections but evolutionary adaptations. They are not imperfections in the sense that their removal would take us closer toward perfection, but rather they are evolutionary adaptations, and without *a priori* status.

In other respects it is also not a completely novel point, and has been previously stated in terms of the stability of a decomposable system (Simon 1981). This relates to the construction principles of a system that can exhibit order amidst environmental turbulence by localization of effect by decomposition (see Heiner 1983: 583–5). The notion of decomposability is then associated with hierarchical structure and modular systems (Langlois and Robertson 1995), so establishing a theoretical basis for order witnessed in organizational systems. This theme is also found in Cyert and March (1963), who conceive of organizational slack as a systematic way of coping with uncertainty and environmental turbulence. Furthermore, hierarchy may be seen as a device for decomposing information or task complexity into manageable units (Mintzberg 1979, Kay 1997). Foster (1993) argues that this basic conception is clearly evident in Marshall's understanding of the fundamental importance of temporal irreversibility in the nature of the economic process. He cites Loasby (1978: 2), who explains that 'Marshall's endeavours to incorporate time as an essential component of his analysis are responsible for much of the careful imprecision so characteristic of the Principles'. Loasby's phrase, 'careful imprecision', captures elegantly the emphasis of the importance of historical, situational and institutional factors that Marshall attributed to the determinant of the economic outcome. The footnotes that Samuelson et al. were later to elevate to the status of essence were, it would seem, regarded by Marshall as overly precise. Which is to say that the rigour such techniques afforded did so by overtaking the factors that were the primary determinants of the actual process. As Loasby summarized (1989: 148),

> if actions are to be based on reasons . . . then the knowledge requirements must be reduced. Decomposability of the systems within which the decisions are made is a principal means of reducing these requirements, . . . Economies are stabilised by their institutions, in the widest sense of that word.

But these ideas are still very much in the realm of the particular, or rather, the implied generality (and typically the basis of inspiration) yet remains implicit. In other words, it is not *prima facie* evident that they are all ultimately speaking of the same thing, refracting into particular domains the same general principle. If so, then it would be this: modularity, decomposability, organizational slack, specific institutions and suchlike are all in abstract the same thing—they are all expressions of geometric incompleteness, and furthermore a particular state of incompleteness that, it would seem, corresponds to structural complexity.

### 4.4.3 An Illustration: Incomplete Contracts and the Complexity of Organization

The burgeoning literature on the new 'incomplete contracts framework' (for example, Grossman and Hart 1986) theory of the firm serves to illustrate this point. Coase (1937), Williamson (1975), Alchian and Demsetz (1972) and Simon (1959) may all be credited with initially establishing the link between bounded rationality, uncertainty, imperfect information, contractual incompleteness and the rationale of the firm. In further instance, Loasby (1976: 135) writes of the 'imperfectly specified contract which characterizes the firm'. The modern (and highly formal) incarnation of the incomplete contracts theory (see Hart 1995) defines the boundaries of the firm in terms of ownership rights to physical assets. The significance of incompleteness relates to incentive conflicts solved by the distribution of property rights. Property rights matter, in this theory, because they are sources of power (implementation of decisions) when contracts are incomplete. The rationale of the firm, thus, is the assignment of property rights solving incentive problems in the event of contractual incompleteness. Yet as Foss (1999) argues with reference to the work of Brian Loasby, contractual incompleteness can be seen in a very different way. Foss suggests that Loasby's view of incompleteness is related not to incentive conflicts, but to the building of capabilities through organizational learning. The point here is that incompleteness can be perceived in two fundamentally different ways: as a problem to be solved (Alchian and Demsetz 1972, Grossman and Hart 1986) or as the solution to a problem (Loasby 1976, Foss and Knudsen 1996).

Oliver Hart (1995: 1) suggests that 'the basic idea is that firms arise in situations where people cannot write good contracts and where the allocation of power and control is therefore important'. He later notes that (*ibid.*: 21) 'one important factor missing from the principal–agent view is the recognition that writing a (good) contract is itself costly', thus inducing the property rights approach. In the situation where complete contracts cannot be written, negotiation must occur after the contract is written and thus creating a function for residual ownership of factors. As property rights, these are the source of power when contracts are incomplete (Grossman and Hart 1986). Theory is then concerned with the efficient distribution of property rights (Hart and Moore 1990). The incomplete contracts literature thus tells a story of the boundaries of the firm, equating ownership of assets with the boundary of the firm, or, more specifically, property rights emerge to protect knowledge-based rents which arise in the context of incompleteness. So if there was perfect knowledge and it was not costly to write good contracts, firms, as governance structures, would not emerge. The orthodoxy is thus preserved.

Simon (1991: 26) has doggedly criticized the new institutional literature and related approaches for blindly retaining the centrality of markets and exchanges when pretending to deal with the theory of the firm. He explains,

> The idea behind these ideas is that a proper explanation of an economic phenomenon will reduce it to maximizing behaviour of parties who are engaged in contracting, given the circumstances that surround the transaction. . . . Access to information, negotiation costs, and opportunities for cheating are most often treated as exogenous variables that do not themselves need to be explained. It has been observed that they even introduce a sort of bounded rationality into the behaviour, with the exogeneity of the limits of rationality allowing the theory to remain within the magical domains of utility and profit maximization.

His criticism of such theoretical developments hinges about their explanation of organizational behaviour entirely in terms of 'concepts drawn from neoclassical economics [and] ignore key organizational mechanisms like authority, identification, coordination and hence are seriously incomplete' (*ibid.*: 40). In other words, these theories of incompleteness are still not engaging with the concept of a firm as a system (a behavioural system, as an information-gathering and -processing system). That is, they are endeavouring still to retain the allusion of integral space in dealing with incompleteness by loading all discrepancy onto the residual. For Grossman and Hart, it is not residual returns that is the heart of ownership but residual control (see Stiglitz 1994: 165). Residual control is the right to do with an asset anything which is not expressly forbidden by the contract associated with the asset. The fact that such a contract can never be perfect thus establishes the rationale of property rights. As I emphasized in Chapter 3, the employment of a residual enables the aggregate to be, by definition, the sum of the parts and therefore independent of how the parts are summed. Yet different governance structures are essentially different ways of summing the parts. The choice of different governance structures would presumably reflect the method of summation that is expected to result in the greatest aggregate given the different organizational (and psychological) properties of different systems.

This, essentially, is Loasby's (1996) point. Agents choose particular governance structures not primarily because they reduce transaction costs but because they expect to generate higher knowledge-based benefits. Which, as Foss (1999) emphasizes, is to be associated with the building of knowledge-based competence. These competences are assets ('knowledge capital', Foss 1996: 10), but not in the sense inferred by Hart et al. which necessarily attaches property rights. They are dynamic assets that exist in the context of an organizational system and do not exist independently of some embedding structure. The firm, then, is not a residual phenomenon but the antecedent to the existence of dynamic competence. Competence does not exist in the integral context because there is no rationale for the firm to exist as an embedding structure. The existence of the firm induces the existence of competence. At its logical conclusion, competence emerges because of (not in spite of) incompleteness.

## 4.5  Equilibrium, Coordination and Complexity

[T]he dominant feature of a holistic inquiry is the choice of the unit of analysis including the totality of its parts: this is the switch in metaphors which is going on in biology, from reductionism to holism, from the notion of survival to autopoeisis, from inheritance to emergence. Necessity and contingency: complexity, in one word.

(Francisco Louçã 1997: 99)

## 4.5.1 A Tale of Two Paradigms

The laws of mechanics describe reversible time: order is, was, and always will be. The laws of thermodynamics describe irreversible time: from order, disorder; and what is and was will no longer be. But something basic is missing. From where comes the is and was? In both mechanics and closed-system thermo-dynamics, order—the Newtonian clockwork, the 0th law of thermodynamics—is initially regarded as a self-evident fact or an axiom. In neither theory is there an internal explanation for the prior existence of order (Bunge 1959), which then respectively stays or goes. Evolutionary biology, in the form of the Darwinian revolution, was the first modern science to see through this stage, introducing the innovation of an internal explanation for the emergence and continuity of order. This explanation consisted of a coupling of two mechanisms, one divergent (the tendency to variation) and the other convergent (natural selection), to create a theory that accounted for the order observed in natural phenomena. This attribution of order wholly to the mutual workings of these two mechanisms is, when a mechanism of replication is also added, known as orthodox Darwinism (for example, Dawkins 1976). Order is the product of incremental and random modification honed and shaped by the force of selection. This is the story of 'descent with modification', a theory of random variation and natural selection. It is a story of orderly change, 'the supreme achievement of chance, operating under conditions of free competition and *laissez-faire*', as Keynes wrote (1971, IX: 276).

The Darwinian story has been challenged on many points, but the most persistent problem is the strict dichotomy in the twin mechanisms between randomness and determination, or, in Monod's (1972) more poetic phrase, which is the title of his book, between *chance and necessity*. The problem, and despite the theoretical elegance of such treatment, is that it is not at all clear that these mechanisms are independent. This problem has been highlighted by the contemporary study of complex autocatalytic systems (Schweitzer 1997). In such systems, randomness and determination, chance and necessity, are simply different aspects of the same thing. That same thing is complexity and self-organization.

There is an irreducible complexity in nature and society, in living systems, whereby the mechanism that induces variation and the mechanism that selects from that variation are both aspects of the process of self-organization. In this sense, Kauffman (1995: 25) argues that 'much of the order in organisms may not be the result of selection at all, but of the spontaneous order of self-organized systems'. And by the same token, much of the order (and supposed equilibrium) in an economic system may not be the result of 'market selection', which is the total presumption of the modern neoclassical school, but a spontaneous order of self-organized systems (Anderson et al. 1988, Arthur et al. 1997). Hayek (1974:

24) also argued that the subject matter of economics 'deals with essentially complex phenomena', providing an early version of economics as the study of organized complexity. Hayek, like both Schumpeter and Keynes, clearly perceived the problem: small effects can sometimes produce large consequences, and typically these come from within the system. It is not the case that the economic system is internally determinate, buffeted only from the outside; rather, change continuously erupts from within, feeding self-transformation and self-organization. In such cases, the supposed random component is endogenous and the determinant component is a mostly non-linear relation, feeding back in often surprising ways. And this is precisely what complex systems theory tells us to expect: complexity is neither random nor determinant, but both simultaneously and inextricably.

The point is that static equilibrium, being an atemporal field concept, tells us nothing about the nature of order in an economic system. The question of order is a question that asks of the emergence and stability of patterns of connectivity between elements, or, more directly, asks how coordination actually comes about. General equilibrium theory is not an explanation of why economic systems work as coordinating devices (Loasby 1991). It is the mistaken belief that GE theory is such an explanation which has arrested the development of a general framework of economic coordination (for example, in the vein of Richardson 1960, or Leijonhufvud 1973) and conspired to misrepresent many pivotal contributions and insights to this question as *prima facie* irrelevant. It is perhaps a rather uncomfortable thing to admit, but admit it we must: we, as economic theorists, have not yet furnished a comprehensive and deep understanding of how economic systems work, in the sense of the way in which they function as coordinating devices and the principles by which order is achieved in a turbulent environment. We have many important insights, and general equilibrium theory is of course part of this, but we do not yet have a coherent explanation. The question 'What is the nature of the order in an economic system?' simply does not make sense within the equilibrium-based paradigm of a field. In this context, equilibrium *is* order. Similarly, the question 'How is an economic system coordinated?' neither makes sense. For it is implicit that equilibrium *is* coordination (*pace* Debreu 1959).

Yet the study of such phenomena as dissipative systems (for example, see Prigogine and Stengers 1984), whereby a spontaneous order arises far from equilibrium, reveals plainly that the question of the nature of order is a very different question from that of the nature of equilibrium. On this distinction a new paradigm in science has emerged.

### 4.5.2 The Paradigm Shift

The Cartesian paradigm of science investigates the nature of order as the nature of equilibrium by posing the question in terms of organized simplicity. Observations and identifications of order are perforce associated with equilibrium phenomena such as cyclical or harmonic motion (planetary orbits, periodic waves, pendulums) and therein associated with a clean distinction between deterministic and stochastic forces (and, in turn, the wholesale use of the *ceteris paribus* clause to keep this distinction clean). In this way, order derives from the deterministic component of action and is uniquely associated with the equations of motion. Any departure from determinant motion is therefore the result of stochastic and exogenous shocks. The culmination of this paradigm is the Hamiltonian equation (or, similarly, the Lagrangian formulation), where dynamics are fully specified in terms of a vector of initial conditions and a set of dynamical equations constructed in terms of some conserved quantity. This extreme form of mechanistic determinism, as exalted by Laplace (and echoed by Friedman 1953, who then quite falsely invoked prediction as the ultimate goal of science), eventually proved untenable in physics for a number of fundamental reasons. Notwithstanding the impracticality of perfectly known initial conditions, in both measurement (identification) and computation, it soon became apparent that none of this mattered anyway because of the logical impossibility invoked by quantum indeterminism. However, the more subtle aspect, which has ultimately been revealed to be the most significant, is with respect to the nature of the dynamical equations themselves.

If dynamical equations are coupled to each other, such that there exists irreversibility and feedback, then a number of criteria are weakened: (1) stability is not guaranteed; (2) convergence is not guaranteed; (3) a unique path from cause to effect cannot always be defined (see Mirowski 1988a: 16–22). Lorenz (1963) demonstrated that deterministic equations could produce chaos, a state of nature mostly indistinguishable from the product of a purely stochastic process. Essentially, the clean distinction between determinism and random factors is a very special and artificial case, and something not to be found anywhere in the realm of complex organization.

Yet orthodox economics is totally committed to the logical structure of an absolute distinction between deterministic and stochastic forces (Louçã 1997), and every endeavour to transcend this mechanical reductionist approach has induced only further strident commitments to entrench axiomatisation and extreme reassertions of agent rationality (for example, Debreu 1959, Lucas 1975). And for the greatest part this has misunderstood the implications and theoretical context of a melding of determinist and stochastic events. The underlying fact of the matter is that the distinction between stochastic and deterministic forces is a necessary consequence of the field abstraction.

For instance, a most fundamental result in mathematical economics is the existence proof of a general equilibrium, which makes use of a topological argument known as Brouwer's fixed-point theorem (for example, see Mas-Colell 1985). This result has absolutely nothing to do with dynamics, concerning only the topology of initial conditions. The existence proof is that given a field of all possible initial conditions, if we treat this as a topological space then somewhere in that space is an equilibrium vector. Dynamics have been developed along a mathematically somewhat separate path (Smale 1980; Goodwin 1982, 1990; Day and Chen 1993). This distinction is important. The neowalrasian analysis involving several time periods is not dynamics, but topological analysis of initial conditions. All states are in a topological sense equal (all of the same homeomorphic group, as all points in the space can be continuously transformed into one another) and hence there is no distinction between ordered and disordered states.

Moreover, because of this equivalence, there is no meaningful conception of time; continuous transformations are reversible transformations. Because all states are in this sense equal, all modes of disturbance or propagating forces or whatever must necessarily be located outside the system. Outside of the system means outside of the theory, and therefore to be treated as stochastic exogenous shocks. The system itself is presumed orderly and coordinated. But order and coordination have entirely empty meanings in this setting. 'For decades, coordination has been identified with general equilibrium' observes Louçã (1997: 352) and 'soon coordination became just a logical game for orthodox economics'. Coordination is read in its mathematical meaning, that is, a vector co-ordinate, and not in its verb sense, which as defined in the *Collins* Dictionary is 'to bring into order as parts of a whole'. This latter conception was what the issue of coordination meant to Hayek (1933: 129–31), and his notion of a 'spontaneous order', as also to Richardson (1960, 1972) in recognition of the coordination problem of both competitive and complementary investment. The Austrian and Shacklean notion of coordination, as associated with the entrepreneur, is also interpreted in this sense (Shackle 1972, Kirzner 1973, Buchanan and Vanberg 1991).

This issue is wider than economics. There is increasing recognition that a single principle may be behind the existence and nature of order in many phenomena of complex organization. This single principle is, essentially, self-organization and complexity as a critical balance between order and chaos. It is being recognised that for the domain of the chemical, biological and social sciences, existence and change cannot be parsed into representation as equilibrium statics and exogenous dynamics without destroying the very essence of what they are trying to represent. In these domains of complex organization, existence and change are one and the same thing. In other words, what is meant by coordination is a selection of connectivity—of which elements are connected to which others—and that this occurs with respect to the requirements of both existence and change at once. The balance is complexity.

Indeed, a contemporary revolution in our understanding of the basic dynamical principles of natural law is presently emerging a new paradigm of science, the science of complexity.[8] This contemporary revolution is occurring in most domains of science, from cosmology and particle physics, through chemistry, geology and biology (see Nicolis and Prigogine 1989), to the study of socioeconomic processes and cultural dynamics (for example, De Vree 1997). Mirowski (1990: 289) rightly points out that

> We are living in the midst of a profound rupture between older and emergent notions of scientific explanation. The very meanings of order and chaos, the deterministic and the stochastic, are being reconceptualized in this decade, and it is fair to presume that things will never be the same.

Louçã (1997: xi–xii) concurs, observing that

> In the recent decades, the scientific discontent with traditional positivism has mounted to unprecedented levels, opening a major paradigm shift. New research programmes have been developed in the direction of the incorporation of change, choice, contradiction and dialectics; causality could no longer be restricted to deterministic processes, and the very pretension of natural sciences to be the purest form of cognition has been weakened in a broader concept of the plurality of knowledge.

The new paradigm of complexity and self-organization deals squarely with the question of the nature of order in complex systems. And this is of rudimentary importance to the methodology and theory of economics, which, perhaps more than any other subject (and despite the field-theory foundations of neowalrasian microtheory), is phenomenally concerned with the dynamics and emergent order of complex systems.

In sum, equilibrium and order are not the same phenomenon. Equilibrium and coordination are not the same phenomenon. Disequilibrium processes can generate order, and coordination can be the result of self-organization and complex feedback. Coordination means order only when both are interpreted to mean equilibrium. It is true that equilibrium is equilibrium, but not much else follows from that. As indicated, there is currently something of a contemporary scientific revolution in the making, and its centre is to reinvest coordination and order with analytical meaning. This is achieved by interpreting both concepts with respect to complexity. Complexity is not equilibrium, but in certain contexts complexity does mean coordination. The upshot is that order and coordination are meaningless and dead concepts in relation to equilibrium.

However, with respect to the concept of complexity, these notions are reinvested with meaning and analytical significance.

## 4.6   Complex Economic Behaviour and Efficiency

Our treatment of first principles is almost done, but there is one final concept to consider. If the economic system is a complex hyperstructure of systems of connected elements, what does this then imply about the nature of economic behaviour within such systems, and what, then, is the economics of such behaviour? Presently, I shall only cut a somewhat impressionistic outline, yet this nevertheless indicates the basic principle. It is this: in the context of a changing or otherwise complex environment, efficiency is complexity.

Immediately, we must circumscribe and qualify this statement. Efficiency, in both the pedestrian and technical meaning of the word, denotes a quality of a behavioural outcome that minimizes waste or lost opportunities. More broadly, efficiency is often attributed to be a quality of markets, in the sense that a market can, under certain conditions, be said to effect an efficient allocation of resources. It must of course be stressed that it is the allocation that receives the metric of efficiency, not the market. The reason is simple, there are no markets in the theory that defines such outcomes (Clower 1995).[9] This claim to the effect that an allocation is efficient is known as the Pareto efficiency condition. We need not go into the subtleties and profundities of this matter, we simply note that the allocation and the Pareto condition both apply to a single state interior to a very high-dimensional manifold of possible states. Of the many, only one is efficient.

The logic of complexity challenges this presumption, a presumption that is a direct consequence of the analytical scheme of a field. Dynamic efficiency, however, is not a single point but a region of space. I discussed this above and talked about 'the smudge of efficiency' and praised 'incompleteness', but still, I left unanswered the issue of what actually constitutes efficiency.

Above I claimed that 'Complexity is a dynamic optimum in the sense that departures from complexity, towards either the extremes of order or chaos, are in general to be associated with a loss of dynamic efficiency'. The implication is that a system can achieve complexity or not be complex, just as a system can achieve equilibrium or be in a state of disequilibrium. Yet these respective concepts are defined over different domains. Equilibrium is defined in terms of an allocation, which may be represented by a set of vectors; for example, the set $V$ in an integral space. Equilibrium is a special vector $V^*$ in the space of $V$. Complexity, however, is defined with respect to the set $E$. The choice problem for the orthodox framework is the selection of a bundle of goods, or some such, with the set of all bundles defining the allocation. The choice problem for the evolutionary microeconomics is the selection of a set of connections, in $E$, and it is suggested that an efficient set of connections will be a complex set of connections.

The reason for this suggestion, or hypothesis, is conceptually the same as that advanced by Kauffman (1993: 279–81). In essence, the requirements for successful behaviour by agents in both the biological and the economic environment involve two mutually conflicting constraints: order and change. Order means efficiency at a point in time, which in the biological realm means being well adapted to the conditions of the given environment, and in economics means an optimal allocation. Change means efficiency at future points in time, and in the biological realm means the ability to adapt to changes in the environment, and in the economic realm it means much the same thing. The field construct in economics in fact defines this change to be, effectively, instantaneous and frictionless. The plain fact, however, is that change is not easy. This observation is all too apparent in ecology. Panda bears, for instance, need not become extinct, they simply must substitute to other food sources and other living conditions. But for Panda bears this is not so simple; they are very much locked in to a particular environmental circumstance. They cannot change in short order. The economic world is, in significant part, very much of the same nature.

Order and change must be traded off against each other, we cannot have both (again, *pace* Debreu 1959). The more we adapt ourselves to a given circumstance, the less we are suited to changed circumstances. The more we prepare for all possible contingencies, the less we have devoted ourselves to the extant circumstance. This is a fundamental economic problem, and one that does not exist in the orthodox framework. The question is how do we decide what the balance between the known present and the set of all possible futures is when it is impossible to know the set of all possible futures? Nature itself has answered this question: complexity. Overconnection, when the state of our lives is a function of almost everything causes chaos, literally. Underconnection, when our being is a function of only a few things locks us in too much; unexpected changes leave us stranded, frozen. Neither extreme is a universally viable strategy.

The underlying principle is that each agent, each semi-autonomous system, will be dynamically efficient if its connective structure is complex. It remains for us to refine what this means in empirical terms; certainly it will be somewhere intermediate between the null state and the complete state, but it will require comprehensive investigation to shed light on the approximate position of this regime of efficiency along the spectrum of state-space, and upon what factors, if any, it crucially depends. All I have endeavoured to do at this point is to suggest the nature of the problem, and the scheme of the solution. I have asked 'what is dynamic efficiency?' and answered 'complexity'. We now pass this concept forward from first principles into the research programme of an evolutionary economics, and to the study of the phenomenal nature of complexity.

## 4.7  Conclusion

> Equilibrium is a fascinating intellectual toy. But it is irrelevant to the real problems of economics, and should be dropped from our vocabulary.
>
> (Jack Wiseman 1983a: 23)

In Chapter 2, I argued for a fundamental distinction between economic theory in terms of an integral and a non-integral space. This established the necessary framework to define a system as a geometric object in non-integral space. In this chapter I have been concerned with a basic question: where within the total domain of a non-integral space would we expect to find economic systems? The first point was that we would not expect to find them at the extremes (a null or complete system). But this is not to say that the extreme points are not without identifiable qualities. Extreme order, the null system, is absolutely stable, and a system thus composed will not be affected in any surprising ways by point changes in any of the particular elements within the system. If it is at an optimum in the neighbourhood of state-space, it will not easily be displaced from it. Extreme chaos, the complete system, is a full-blown search of the set of possible states. If there is a global optimum in the neighbourhood of state-space, the complete system will find it. Yet these qualities are only part of the story. If the null system is not at an optimum, it will not be able to get to one. If the complete system finds an optimum, it will not be able to lock onto it. Each extreme state can be improved by tending towards the other extreme. The working expression of this is the hypothesis of evolution towards complexity. Abstractly considered, a system will require properties of both extremes if it is to be able to adapt to a changing environment, but yet make use of the good adaptations found along the way. This balance is achieved within or near the regime of complexity, and thus, as a working hypothesis, we may then associate this regime with the concept of dynamic efficiency.

The hypothesis of evolution towards complexity is a connecting principle that gathers together prima facie separate and disparate investigation of systems in the context of the economic process into the same analytical framework. Firms are systems, as are markets, agent's heuristics, technologies and institutions, and the principle by which order, as coordination, arises in all is the same: low connective structure. We expect, by hypothesis, that the specific connective structure will tend towards the regime of complexity as the system adapts itself to bring stability and flexibility into balance. This process occurs entirely within the non-integral domain of the set $E$. The hypothesis, then, gives us a basis from which to reason how changes in the structure of one system may impact upon other systems in a web of interactions. The hypothesis of evolution towards complexity therefore suggests that the total economic process will, in time, attain some kind of overall critical state balanced between extremes.

The ideas sketched above are first principles. There is an enormous amount of work yet to be done, but the outlines of how we are to proceed can, I think, now be discerned. This, I suggest, makes up a subset of the positive heuristics (derived from first principles) of the evolutionary microeconomics research programme thus:

Some Heuristics of Evolutionary Microeconomics

PH1: Recognize economic problems as involving both allocation and coordination dimensions, but separate these dimensions with respect to the set $V$ and the set $E$. Focus on the set $E$.

PH2: Attempt to locate the system under investigation within a hyperstructure. Identify the systems nature of the elements and the elementary nature of the system. Extract, then, the three different levels of connections.

PH3: Locate the system, in terms of its connective structure, on the axis of coordination. Furnish reasons for its seeming location in terms of the requirements of stability or flexibility. Attempt to find exceptions that would refute the hypothesis of evolution towards complexity.

PH4: Focus upon discontinuities in the behaviour of the system that seem indicative of phase transitions. Identify the direction of the transition. Search for simultaneous points of flexibility and stability in different dimensions of a system's behaviour. Hypothesize that these will be in balance.

PH5: Identify dynamic efficiency with complexity. Search for cases where allocative efficiency implied dynamic inefficiency. Search for cases when allocative inefficiency implied dynamic efficiency. Investigate the linkages between dynamic efficiency and change, broadly defined, in different species of system. Link dynamic efficiency to bounded rationality, uncertainty and knowledge.

# Notes

---

[1] The number of 'complexity measures' is quite staggering, as it seems every other research scientist or theoretician who enters this field produces their own definition and measure. For physical systems, see Crutchfield (1994) and Gell-Man and Lloyd (1996). For 'human systems', Biggiero (1998) identifies three main classes of complexity: logical complexity, gnosiological complexity and computational complexity. Horgan (1997: 303) chronicles over 60 measures. Edmonds (1999) contains a detailed discussion of 48 different *types* of measures, and includes a bibliography listing hundreds of papers on this topic. In economics, there has also been a surfeit of classifications. Andersen (1994), for instance, distinguishes between data complexity, problem complexity and system complexity, which, he regards, can equally be distinguished as entropic complexity, logical depth and organizational complexity. And still there is no end in sight.

[2] Entropy is a concept that applies to both energy and information. According to the classical statistical interpretation (of Boltzmann, Gibbs and Shannon: see for example, Georgescu-Roegen 1972), entropy is taken to be a measure of disorder. In this sense, information is a decrease in entropy so that maximum entropy is associated with zero information when the system is completely random and maximally disordered. In this way order and disorder are laid out along a spectrum, graduated by the measure of entropy (where entropy is of the standard form $S = \Sigma\, p_i.\ln p_i$).

[3] Note that in the terminology of graph theory a complete system (graph) and a connected system (graph) are different concepts. For a system to be connected, it is sufficient that from any element there is a *path* to any other element, irrespective of how many edges make up this path. In a complete system, every element is connected to every other by one and only one edge.

[4] For discussion of the relation to economics, see Scheinkman and Woodford (1994).

[5] For a sociological take on this phenomenon, see the very interesting book by Burt (1992).

[6] A further, and much overlooked, point we might recognize is that if all resources are allocated efficiently in a neowalrasian equilibrium with zero transaction costs, then no resources will be allocated to the management of change.

[7] Compare Cohen and Axelrod (1984) with Stigler and Becker (1977).

[8] Key references tracking the development of complexity theory can be found in: Bertalanffy (1962), Simon (1962), Lorenz (1963), Emery (1969), Nicolis and Prigogine (1977), Eigen and Schuster (1979), Jantsch (1980), Prigogine and Stengers (1984), Clarke and Crossland (1985), Mandelbrot (1987), Anderson et al. (1988), Ebeling and Ulbricht (1989), Kauffman (1993), Stonier and Yu (1994), Bak (1996), Mainzer (1996), Stocker et al. (1996), Arthur et al. (1997), Schweitzer (1997), Bossomaier et al. (1998), Rosser (1999).

[9] For an evolutionary approach to markets as complex computational systems, see Mirowski and Somefun (1998).

# 5. The Microeconomic Agent

## 5.1 Introduction

The overarching failure of orthodox microeconomics is that it has not engendered a plausible and scientifically interesting model of economic agency. *Homo economicus*, otherwise 'rational economic man', is an entirely one-dimensional, purely hedonistic stimulus-response function.[1] *Homo economicus* is not the result of the study of human behaviour but a derived mathematical artifact, with every compass point of its being dictated by the requirements of the axiomatic framework in which it is embedded. There are literally scores of critics and volumes of criticism directed at the unreality of the neowalrasian model of economic agency, but despite this there has not yet emerged a general alternative model that satisfies both an account of the main dimensions of human economic behaviour and then locates this within a general framework. In this chapter I construct an alternative model: *hetero economicus*.

The conception of human agency I shall assume derives from Voltaire, who, in the context of introducing the concept of 'civilization' (in *The Universal History*, 1752) postulated an irrepressible drive to creativity and search in the ambit of human behaviour. In short, Voltaire argued that civilization was the product of individual human imagination. This was a radical idea, and although in accord with a number of contemporaries of the Enlightenment—such as the encyclopaedist Deridot, the travelling Scot, Adam Smith, and fully presaging the French Revolution—this notion ran directly counter to the ecclesiastical and political forces of the day, which insisted that society was the product of obedience and submission to the power of authorities. (Delightfully satirized in Voltaire's 1759 novel *Candide*.) So the concept of the power of human imagination to create higher-level social order (that is, civilization) presaged and deeply influenced the writings of Adam Smith, who then developed a particular mechanism—specialization and the division of labour—as the starting point of his theory of *The Wealth of Nations* (1776). This basic motive force sits very deep within economics, yet the development of axiomatic economic theory has now effectively buried it. Yet it has not been easily buried. Veblen forcefully argued that this quality was fundamental to the nature of the economic process, as also did Keynes in the *General Theory* (with his seat of psychological variables underpinning the determination of the level of output) and

111

Schumpeter, in his vision of the nature of the capitalist process (similarly, but as a basic motive of the entrepreneurial agent to prefer action to inaction).[2]

The static basis of the model is a graph-theoretic conception of the agent as a set of elements and a set of connections as a system $S = (V, E)$. These elements will be the basic resources and the connections will be the technologies that can be made with these resources. I construct the general model of an agent in the context of a multiagent model. The economic problem, then, becomes the choice of technology (compare, an input, output or consumption bundle aggregated into an allocation). In a non-integral framework, it is technologies that are scarce, not resources. The model develops as we consider the mechanisms by which these choices are made. This takes us from statics (graph theory) to dynamics (string theory). Thus I shall frame 'the economic problem' as a choice problem over the set $E$. In the neowalrasian framework, choice occurs over a set $V$. Our starting point, then, is to conceive of the human agent as an inquisitive being prone to experimentation over the domain of connections. I shall term this agent *hetero economicus*, active in a non-integral space, and in contrast to *homo economicus*, who operates in the integral space of the real field.[3]

This chapter is set out in two parts. In Section 5.2, I construct a model to describe the economics of a single agent alone on the planet, as it were. The key idea is that a single agent's economic problem is the choice of technology, and to cope with the complexity inherent in this choice the agent evolves what I term schematic preferences. These are high-level rules that make use of abstraction, and form the basis of a model of agent interaction. In Section 5.3, a general model of an agent is constructed as a set of resources, technology and control function, all of which emerge in the process of the choice of technology, and also a set of tags enabling the agent to exchange resources and build complex multiagents to form higher-level technologies. This general model emphasizes that the fundamental economic problem is not the allocation of resources but the choice of technology in the context of imperfect information. The choice of technology, in the abstract graph-theoretic expression, is an equivalent firm and consumer problem. Section 5.4 concludes.

## 5.2   The Agent: *Hetero Economicus*

The sentiments of human behaviour engaged in economic action are, of course, wider than rational self-interest. For Adam Smith, the principle of self-interest as the behavioural mechanism behind the 'invisible hand' was perforce only one aspect of human economic behaviour and functioning in parallel with moral, tribal, emotional and ethical sentiments. Such concern, however, has been marginalized (compare, Etzioni 1988, Ben-Ner and Puttermann 1998). A different tack was taken by Herbert Simon, who instead of attempting to locate the various motive forces underlying economic behaviour (the Bentham/Mill/ Marshall strategy) inquired of the processes by which any such force must work. Simon thus exposed the cognitive and heuristic dimension of the economic agent, and by implication the theoretical impossibility of the feats of maximization attributed in the axiomatic conception of *homo economicus*. What Simon achieved, along with the many economists who have followed his line of inquiry, broadly or narrowly (Conlisk 1996) was a theoretical dislocation of the economic agent from the field context. Those orthodox economists who have responded to Simon's concept of bounded rationality have often attempted to restore the field context by regarding this as an additional constraint interior to the general model (for example, Sargent 1993). But this misses the main point. The rationality constraint is not a parameter, as such, but a wholly different way of looking at the economic problem faced by agents. Agents must, effectively, choose how to choose. I aim to generalize this problem, linking choice heuristics and other such cognitive technologies with the full domain of consumer and household technologies. I do this by generalizing Simon's heuristic model of the economic agent, whom I shall call *hetero economicus*.

### 5.2.1 From *Homo Economicus* to *Hetero Economicus*

Scarcity, opportunity cost and consumer choice are three absolute rudiments in the logic of a microeconomic model. In this section, I offer a reconstruction of microeconomic first principles wherein these are not the main conceptual building blocks, but derived boundary conditions from a model of an economic agent following simple rules of search and experimentation. In the process of these rules becoming more complex we then witness the emergence of scarcity as a boundary condition, and choice and opportunity cost as the set of pathways between points. Further, we shall witness that technology and preferences are equivalent internal constructs that emerge as separate phenomena in the course of an increase in system complexity. This dynamic process is driven primarily by the feedback and construction of the rules of search and experimentation in state-space. *Homo economicus* is a set of elements in a preference and technology field. *Hetero economicus* is a set of elements plus a specific set of connections between them. These differences are profiled in Table 5.1.

*Table 5.1* Two models of the economic agent

|            | *Homo economicus*          | *Hetero economicus*              |
|------------|----------------------------|----------------------------------|
| *Space*      | $R^n$                        | $Z^n$                              |
| *Variables*  | Commodity bundle ($V$)       | Preferences, Technology ($E$)      |
| *Parameters* | Preferences, Technology    | Rules of Search                  |
| *Limits*     | Scarcity in $V$              | Scarcity/Complexity in $E$         |
| *Objective*  | Optimize over $V$ in $R^n$     | Satisfice over $E$ in $Z^n$          |

We begin with just a single agent in an environment stocked with resources (a Robinson Crusoe formulation, as such). The model is then initially of two sets—an environment state set $V^*$ and an agent resource set $V$—where we shall initially define $V^*$ as an infinite set of elements in the environment from which we draw a subset as the resource elements held by an agent (see Figure 5.1). The assumption of infinite resources may perhaps seem dubious, as it would surely negate the economic problem (the allocation of scarce resources) at the outset. But this is not the case if we then add a further assumption, namely that none of the resources can be used directly and all must be transformed in some way to obtain value in use (see Georgescu-Roegen 1970, 1975). Strictly speaking, we do not actually require for the purposes of the theory an infinite abundance of primary resources, as $V^* \gg V$ is sufficient. The presumption of an infinite set in the initial instance is to highlight the methodological shift in emphasis, from the domain of scarcity in the set $V$ (an axiom in the neowalrasian framework) and towards scarcity in the set $E$. The shift is from scarcity of resources to scarcity of knowledge. This shift reveals that the solution to the allocation problem (as a vector in P–Q space) is not in fact a complete solution to 'the economic problem'. Rather, there is a further dimension, an aspect of which is the coordination problem. The special concerns of coordination as elaborated by Coase (1937) and Richardson (1960) on the nature of the firm and the industry can now be further generalized. Loasby (1991) has circumscribed the full extent of this in terms of the growth of knowledge, which we now define as a general microeconomic problem. The primitive economic question is, what are the principles of choice that continually allocate the set of resources in an optimal way? From the evolutionary perspective, the primitive economic question is, what are the principles of choice that allow the continual growth of knowledge?

The set $V^*$ is our abstracted environment, and we may understand the elements {a, b, c, ...} as nature's endowments. For Robinson Crusoe these might represent clams, rocks, firewood, coconuts and suchlike, but the assumption must be that none are of any use in themselves, but must be combined with other elements to obtain value. For instance, Crusoe cannot eat raw unopened clams, but he can open them with rocks and cook them with fire. Supermarkets are somewhat like this, in that much of what is sold cannot be consumed directly (for example, flour, eggs, tinned food) but requires further processing in order to obtain value (for example, see Bianchi 1998, 1999 on this point). For the sake of the argument, let there be such an abandoned supermarket for Robinson Crusoe.[4] Let us call it Friday's, and denote it $V^*$.

$$V^* = \{a, b, c, d, c, b, a, b, a, a, a, c, b, c, a, c, b, b, c, c, a, d, d, d, \ldots \}$$
$$\downarrow \ \downarrow \ \downarrow \ \downarrow$$
$$V = \{a, b, c, d\}$$

*Figure 5.1*  Environment and agent resource sets

Robinson picks {a, b, c, d} from the shelves at Friday's and returns to his camp to ponder what to do next.[5] Generally, we represent the agent thus as a resource subset <resource>. The set of resources (or endowment, if you prefer) is a set of elements, so we define these as the set $V$, such that

$$agent: <V> \qquad (5.1)$$

While we assume that none of these elements are immediately useful to the agent, we allow that specific combinations possibly will be. This is what Crusoe is pondering.[6] The agent's problem is to find the good combinations, so that a single agent is charged with the creation of 'value in use'[7] by the discovery of specific combinations of primary resources. The agent must therefore engage in experimentation by combination, searching through the space of possibilities for useful combinations. This is a search in state-space (compare, a technology field, see Mirowski 1989). Robinson would thus map the set of possible pairwise combinations as in Figure 5.2.

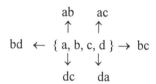

*Figure 5.2.* Adjacent technologies

All of these combinations are adjacent in state-space to the initial endowment set, such that by a single step (as a single connection) the agent can attain any pairwise combination. The set of possible combinations is the state-space of the set $E$, and thus the agent is engaged in the process of selecting a particular connection or set of connections in $E$.[8] For instance $a$ might be canned beans, $b$ a can-opener, $c$ soap and $d$ razor blades. It is evident, I trust, that only one of these combinations will produce food, and despite the fact that there are three combinations that contain an element of food. So if Crusoe is concerned with food technologies we might represent his situation as a set of ingredients and a viable[9] technology thus:

*Robinson Crusoe* < a, b, c, d > < ab >

Generally, this is the framework of an agent as a resource endowment ($V$) and a set of connections as technology ($E$) as represented in (5.2).

$$agent: < V > < E > \qquad (5.2)$$

So far, our model is not unorthodox, just differently expressed. Elements are endowments and technology refers to the different combinations the agent can make with the endowment set. We may also then suppose that the agent's rankings of these technologies is an expression of the agent's preferences. The agent's preferences, of course, are engaged only after all technologies have been sampled. There is a subtlety amidst this, however, that is crucial to all that follows. In ranking the combinatorial possibilities, for example, {ab, ac, bc, ...}, Robinson has selected two things: a commodity system (the compound element, a.b) and a technology system (the connection, ab). In this fully defined and therefore effectively integral space, these are identical. However, once we move into non-integral space (where not all connections are made, and thus the sample is incomplete) it will become apparent that these are not the same.

In a framework where the agent cannot utilize the fruits of the environment directly but must transform them to obtain value, we model the logic of a technology-using and knowledge-creating agent.[10] The component of choice in a single-agent model is choice of technology, where by technology we mean the set of possible connections (useful or not, which is to say that a poorly ranked technology is still a technology). This establishes the basic ontological platform of agent statics: an agent exists as resources and technology, as elements and the connections between them. Our dynamic concern is with how this choice process is made, which we model by constructing a simple set of rules that would generate such an outcome.

### 5.2.2 *Hetero Economicus*: Algorithmic Man

The process by which *homo economicus* enacts the behaviour of choice (expresses preferences) is formally defined over a field. Typically, there are tales told to suggest how this field equilibrium may be enacted, (for example, Walras's 'tatonnement', Edgeworth's 'recontracting', or the neowalrasian 'auctioneer') but these stories which accompany the theory are not part of the theory. There is no such thing as a theory of a choice process in the neowalrasian microeconomics, but instead there are equilibrium configurations of resources in commodity space that under a change in the parameter settings produce a different equilibrium configuration. No choice actually takes place, and thus there is no theoretical need to account for how this might actually occur. In the evolutionary microeconomics, the phenomenon of choice occurs as the outcome of an algorithmic process. This is defined as a set of sequential and conditional operations, such that we refer to a decision algorithm or a choice heuristic (see Simon 1959, Holland 1995). As a first approximation, and as a theoretical expression of the sequential heuristic concept of a 'decision cycle', we break the set of operations describing the choice of technology into four separate components: LIST, CONSTRUCT, RANK, SELECT.[11]

The first operation, LIST, consists of the identification of all adjacent combinatorial possibilities from the set $V$. The LIST operation defines the set of theoretical possibilities for the next iteration, which Crusoe then maps in his mind {soap—can-opener, soap—canned beans, and so on}. Following from this conjectured mapping the agent would proceed to CONSTRUCT the possibilities. Crusoe tries these possibilities. From the set defined by LIST a fraction will be worthless or grossly inapt,[12] and so from these two operations will emerge a set of viable technologies. The agent is now in a position to engage in a selection process that begins with the assignment of RANK to all viable technologies, and so ordered, a SELECTION operator then identifies the technology to be chosen. Crusoe ranks these sets and then chooses the {canned beans—can-opener} product and thus the technology pathway {ab}.[13] The exhaustive set of search operations as the heuristic process of the agent is represented below. For the sake of later formalization we define this algorithm (which we may suppose to be an innate property of an autonomous agent) as $< Y >$.

$$< Y > = < \text{LIST} : \text{CONSTRUCT} : \text{RANK} : \text{SELECT} >$$

These four sequential operations are the algorithmic components that construct the behaviour of choice. In this way, an agent is defined as a set of resources, a set of behavioural algorithms governing search of adjacent possibilities, and a set of chosen technology or technologies. We gather this set of heuristic rules as the CONTROL set. The set of resources, the set of technology and the heuristic set then represent the analytical scheme of *hetero economicus*, such that:

$$\text{agent: } < V > < E > < Y > \tag{5.3}$$

### 5.2.3 Hyperstructured Technology: Capital

Capital is hyperstructered technology. It is elements connected in particular ways to make a system that then becomes an element in a higher-level set.[14] For the sake of the argument, allow that there also exists an abandoned hardware store on the island (Saturday's?).[15] The set of connections is now part of the agent's endowment. In this sense Robinson now possesses the can-opening technology, which is a connection between elements. In the language of the theory, the control algorithm $Y$ acted on the resource set $V$ to produce a technology in $E$.

The set-theoretic foundations of graph theory allow us to formulate the concept of a system—as $S = (V, E)$—as a nested hierarchy (see Simon 1962). For this we combine the notions of emergence and hierarchy into a single construct—hyperstructure—by recognizing the principle of system-element duality. System-element duality is the principle that a system can itself be an element for a higher-level system and symmetrically, an element may itself be a system at a lower level. In this way routines build skills, skills build competence, competence builds firms, firms build industries, industries build economies and so on. Following Baas (1994, 1997), and as outlined in Chapter 3, this geometric conception is a hyperstructure. The formalisms are straightforward. For example, if $S^1 = (V^1, E^1)$ then, $S^2 = (S^1, E^2)$. System-element duality then is: $S^n = V^{n+1}$. This defines that connections between elements build systems which may then become elements in higher-level systems. The technology made by the emergent connection, (*ab*, in the above) may then be treated as a system $S^n$ and equivalently $V^{n+1}$, which may then feed back into the algorithm $Y$. It is the emergence of a connection between two elements that transforms the two elements plus the connection into a system. Technology builds capital as a higher-level system, which may then act as inputs for further technologies and thus higher-level systems still. In this way, the iterations (in $Y$) proceed as these new elements {ab, aa, ac}, which are $S^1$ systems or $V^2$ elements, then feed back into the same process.[16] By this process, Crusoe builds ever more complex technologies.[17]

The agent so far is a set of resources ($V$), a set of technologies ($E$) and a control function (the behavioural axiom of *hetero economicus*). However a single set $E$ is not sufficient to represent the analytical scheme of the evolution of technologies, and so we shall represent $E$ as an adjacency matrix, $S(A)$, which we can then express in hyperstructured form. The technology set begins, then, with a single iteration which results in $S(A)^0$. This then becomes $V^1$, and enters a second round of iterations to produce $S(A)^1$, and so forth. Thus, for each iteration there exists a matrix $S(A)^t$ the size of which grows proportional to the feedback at each iteration.[18] A set of these we shall describe as the technology string, which is of the form:

$$< E > = < S(A)^0, S(A)^1, ..., S(A)^t, ..., S(A)^i > = < \Sigma \, S(A) > \qquad (5.4)$$

Reading the string from the left to the right, the first entry describes the transformations from the initial state, then the second entry the transformations from the second state which now includes as elements the product of the first transformations, and so on to the $i$-th iteration. The constraint we shall impose, as above, is that the string is finite of length $i$. For new technologies to enter, as the transformation $i+1$ ($Y^{i+1}$) the agent must remove another technology. Given the necessary ordering, the only way the agent can include $S(A)^{i+1}$ is to drop $S(A)^0$. It seems fair to ask how this could be done without undermining the logical integrity of the system. A simple answer I suggest is that this becomes our definition of capital.

Capital emerges when an element of the technology set is able to be pushed outside the agent to become an external element. A single agent thus evolves capital as a way of allowing the technology set to incorporate new technologies. We imagine, then, that technology is like a pool, with an inlet $S(A)^{i+1}$ (new knowledge) and an outlet $S(A)^0$ (capital). Capital, in this model, is the derivative of knowledge when knowledge can be wholly constructed as an autonomous system independent of any particular agent.

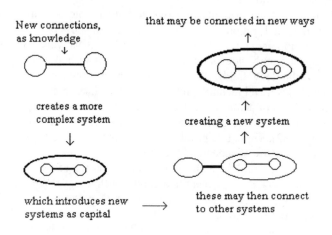

*Figure 5.3* The circular flow from knowledge to capital

This model of capital is still very much conceptual. But its key logic I hope is clear: capital is the byproduct of the growth of knowledge, but, insofar as capital can be released as an autonomous system— $S(A)^0$ above—then it is able to feed back into the process of the growth of knowledge. This feedback process, I hypothesize, is the underlying dynamical principle accounting for the phenomenon we may term supercritical economic growth (for example, Kauffman 1993: 397; Romer 1994), as underscored by, say, the industrial revolution or the microelectronic revolution (Mokyr 1990). In both cases an initial knowledge breakthrough (in $E^1$) fed into the development of particular machines (as $S^1$, for example, a steam engine or a transistor) and these then enabled further leaps in knowledge, as these systems were combined with other elements. A good example of this phenomenon (bootstrapping, or the production of commodities by means of commodities) is that computers are now used to make computers, and the development of new generations of computers ($S^{n+1}$ systems) makes use of $S^n$-level system to discover the particular connections sought at the $E^{n+1}$ level.

### 5.2.4 Schematic Preferences

Previously, we treated the control function in terms of a small state-space, where the agent can effectively undertake all operations in $Y$ on all adjacent states. This was the topographical equivalent of an integral space ($R^n$). We now depart from this model, and enter non-integral space.

A non-integral space presents two overarching problems. The first is the problem of bounded rationality, where the set of possible combinatorial technologies is too large for the agent to search exhaustively (Simon 1959, 1982). The agent simply does not know the extent of technological possibility (compare, a technology field). The second problem concerns how the agent ranks and evaluates novel technologies. The agent is faced with the problem of reducing the process of actually constructing, testing and evaluating all adjacent technologies. This becomes increasingly costly as the number of possibilities escalates (Hey 1982). These two problems, as it turns out, have the same general form of solution: the use of schematic preferences.

We formulate the problem with respect to the choice of new technologies (combinations in state-space adjacent to a current technology). We also presume that the number of adjacent states is far greater than the agent can hope to explore (in finite time, Velupillai 1995a). This is both a consumer and producer problem (for example, Earl 1986, Swann 1999). Equivalently, and without a bounded rationality constraint, we may argue that it will simply be inefficient for agents to engage in an exploration of all states if they can find some way of forming a theory of which states are more likely to contain good solutions.

Following Loasby (1991), we assume the agent will attempt to form conjectures as a solution. These may be thought of as rules of thumb, or subroutines, or any such way of shaping the phenomenon of choice with cognitive tools. Such conjectures or theories (cognitive tools) are not logical relationships, which is only a sensible proposition when the analysis has no temporal context, but are conjectural relationships. The critical synthesis that I add to this is that these conjectures *are* the agent's preferences. When preferences are placed within the stream of time then they must cease to be logical relationships and reassert themselves as conjectural relationships that are, moreover, capable of being falsified. It also follows that hypotheses, by definition, are necessarily incomplete. Hence these schematic preferences cannot be neowalrasian preferences which are by definition complete. But the neowalrasian scheme of preferences, by this same token, cannot cope with novelty. Thus the general case of preferences are hypotheses which contain the standard model of preferences as a special case in the absence of novelty. The neowalrasian model of preferences is thus a special case of what I shall term schematic preferences.

Schematic preferences address the problem of the choice of technology where it would be either impossible or highly inefficient to CONSTRUCT all adjacent possibilities. To reduce the cost of the CONTRUCT : RANK phase, which is the phase of information gathering, testing and evaluating components up to the moment of choice (SELECT), the agent will form higher-level search rules.[19] It is these I identify as the substance of an agent's preferences, and they are living, adaptive things that can never be photographed as Edgeworth insisted of the classical type. Schematic preferences are the general form which collapse to neowalrasian preferences when we assume an integral space.

Schematic preferences are high-level rules governing choice when complete information is not available, which in most non-trivial situations is always. The model follows from original work done by John Holland (1975, 1995) towards an algorithmic approach to machine learning (see also Scarf 1989). He defines a method of search he calls *schemata* (hence schematic preferences), which are rules for conditional acceptance of the IF < ab## > THEN < ... > form. Obviously, these rules are components in a production system (see, for example, Gilbert and Troitzsch 1999: 164).

These rules form a set of schematic preferences, which I denote $P$, where an individual rule is $P_s$. The symbol '#' essentially means 'don't care', such that this rule will accept a pathway beginning with *ab* but it does not matter what comes after that. Schematic preferences are a set of incomplete rules that enable the agent to deal with either novel situations, by searching for partial matches,[20] or to deal more efficiently with familiar situations by making use of abstraction. Schematic preferences collapse to neowalrasian preferences when there are no '#' symbols anywhere in the preference set. In this case the agent has thus either obtained omniscience (a particular string $P_s$ for every conceivable situation) or is constrained to function in a world without change.

In this way, a schematic preference is like a hypothesis, in that it contains a necessary amount of abstraction (the '#' places). The complexity of an agent's preference set increases as '#' symbols are dropped, which occurs as the agent learns more distinctions and recognizes, or experiments with, new rules. New rules evolve by modifying existing rules, and for this we define a further operator in the control set, as $X$. The set of operators $X$ are endogenous rules that function to change other rules, that is, the set of schematic preferences. We denote the set of operators $X$ and the set of schematic preferences $P$ such that,

$X = \{X_1, X_2, ... X_q, ... X_r\}$ (Operators defining change in strings)
$P = \{P_1, P_2, ... P_s, ... P_t\}$ (Schematic preferences as strings)
$Y = <$ LIST : CONSTRUCT : RANK : SELECT $>$ (Platform of search algorithms)

$$< Control > = < X, P, Y > \qquad (5.5)$$

Several points may now be further clarified. First, the standard model of a preference function is fully a preference field (Mirowski 1989), and not a set-string, as in $P$. The field axioms (transitivity, reflexivity, continuity, completeness and monotonicity) define neowalrasian preferences as singular (a preference function) which has no holes in it, as it were (Etzioni 1985).[21] Preferences in $P$ are both multiple (there are $t$ schematic preference strings) and they are full of gaps, as the # positions. This is a more intricate formulation but it allows a fundamental advance. Individual preference strings within an agent can then compete with one another; they are like a set of competing hypotheses concerning which procedure, strategy or choice will best produce utility or some such. These strings $P_s$ make a population $P$ and the members of the population compete with one another for application and evolve by the effect of the operators. By this internal process, an agent can evolve good preferences that work well in most situations and can adapt to new information (see Darley and Kauffman 1997). Moreover, the parallelism implicit in this formulation enables the agent to hold inconsistent (intransitive) preferences in different strings and draw upon these different strings in different contexts (as a complex system).

Second, the number of different preference schemata in the set $P$ and the number of # places in the schemata $P_s$ provide us with a relative metric of the sophistication of the agent. In the course of experience and experiment, the agent will fill out the set $P$ by the process of learning (see Velupillai 1994). Specialization, skill or commercial expertise, for instance, can be represented by the significant filling out of a particular set-string. Two internal possibilities follow. Either this is achieved at the expense of other strings, which would suggest the application of equimarginal principles of optimality to define the active length of strings (or the application of a constraint that cognitive psychologists call 'chunking'), or there is the possibility of transferal effects. In other words, if agents commit all their learning resources to a single string then they may neglect other strings on the basis that principles can be transferred.

As such, evolving schematic preferences is, in terms of this framework, the phenomenon of learning. And from this perspective, it is the set of operators $X$ which enable the process of learning to occur by generating changes in the set of schematic preferences. These preferences enable the agent to search through high-dimensional space.[22]

According to Romer (1992: 69),

> The potential for continued economic growth comes from the vast search space that we can explore. The curse of dimensionality is, for economic purposes, a remarkable blessing. To appreciate the potential for discovery, one need only consider the possibility that an extremely small fraction of the large number of possible mixtures may be valuable.

And to which Velupillai (1995b: 7) counters,

But the problem is that no effective procedure can be constructed to know which 'extremely small fraction to search'. It is as if the space is full of hills and valleys and there is no way not only of knowing whether there is a global optimum or optima, but also one has no way of knowing which little, local hill to start the search from. The use of local scouts, sherpas and the like will be the only hope. There will be lots of scope for the Tontos and Tensings of this world, without whom the Lone Rangers and Hillarys might as well stay home.

## 5.2.5 Dynamic Operators: The set X

A preference schema, then, is like a chromosome, in that the dynamics of schemata can be constructed in terms of a small set of transformation functions. These we term dynamic operators (as genetic algorithms), which are functions (strings) which are not subject to evolution—they are hard-wired into the control set—but rather are the mechanisms governing the process of evolution. The operators $X$ act on the strings $P$. In biology, the classical genetic operators are mutation and crossover. Mutation is simple and random, operating on a single string to produce a variant that is adjacent in state-space to the original. Crossover works on two strings, allowing the possibility of a jump in state-space to a state that is not adjacent to the initial state. In *evolutionary computation*, mutation and crossover are the fundamental search operators, as operators that generate new candidate solutions. For an excellent introduction to genetic algorithms and evolutionary computation, see Mitchell (1998). Below I sketch eight ways (compare, Holland 1995, Dosi et al. 1999) in which the schematic preference strings may evolve 'genetically'.[23]

$$X = \{X_1, X_2, ..., X_q, ..., X_r\} \quad \text{(for } r = 8)$$

$X_1$: Point-mutation: A single string 'mutates' at a point to produce a daughter string.

$$< aaab > \ \rightarrow \ < aaaa >$$

$X_2$: Cross-over: Two strings 'splice' taking part of one and part of the other to produce a daughter string. The consumption basket of a married couple is an example.

$$< aabc > <bbcc > \ \rightarrow \ < aacc >$$

$X_3$: Inversion: Between two points the operator inverts the ordering. This operator applies to a single string and would describe a 'rethink' of preference orderings. We may imagine that advertising or other such peer references would be the 'cause' of this operator.

$$< abca > \ \rightarrow \ <acba >$$

$X_4$: Slide: A shift up or down the string, as may describe a sudden large change in income, for example, a lottery win or a significant uninsured loss by theft or taxes, as well as a marginal change.

$$< \#\#aabbcc\#\# > \; \rightarrow \; < aaaabb\#\#\#\# >$$

$X_5$: Reclustering: A reclustering operator would shift commodity sites into new clusters as the working out of a change in technologies or following consumer innovation. This makes sense of the distinction between core and peripheral technologies, such that a change in a minor technology (a new toothbrush design) would have an effect perhaps best described by a point-mutation, but a core technology (say, the introduction of the cellphone) would have a reclustering effect, as a great many other commodities are affected.

$$< abcabcabc > \; \rightarrow \; < aaabbbccc >$$

$X_6$: Emergence/Closure: This operator makes more direct sense in the production aspect, as the formation of a closed loop that we may recognize as a competence. However, Swann (1999) has illustrated that consumer behaviour such as collecting exhibits this quality, where a complete collection has an emergent the-whole-is-more-than-the-sum-of-the-parts property. This operator may provide the basic logic for decomposition.

$$< aaaaa\#\#\#\# > \rightarrow < aaaaa >$$

$X_7$: Higher or Lower Specification: In many respects this will be the most common operation on schematic preferences. Higher specification replaces a don't care symbol with a specific requirement, as occurs in the process of learning. Lower specification occurs in the process of simplification, which may also be a product of learning, or reflect a decreased importance of the decision or an attempt to isolate which are the key elements in the tag.

$$< aabb\#\# > \; \rightarrow \; < aabbc\# >$$
$$< aabb\#\# > \; \rightarrow \; < aab\#\#\# >$$

$X_8$: Birth or Death: Simply, an operation that either deletes a complete string or brings into existence a new string. Forgetting and imagination suitably describe this context.

$$< ... > \; \rightarrow \; < aabbc\# >$$
$$< aabb\#\# > \; \rightarrow \; < ... >$$

## 5.2.6 Recapitulation

The model so far is represented in (5.6) below.

$$agent: < V > < \Sigma S(A) > < X : P : Y > \qquad (5.6)$$

The resource set is orthodox, and ought not to be problematic. The technology (and capital) set involves a hyperstructured analytical representation, which is an alternative concept to the orthodox representation of technology in a field. The set of dynamic operators $X$ and the platform of search algorithms $Y$ are simple rudiments of, respectively, the theory of genetic algorithms and heuristic decision-cycle theory recast into the scheme of the present framework. These two concepts are well-founded components of research into complex systems.[24] Amidst this, it is the concept of schematic preferences that is the innovation.

Schematic preferences are the preferences of an (automata) agent in a lattice space. They are a scheme for coping with what is otherwise termed bounded rationality, they are the locus of learning, and the defining characteristic of agents. Agents differ in their resource and technology sets certainly, but they also differ in their set of schematic preferences. Schematic preferences, as such, are a product of experience and experimentation (the locus of history and imagination) and are structurally complex for reasons of expediency. They are the expression of adaptive rationality.

I develop this concept with a specific intention: schematic preferences provide the essential analytical logic to bridge us from a model of an adaptive agent to a model of agent interaction. Agent interaction, then, is defined with respect to the active or inactive sites over sets of schematic preferences, which provide, as such, the points of contact. We proceed to model agent interaction by generalizing the function of schematic preferences. That is, for the single agent, schematic preferences evolved for the purposes of choosing interior technology over a very large state-space. This same scheme is generally applicable to interaction with other agents as well. For in the process of learning and dealing with internal complexity the agent has attained the ability to be affected by discrete chunks of information, that is, the agent has evolved a set of condition-action rules (schematic preferences) where the conditional part can be defined with respect to another agent. Mutual schematic preferences make possible the phenomena of agent interaction.

## 5.3 Agent Interaction

How do agents interact with other agents? The problem that agents now face is the decision of which other agents to interact with. It seems reasonable to presume that interaction between agents will be engaged according to the same logic by which the agent interacts with the environment. I propose, then, that agents mutually decide whom to interact with by utilizing their schematic preferences, and therefore interacting locally with partial information.[25]

A schematic preference of the form $<$ ab##... $>$ is a conditional for action internal to the agent (a component of a production system) such that the SELECT function may be operating IF < ab##... > THEN : *engage* SELECT *rule*. The matching of the active sites, the 'ab' in the first two places, triggers the rule to action. Without this matching, in the space of the agent's own technological possibilities, the rule would remain inactive. However, this same rule may be triggered by a technology in another agent. This is simply to say that the agent's environment consists of the resource and technology sets of other agents. Agents may variously display these sets, such that they act as triggers for interaction. When there is a symmetrical and respective triggering of a conditional for action between two agents we suppose that the necessary condition for agent interaction has been made sufficient. Unless this happens, interaction does not occur.

Following Holland (1995: 12–5), I propose to call the active sites in a set of schematic preferences 'tags'. Tags are combinatorial sequences that when matched with a rule (as a string in the set $P$) activate that rule.[26] As Holland explains,

> Tags are a pervasive feature of complex adaptive systems because they facilitate selective interaction. They allow agents to select among agents or objects that would otherwise be indistinguishable. Well-established tag-based interactions provide a sound basis for filtering, specialization and cooperation. This, in turn, leads to the emergence of meta-agents and organizations that persist even though their component parts are continually changing. Ultimately, tags are the mechanism behind hierarchical organization.

A rule is activated by a tag, and thus a tag is a conditional for action.[27] An agent thus interacts with another agent by proposing a tag that is then accepted by the other agent, so that the tag in one agent acts as the conditional for action in the other agent. Without this matching of tags, then, no interaction takes place, and, indeed, all interactions in an economic system necessarily occur by the matching of tags. Tags are made by the agent from resources in the set $V$.

I assume that interaction takes place for only two reasons. First, for the exchange of resources, and second for the creation of new technologies. In the first mode of interaction, two agents come together for the purposes of a reciprocal exchange of elements from their respective sets $V$, then disengage. In the second mode of interaction, agents come together to combine their resource and technology sets $V$ and $S(A)$. The first form of interaction modifies each agent, the second form of interaction creates a new agent (a multiagent, such as a firm or a household). In both cases it is the set of schematic preferences $P$ that governs interaction. In each case, we assume that the set of agents makes a population within a bounded space.

### 5.3.1 Exchange

A model of exchange requires that each agent employ two tags, a proposal tag and an acceptance tag, which I shall denote respectively by the symbols $\pi^+$ (proposal) and $\pi^-$ (acceptance). For two agents, then, the proposal tag of one agent is matched to the acceptance tag of the other agent and vice versa, wherein an exchange will take place only if both pairs of tags match. If only one set of tags is matched or neither set of tags is matched then no exchange will take place. When a bilateral matching of proposal and acceptance tags occurs, an exchange of resources will then take place, with a reciprocal switching of a quantity of an element in $u_i{:}V$ for a quantity of an element in $u_j{:}V$. The crux of this model, and therein the nature of its departure from the field logic, is that exchange occurs as intermediated by the matching of tags.[28]

In this simple model of exchange, the proposal and acceptance tags ($\pi^+$ and $\pi^-$) are strings such as $<$ abb### $>$. Exchange, then, involves reciprocal proposals, each of which is checked against acceptance conditions. Agent $i(u_i)$ proposes to agent $j(u_j)$, who then vets the proposal, and vice versa:

$$u_i : \pi^+ \to u_j : \pi^- \text{ and } u_j : \pi^+ \to u_i : \pi^-$$

A proposal $u_i : \pi^+$ as say $<$ abb### $>$, is accepted by $u_j : \pi^-$ *iff* there is pairwise mapping of the active sites in the proposal tag map to either exact matches or # sites in the acceptance tag. Thus, $u_j : \pi^-$ $<$ abb### $>$ obviously accepts, but so to would $<$ ab#### $>$. However, $<$ abba## $>$ would not accept, because it has an extra conditional (in the fourth site) that has not been satisfied. In this case, $u_j$ would seek further information, given that this site is inactive in the proposal and may potentially be satisfactory. The same mapping must occur for $u_j : \pi^+ \to u_i : \pi^-$.

Three logical implications follow. First, it is apparent that exchanges are more likely to occur, the less specific the acceptance strings. In the extreme case, the acceptance tag $<$ ###### $>$ accepts every proposal. Similarly, exchanges are also more likely, the more specific the proposal string. This was illustrated in the above instance of the agent who required more information. Thus we would expect, according to this model, the growth of exchange interaction to effect two emergent patterns: (1) generalized acceptance criteria, and (2) the tendency towards ever more detailed proposals. Both facilitate exchange interaction.

An obvious generalized acceptance criterion is a common currency. Money enters as a universal acceptance condition, whereby $\pi^-$ is in terms of a metric known to all agents. Money then becomes a further class of element in $V$ (in the sense of Wicksell's triangle) with the unique property that when advanced as a proposal tag $\pi^+$ it will be universally accepted by all $\pi^-$ tags, subject only to quantity conditions. More detailed proposals obviously incorporate such aspects as more detailed product information, in the sense of, say, a categorical list of ingredients; this trend is plainly evident in modern consumables. Other important aspects include the relation of the element to other elements in the context of a system,[29] and the domain of input substitution.

The acceptance condition will be the set of elements that will satisfy the requirements of input into the technology. This set, then, is a set of substitutes. An agent may search for a set of inputs using a schematic process, whereby a schema, say < abba## >, specifies the acceptance condition, and will accept, for instance, both < abbabb > and < abbaaa >. These are therefore substitutes according to the schematic preference function, they are equally acceptable. The agent will discover other substitutes by experimentation with the form of the schema. For example, a wider schema could be applied as < abb### >, or a narrower one as < abbaa# >. These schema are modified by the same function that modifies the technology schemata, the set of operators $X$.

Second, the agent commits resources from the set $V$ to produce these tags. As such, there are 'transaction costs' associated with the interaction of exchange and these costs are individually met by each agent. The more resources the agent devotes to the facilitation of exchange,[30] the more likely that the agent would be party to optimal exchange. But such optimal exchange may, by the same token, be very costly to the agent. This is an area that, despite the apparent orthodoxy of the question, has been afforded little treatment in the economic literature.

Third, a population of agents will differ in their tags, and this differentiation is the basis of competition for the exchange of resources. Competition arises, as such, when the same tags are present so that the mechanism of competition becomes tag differentiation. This model, then, suggests an evolutionary theory of monopolistic competition in which tag differentiation is effectively a process of adding more information to the interaction conditionals. This notion of competition is thus based upon an incentive structure to create more information, and accords broadly with Austrian accounts of the nature of the market process.[31] The basic mechanism, then, is a growth of knowledge by increased definition of the proposal tag $\pi^+$.

This string theory model of exchange is non-compensatory, representing the general form of an algorithmic choice process. Higher-level rules may modify this in many ways, for instance constraining it to a lexicographic process, or, by adding further rules for comparability, a compensatory form may be derived. The compensatory model is, however, very much a special case of the generalized non-compensatory scheme presented here. We make sense of this by recognizing that the motive for exchange is to obtain specified inputs (as an element $V_i$ in $V$) into the technology system (household or firm) described by $\Sigma S(A)$. Only in the limiting case that $V_i$ is represented by the string < ##### > in

$P$, such that effectively anything will be accepted as an input, will the pure compensatory model over $n$ goods be applicable.

Exchange occurs for the purposes of obtaining particular resources that are in some other agent's resource set $V$, and we augment our model of the agent so as to incorporate this interaction as in (5.7) below.

$$agent: <\pi^+ : \pi^- > < V : \Sigma S(A) > < X : P : Y > \qquad (5.7)$$

### 5.3.2 Combination

Combination occurs, however, for the purposes of obtaining other technologies that are in another agent's technology set $\Sigma S(A)$. While resources are separable, capable of being moved between agents, technologies are not. It is only the limit of technology, as capital $S(A)^0$, that is capable of moving from one agent set to another. So to obtain the technology set of another agent, combination must occur, such that two or more agents form a composite agent. Following Holland (1995: 126), we shall call this a *multiagent* in the context of string theory.

Combination occurs as the product of interaction, and we shall again presume that this is mediated by tag matching. We shall term these tags combination tags, and like exchange tags they have two forms, which we shall term offence and defence denoted by $\Omega^+$ and $\Omega^-$, respectively. The mechanism of tag matching in the case of combination is conceptually identical to the case of exchange. If there is reciprocal tag matching, then the agents will combine into a multiagent, if not, they will proceed as free agents. The same three logical implications apply, regarding the specification of the tag sequence, the cost of the tag sequence and the nature of competition.

In a multiagent, interaction occurs such that the resource sets $V_i$ and $V_j$ are merged into a single set $V_{ij}$. A firm, for instance, is such a thing, drawing the skills of employees and elements of capital into a single multiagent. The technology sets cannot merge directly, but they can enable the formation of higher-level technology. It is this possibility of emergent technology that I identify as the analytical form of the phenomenon of 'competence', where competence is a phenomenon unique to multiagents. Competence, as such, can emerge in the household or the firm, as both are phenomena of production systems made by combining lower-level systems. Competence, then, is the connections that form between the resource sets of two or more agents. They are conceptually the same as the technology pathways that form within the agent (as Robinson Crusoe learned to connect canned beans and can-opener), but these technologies, as competence, occur between complete agent systems. For the competence to exist, the agents must be part of a higher-level system, a multiagent. Multiagents form by a process of tag matching, wherein the tags display the resources and skills or technologies that can be contributed to a multiagent. The multiagent combines resources to build higher-level technologies, which we term competence.

The boundary of a multiagent, therefore, is determined by the competence that emerges from the multiagent. Thus a multiagent that does not advance the technology system brought by the union of the sets $(u_{ij}:\Sigma S(A)^n)$ into some new region of state-space, which is to establish new connections at the $E^{n+1}$ level (thus building a 'competence' as a system at $S^{n+1}$) will be unstable as a multiagent. A firm where the combination of agents produces no more than each could produce individually will not be stable as a firm; and similarly so for a household. In such instances, the combined resource set $V_{ij}$ will be the only basis for the multiagent boundary.

When a multiagent forms, so combining resource and technology sets, then so too would the schematic preferences—$P_i$ and $P_j$—combine. This may well constitute a significant proportion of the gains of specialization afforded interior to a multiagent. The mechanics of this is an issue to be confronted at the level of the constructed model, yet the basic principle would be that they do not aggregate, but merge. That is, a single schematic preference would result. Obviously for firms, this is associated with the function of operational and representative management (see Kollman et al. 1997). In a household this process does not typically occur, but rather there may exist consensus or specialized decision making. These are difficult issues that will require much further theoretical and applied investigation. Needless to say, when schematic preferences fail to merge into either a single schematic preference or a systematically partitioned schematic preference, the multiagent will be unstable due to the live possibility of internal contradiction and/or decision conflict.

We may thus add the set of combination tags to our general model of agency, as in (5.8) below.

$$agent: <\Omega^+ : \Omega^- > < \pi^+ : \pi^- > < V : \Sigma S(A) > < X : P : Y > \tag{5.8}$$

## 5.4 Conclusion: The Agent as a Complex System

To summarize. Our agent *hetero economicus* is a complex system composed of three subsystems:

- A set of resources and technology,　　　　　$< V : \Sigma S(A) >$
- a set of control algorithms and schemata,　　$< X : P : Y >$
- and a set of tags for interaction　　　　　　$< \Omega^+ : \Omega^- > < \pi^+ : \pi^- >$

*Hetero economicus*[32] makes use of abstraction to live in a changing environment populated by other agents. This agent does, effectively, three things. It searches through the adjacency structure of state-space for technologies that can be made with its resource endowment. It then attempts to select and effect new or better technologies. It engages in exchange interaction with other agents for the purposes of obtaining inputs into extant technologies. And it engages in combination interaction with other agents for the purposes of building higher-level technologies than it could obtain by itself. It is evident that it is the dynamics of technology (the growth of knowledge) that is the key and driving aspect of this model.

The main aspect of the evolutionary microeconomic model of economic agency is to elevate technology, broadly defined, to be the pivot of the economic problem. Technology is a general abstract term encompassing the connections made by consumers and producers, households and firms. The agent's problem is the discovery of good combinations of resources, as those combinations that produced value to the agent. In this respect, preferences emerge as a mechanism for learning. In this way, preferences emerge as a special case of technology and in the general form of schematic preferences. These, essentially, are a heuristic technology for finding further technologies (both heuristic and phenomenal). Preferences, then, are incomplete evolving rules that can be modelled as a number of schemata operating in parallel. As strings, these begin initially as very approximate and in the course of experience and experiment become more complex and specific.

The two key components of this synthetic model are: (1) parallel architecture, as the set $P$; an internal mechanism for adaptation, as the set of operators $X$; and an innate algorithm for discovery, $Y$, and (2), the use of abstraction as the way of coping with information overload. Agents will form action rules triggered not by every piece of information but by particular tags which appear as the active sites in the schemata. The operators $X$ experimentally modify these as $P$ evolves. Consequentially, the dynamics of an economic system then turn on the nature of these tags. As such, agent interaction occurs with respect to and in the context of these tags. This reinstates the coordination problem, signalling problems and information problems generally at the centre of microeconomic analysis. A clear consequence is that the analysis of the microeconomics of a dynamic economic system requires far more accord with other behavioural and organizational sciences than has previously been extended.

# Notes

[1] For example, Veblen (1898, 1899), Georgescu-Roegen (1971), Hollis and Nell (1975), Scitovsky (1986), Cowan (1989), Frey (1997).

[2] See also Foster's (1987) economic agent *homo creativus*.

[3] The Latin sense of *homo economicus* is of the genus 'hominoid', which is presumably the quasi-anthropological posturing of the concept. Anthropologically speaking, the use of tools (*Homo Habilus*), and the application of reason to the development of such tools, defines the arrival of *Homo Sapiens*. *Homo economicus* is a restricted version of *Homo Sapiens*, neglecting the imaginative component that makes new tools. From this perspective *hetero economicus*, then, is an economic agent that both uses tools and makes new tools. But in the Greek, *homo* means 'same', which seems to accord more with Marshall's representative agent and the neowalrasian social atom. '*Hetero*', in the sense I use it above, is to align with the Latin and to contrast with the Greek prefix, suggesting an agent that both makes and uses tools, and which is not the same as all other agents.

[4] 'Then it occurred to me again, how well I was furnished for my subsistence, and what would have been my case if it had not happened that the ship floated from the place where she first struck, and was driven so near the shore that I had time to get all things out of her . . .' (Defoe 1719: 44). See Wiseman and Littlechild (1990) for a further reading of Defoe's novel in terms of the economics of production.

[5] '. . .But what need I have been concerned at the tediousness of anything I had to do, seeing I had time enough to do it in? Nor had I any other employment if that had been over, at least that I could foresee, except the ranging the island to seek for food, which I more or less did every day. I now began to seriously consider my condition, . . .' (Defoe 1719: 45–6)

[6] '. . .I have already observed how I bought all my goods into this pale, and into the cave which I had made behind me: but I must also observe too, that at first this was a confused heap of goods, which as they lay in no order, so they took up all my place . . .' (Defoe 1719: 47)

[7] Note we are still considering a single agent and not yet agent interaction, so that we may define value in use prior to and independent of exchange value. Value in use thus means cardinal utility.

[8] In the above the order of the pairs does not matter (that is, ab = ba). If the order does matter (that is, ab ≠ ba) we define the graph as a *di-graph* (a *di*rected *graph*) in which the connections are drawn in with arrows pointing from *a* to *b*, or vice versa.

[9] See Georgescu-Roegen (1984) on this point.

[10] '. . .And now, in the managing of my household affairs, I found myself wanting in many things, which I thought at first it was impossible for me to make, as indeed to some of them it was; . . .' (Defoe 1719: 49).

[11] The reason I insist upon four separate operators rather than, say, a singular <CHOOSE BEST TECHNOLOGY> operator is that all four operators are themselves decomposable and quasi-autonomous, and, as such, may themselves be subject to specific adaptation and experimentation.

[12] '. . .I had no plough to turn up the earth, no spade or shovel to dig it. Well, this I conquered, by making a wooden spade; but this did my work in but a wooden manner, and though it cost me a great many days to make it, yet for want of iron it not only wore out the sooner, but made my work the harder, and made it be performed much worse . . .' (Defoe 1719: 78).

[13] '...I began to apply myself to make the things as I found I most wanted, . . . So I went to work; and here I must needs observe, that as reason is the substance and origin of the mathematics, so by stating and squaring everything by reason, and by making the most rational judgement of things, every man may be in time master of every mechanical art . . .'' (Defoe 1719: 47)

[14] This is fully in accordance, I suggest, with the Austrian Structuralist definition of capital, which emphasizes the structure of complementarity rather than an aggregative conception of universal substitution. In particular, see Mongiovi (1994: 268–71) and Lewin (1994: 241) who discuss this in terms of Lachmann's theory of capital, and for a more general exposition, see Endres (1997).

[15] '. . .among the many things which I brought out of the ship in the several voyages, I got several things of less value, but not at all less useful to me, which I omitted to set down before: as in

particular, pens, ink, and paper, several parcels in the captain's, mate's, gunner's and carpenter's keeping, three or four compasses, . . .' (Defoe 1719: 45).

[16] This is generally a Markov chain process (see Nelson and Winter 1982, Andersen 1994). In one of the most lucid presentations of the algorithmic logic of evolution, Daniel Dennett (1995: ch. 3) has described this general evolutionary principle with the metaphor of a crane lifting itself through 'design space' (my hyperstructured state-space). A crane can build platforms upon which further or larger cranes can be built, ever upwards.

[17] '. . . these two whole days I took up in grinding my tools, my machine for turning my grindstone performing very well . . .' (Defoe 1719: 54).

[18] According to this logic the pathway forward experiences exponential growth, as at each round the combinatorial LIST is augmented by the products of the previous round adding to the set $V$. This phenomenon is known as bootstrapping, and is the most fundamental expedient of all evolutionary processes. Unchecked, this idealized process would proceed to an explosion of infinite technologies and complex resources. We must therefore constrain this equation somehow to produce more sensible dynamics. Three constraining functions are obvious: (1) the set of resources in $V'$ is in fact finite; (2) the length of the technology string will be finite, thus constraining the growth function; and (3) the feedback parameter is likely to be very small. There are two reasons for (3). First, it is well known from topography that for each improvement step, the number of further improvement steps decreases by half (Kauffman 1993: 70–1). Second, there will be a fraction of the product consumed at each round, thus not all that is produced will feed back into the algorithm.

[19] The problem is overload, or bounded rationality in the orthodox sense of time being a constraint. But the orthodox meaning is deeply confused here, because a rational choice is technically impossible unless agents do in fact survey all pathways so that they then know rationally which ones not to survey!

[20] As such, schematic preferences cannot deal with completely novel situations, where no active site can find a match. But then completely novel situations of this sort are extremely rare.

[21] Nell (1996: 204) facetiously explains that agents 'can rank every conceivable combination of goods, for example, they know whether or not they prefer 23 living room sofas and 786 light bulbs to 13 sofas and 4562 light bulbs . . .'

[22] Hey's (1982) experimental findings suggest that a relatively low number of general search rules may be sufficient for most normal economic behaviours. Epstein and Axtell (1996: 51–2) conclude that 'a wide range of collective structures and collective patterns of behaviour can emerge from the spatio-temporal interaction of agents operating, individually, under simple local rules'. They emphasize that although the emergence of familiar macrostructures grown from the bottom up, as it were, is certainly interesting, the surprising aspect is the 'generative simplicity of simple local rules'.

[23] See also Riechmann's (1999) discussion of genetic algorithms as models for economic learning.

[24] For instance, see Goldberg (1989), Arthur (1991), Holland and Miller (1991), Levy (1992), Arifovic (1994), Epstein and Axtell (1996), Arthur et al. (1997), Birchenhall et al. (1997), Holland (1995, 1998), Gilbert and Troitzsch (1999) for discussion of multiagent-based approaches to economic modelling and the role of dynamic operators and search algorithms therein.

[25] An alternative, and in some ways more direct approach to modelling agent interaction, is to use statistical mechanics techniques (see Durlauf 1993, 1996; Brock and Durlauf 1999). However, it must be recognized that such techniques, although well developed and rigorous, do not model interactions as much as interdependencies, and is therefore primarily of econometric rather than microeconomic concern. Which is to say that such approaches are modelling techniques that eschew what is actually occurring at the level of the agent.

[26] In Epstein and Axtell's (1996: 71–2) *Sugarscape*, they define cultural tags as binary strings to represent the agent's preferences. Preferences change as agents interact. This is achieved in their cellular automata framework by random comparative matching of tags. Changes in tastes and beliefs (preferences) are then modelled as an endogenous outcome of interaction with other agents.

[27] 'Tags are really schemata that appear in both the condition and action parts of rules' (Holland 1995: 90).

[28] This is not the same as the internal mechanism of Edgeworth's scheme of recontracting, in the sense that the scheme of tag matching proceeds entirely by the criterion of sufficiency rather than optimality. If an exchange is agreeable to both agents then it will occur, and irrespective of the general optimality of the exchange. We would further have to add to this framework the presumption that each agent interacts with all agents to afford equivalence. Simulation models of this mechanism are termed 'annealing models' (Kirkpatrick et al. 1983; Aldrich and McMelvey 1991; Kauffman 1993; Kollman et al. 1997). These are also related to 'spin-glass' models (Edwards and Anderson 1975).

[29] For example, the underlying goal of many marketing strategies is to suggest this sort of association, of the generic form 'product $X$ is to be associated with $Y$ ($Y$ being a well-known other phenomenon) to produce $Z$ (a desired outcome)'. In this, the crucial and specific information is on the complementarity of the product in the context of various production systems.

[30] For instance, Klamer and McCloskey (1995) have investigated and argued that one quarter of GDP consists of persuasion. See also Klamer et al. (1988).

[31] In particular, Mises (1949), Hayek (1945, 1978), Shackle (1983), Buchanan and Vanberg (1991) and Kirzner (1997, 1999).

[32] Note that *hetero economicus* collapses to the special case of *homo economicus* when (1) the combination and exchange tags are abstracted into a field context; (2) the search platform $Y$ and dynamic operators $X$ are abstracted into a field context; (3) the technology system $\Sigma S(A)$ is abstracted into a technology field; and (4) the schematic preference set $P$ consists of a complete ordering, and is abstracted into a preference field. Similarly, Velupillai (1995b: 13) argues that 'the rational economic agent is a Turing Machine'.

# 6. Production Systems and Competence

## 6.1 Introduction

The theory of the firm has always been the most overstretched and crudely developed component of the neoclassical analysis. The reason for this is clear: a firm is in essence a combinatorial phenomenon, but coherent expression within the orthodox framework requires that this very aspect be suppressed. The result is a theory of production functions rather than a theory of production systems. In this chapter, I cut some first steps towards a general theory of production systems by introducing an analytical expression of the concept of complex competence.

The theory of the firm is rather disjointed and still professedly struggling with basic questions and standards. There remains much disagreement about basic questions such as why firms exist, where their boundaries are, and what they actually do. The neoclassical analysis has been little concerned with such matters because it is essentially a theory of market coordination, and does not actually require a theory of firms at all. What are referred to as firms are merely placeholders in the theory of markets, and thus a production function serves its purpose by linking the two sides of the equation (inputs and outputs) together.[1] Yet these abstractions have been sufficient and served a remarkably wide domain of application. In particular, Gary Becker (1965) showed that this framework could be applied to the study of households. This was an important moment for economics, because what Becker effectively revealed was that production functions can mean the production of anything. Becker also showed that the concept of a market was just as malleable as he wrote of the market for crime and marriage and other demographic phenomena. The genius of what Becker did was to reframe the question. He exposed clearly what the essential nature of the orthodox framework actually is.

The evolutionary economics framework is largely focused about the nature of the 'supply side' of the economic process, and in particular with the theory of the firm and the theory of technological and institutional change.[2] But, like the orthodoxy before Becker's arrival, it has nevertheless remained somewhat hesitant to state what the essence of the theory actually is. There is as yet no clear counterpart to Becker's illustration of the overriding context of exchange as the essence of 'the economic approach'. The evolutionary theory is of course being shaped by the logic of evolutionary processes, but also by the specifics of its subject matter. It is difficult to separate these out. It would be fair to say that the evolutionary framework is more about production (compare, exchange) but the problem is that unlike exchange, which maps directly to markets and the theory of markets, a generalized concept of production is not so well supported.[3] Firms are enormously protean things.

A recent development is the gathering of all resource-based theories of the firm (as seeded by Penrose 1959) under the rubric of a competence theory of the firm (Foss and Knudsen 1996). This is a most promising development, rich in synthesis and empirical avenues, but it still has some acute problems. Arguably the main one is that it has elevated to the centre of analysis an undefinable quantity. Competence is something that is intuitively easy to comprehend, but seemingly impossible to fix into an analytical framework. It is not clear what competence actually is and how such a concept connects to analytical tools and a microeconomic framework in general.

In this chapter I offer some suggestions on these matters. To do this, I follow Becker's strategy and lift the question to a higher frame. If what we are considering is production systems, then that entails production of anything, not just market goods. In Section 6.2, I develop from the evolutionary microeconomics a theory of production systems in terms of competence. In Section 6.3, this is applied to marriage, which I suggest is a production system. I search for the meaning of competence in this context, and also discuss the sources of complexity in the household system. In Section 6.4, I suggest that this scheme of analysis can carry over to knowledge production in general, whether innovating firms or scientific research programmes. I conclude that the evolutionary microeconomics can give an analytical interpretation of competence and that this concept is the centre of a general theory of production systems.

## 6.2   On the Theory of the Firm and the Theory of Production

### 6.2.1   What is The Theory of the Firm?

Let us begin with Marshall, and then move quickly through the subsequent developments. It is important to note that the theory of the firm attributed to Marshall (mostly by Samuelson, see Moss 1984) is not that which he discusses in Book IV in Chapters VI through XIII, but the principle of substitution defined between factors of production (Marshall 1949: 283–4) leading to the concept of a supply curve (note 2, p. 286). Marshall conceived this abstraction entirely in mechanistic terms, defining an equilibrium between supply and demand as stable, such that 'the price, if displaced a little from it, will tend to return, as a pendulum oscillates about its lowest point' (ibid.: 287). There are two theories of the firm in Marshall, one of which has become the neoclassical production function underpinning the logic of a supply function, and a second more opaque conception of a productive enterprise.

Subsequently, there remained an open question: what and why is a firm? Ronald Coase (1937) argued that the 'why' of a firm lay in its supersession of market coordination, internalizing the transaction costs of using the market mechanism. Williamson (1975) rekindled this idea, as did Alchian and Demsetz (1972), conceptualizing a firm as a governance structure. Edith Penrose (1959) probed the 'what is' question, theorizing that a firm is a pool of resources. Nelson and Winter (1982) deepened this idea, regarding these resources to be quasi-genetic skills and routines that build organizational capabilities. According to Foss (1993, 1996), these concepts are the foundation of the nascent competence perspective. George Richardson (1959, 1972) combined the what and why questions, arguing that firms and markets are both coordinating mechanisms, and that for firms to function as coordinating mechanisms there must exist market imperfections. Richardson recognized that connections between firms matter. Penrose recognized that connections within firms matter. At about the same time, Simon (1959, 1965) and Cyert and March (1963) argued that the sorts of decisions made by firms depend on the connections within firms. So they all recognized that a general theory of the what and why of a firm will effectively be a theory of the what and why of connections.

However threaded through the formal issues of the existence, boundaries and structure of the firm is a deeper issue, on the relation between the firm and the phenomenon of knowledge. This has been a major theme in the works of Brian Loasby (1976, 1986, 1996, 1998a, 1998b, 2000), in which he has specifically enquired of the firm in relation to the coordination of the growth of knowledge. A firm uses knowledge, a concept captured by the logic of a production function for a given technology, but firms also coordinate and create knowledge.

From this basis, we can distinguish two theoretical frameworks of the firm in terms of the treatment of knowledge. These broadly align with the two images in Marshall. The first is a production function, which is defined for a given stock of knowledge and therefore amenable to a field representation. The second is a production system, which acts to coordinate a flow of knowledge (information) and to create knowledge. Knowledge in this last sense must be interpreted very broadly, encompassing a spectrum of meaning spanning tacit knowledge (Polanyi 1967), skills and routines (Nelson and Winter 1982), Schumpeterian creative-destruction (Metcalfe 1998) and the phenomenon of competence (Foss and Knudsen 1996). Competence here is pivotal, standing for all knowledge that exists by specific combination between agents. In this respect, competence encompasses issues such as the organizational structure and boundaries of firms and also the nature of their existence. Competence is itself composed of lower-level systems such as skills, routines and habits. It is the theoretical crux of a production system.

### 6.2.2 Production Systems and Production Functions

The neoclassical theory of the firm, which is a component of the theory of market distribution, can be abstractly represented as below. In the evolutionary microeconomics, the theory of the firm is schematically different.

---

|  | Elements | → | Transformation Function | → | Elements |
|---|---|---|---|---|---|
| or | Inputs $(K, L)$ | → | Production Function $f(.)$ | → | Output $Y$ |
| or | $V$ | → | Technology Field | → | $V$ |

---

*Figure 6.1* The neoclassical theory of the firm

---

Elements + Connections $(V, E)$ → Production System $(S)$
↓
*Competence* → Outputs $(V, E)$
↑
Inputs $(V)$

---

*Figure 6.2* The evolutionary theory of the firm

The fundamental distinction between the two frameworks, then, lies in the treatment of the geometry of economic space.[4] In the neoclassical theory, the firm exists as a mapping between dimensions. Technology or knowledge is embedded in the field, and thus is not a component of the firm. In the evolutionary theory, the firm exists as a production system that, by its particular structure or geometry, produces competence. Competence is then the ability to make further connections, an aspect of which may be the transformation of inputs into outputs.

### 6.2.3 Competence

But what, then, is competence? Foss (1996: 1) explains it thus,

> By 'competence', we understand a typically idiosyncratic knowledge capital that allows its holder to perform activities—in particular, to solve problems—in certain ways, and typically do this more efficiently than others. Because of its skill-like character, competence has a large tacit component, and is asymmetrically distributed. It may reside in individuals, but is in the context of the theory of the firm and strategic management perhaps best seen as a property of organisations rather than of individuals (and therefore hard to imitate and transfer). . . . [F]irms are seen essentially as repositories of competence. And . . . it is firms' ability to accumulate, protect and eventually deploy competences to product markets that is seen as determinative of their long-run competitive advantage. Moreover, firms' competence endowments co-determine their boundaries, notably their degree of diversification.}

In this sense, competencies are the key assets of firms, as knowledge capital, and this asset is acquired and utilized strategically. And as such, firms conceptualized in terms of productive stocks of knowledge capital, as the ability to do things with varying degrees of efficiency, are then clearly the basic unit of analysis.

It is thus clear that the competence perspective does not proceed according to the logical format of a production function, but regards the nature of a firm to be explicable in terms of the emergent and essentially dynamic resources that are acquired as competence. It is this competence that enables a firm to transform inputs into outputs with varying degrees of efficiency, and it is the nature of this competence that determines the sort of activities the firm can diversify into or internalize. Competence, thus, is the working (self-)expression of knowledge; it is knowledge that has acted upon itself to reproduce itself.[5] Knowledge builds competence and competence builds further knowledge. Brian Loasby calls this total process 'the growth of knowledge'.

The nature of the competence determines what does and can occur internal to the firm, distinguishing this from what must either necessarily, or is more efficiently, brought in from outside the firm. This is in part determined by the resources the firm has acquired, as specific capital and the individual skills of labour resources, but also, and arguably more importantly (Wernerfelt 1984, Loasby 1996) by the learning processes that have occurred within the firm. For these learning processes to occur, and be effective as a strategic asset of the firm, it is necessary that there be sufficient stability of the elements involved (specific technologies, markets, employees, as such) for the competence to develop at the level of the firm rather than the individual. Fixed-term contracts, the creation of semi-autonomous teams, a commitment to certain technologies or markets, and other such strategic devices may provide the necessary stability to enable competence to emerge, evolve and embed itself as an enduring asset for the firm.

The point is that competence is a phenomenon that exists as stable or semi-stable connections between elements. It is dependent upon those elements but does not reduce to them. Competence, thus, can only be analytically represented in a non-integral space.

### 6.2.4 Production Functions and Systems in the Theory of the Household

Gary Becker (1976) conceived of a model of marriage as formally equivalent to the neoclassical theory of the firm. This was expressed as the household production function which represented the set of inputs employed to produce the outputs, such as children, status, health and so forth. Yet in the same way that a (market) production function is not a firm, a household production function is not a marriage.

A household production function is a vector field, as is any production function. However in respect of those who have looked inside the black box and then argued that a firm is in fact a system, the corollary is that a household is also a system. We owe to Gary Becker the metaphor that gave leverage into this territory. But that done, the next step is to follow through and re-interpret all of the arguments that apply to the neoclassical production function as a model of the firm to Becker's household production function as a model of marriage. Which is to say that the same basic theoretical questions arise, and we can generalize the concerns of Coase et al. to the phenomenon of a household. Excepting occasional prescient but ultimately passing heterodox comment (for example, Casson 1982, Earl 1986), this has not previously been undertaken from first principles, at least not in the sense by which Becker generalizes the logic of a production function.

In other respects, this can perhaps be thought of as a second wave of imperialism. The model of the household in the evolutionary microeconomics is based upon an abstract equivalence with the competence-based theory of the firm. The evolutionary theory of the firm (for example, Nelson and Winter 1982) and the competence-based theory of the firm both derive from the notion of a firm as a knowledge-creating entity. And it is this basis, of an abstract knowledge-creating system, that I suggest fully generalizes to the non-market context—that is, the household as a knowledge-creating system—and provides the keystone to an evolutionary microtheory of a production system. Which is to say that the theory of the firm and the theory of the household are both derivatives of a general theory of production. In this respect, competence is part of the general theory (of production) and is then manifest in both the special theories of the firm and the household. And as such, a theory of competence can be constructed from the framework of an evolutionary microeconomics.

## 6.3 The Evolutionary Microeconomics of the Household

> Marriage is popular because it combines the maximum of temptation with the maximum of opportunity.
>
> (George Bernard Shaw *Man and Superman*, 1903)

### 6.3.1 On Agents, Marriages and Households

The household can be modelled within the framework of an evolutionary microeconomics. But to do so, we must begin by conceptualizing the household as a combinatorial phenomenon. As a first approximation, consider Figure 6.3, which describes two agents (*M* and *F*, generally $V_i$) forming a connection. The resultant system of elements plus the connection we infer as a marriage.

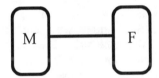

*Figure 6.3* A marriage as a system

Let us suppose that agents enter into such a system by choice, and do so with long term strategic intentions. These intentions relate to the expectation of a stream of benefits associated with the system. These benefits can in part be obtained by other means (for example, sexual or domestic services, equally for both males and females) but not generally (for example, males cannot typically obtain children without such union). The questions of interest are: (1) how do agents choose whom to marry; (2) how does the system then evolve, or, with what specifically is competence associated; and (3) in what sense can we describe the system as efficient? I shall sharpen these questions in conclusion.

We represent each agent in terms of the general model developed in chapter five, in which:

$$agent: <\Omega^+ : \Omega^-> <\pi^+ : \pi^-> <V : \Sigma S(A)> <X : P : Y>$$

Each agent will bring to the union his or her resource and technology set, the control algorithms and schemata as $<V : \Sigma S(A)> <X : P : Y>$. The matching of cooperation and exchange tags will be discussed in the following section. The marriage, as such, is a multiagent ($u_m + u_f$). The basic principles of combination are as such.

The control sets of search algorithms ($Y$) and the set of dynamic operators ($X$) are such that the multiagent only requires one set of each. If we presume that these are approximately the same across all agents, then duplications of either string will be redundant. As such,

$$X_m + X_f = \text{either } X_m \text{ or } X_f \qquad (6.1)$$
$$Y_m + Y_f = \text{either } Y_m \text{ or } Y_f$$

The set of schemata, $P$, can combine in three broadly different ways. The first way would be when one of the strings is dominant and becomes directly the schematic preference of the multiagent. Such a case might be imaged where one partner to a union controls all judgments and decisions, with the other string effectively redundant. Strictly interpreted, this is the neoclassical presumption; like transfinite numbers ($\aleph^1 + \aleph^1 = \aleph^1$), two agents with perfect information and perfect rationality combined makes a multiagent with the same perfect rationality and information (for example, see Samuelson 1956). However, with schematic preferences such that each string is either specialised or incomplete there will be substantial scope for gains in terms of the number of active specialized sites by the operation of crossover, where parts of each string combine into a new string (it will be a situation of a division of labour under increasing returns, compare, Young 1928). This situation is represented in equation 6.2.2, where the first half of string $P_m$ plus the second half of string $P_f$ combine to make a new string $P_j$. In such a situation, the behaviour of the multiagent is partly determined by each agent, with this division according to specialization. A compromise is made, as such, once and for all. A third possibility is that the strings do not combine into a single string at all (as in 6.2a and 6.2b), but remain in parallel. In this case, at each application both strings would engage off-line and the one that was by some criteria more successful at that time would be engaged on-line without modification. Here, everything is argued out, and if a compromise is an outcome (as in equation 6.2b) then it is for that moment only.

$$P_m + P_f = \text{either } P_m \text{ or } P_f \qquad (6.2a)$$
$$P_m + P_f = P_j \qquad (6.2b)$$
$$P_m + P_f = \text{both } P_m \text{ and } P_f \qquad (6.2c)$$

The optimality of each strategy depends upon the context. In the first two cases, the equivalent of one string is made redundant (an entire string in the first, two half strings in the second) and thus information is discarded. In the third case all information is used, but this will be the most costly in terms of processing requirements, as twice as much information is being carried into each application. In a stable environment with low demands on information we would expect the first case to arise, with the best string operating entirely on behalf of the multiagent. Cultural factors would be presumed to be significant in determining which string was selected to represent the multiagent. In a more information-rich, but still mostly unchanging environment we would expect specialization to occur as in the second case, and with the division remaining stable over time. In an information-rich and turbulent environment, the third situation would be more likely to arise due to the need to preserve as much variety and potentially useful information as possible.

The resource sets of each agent will make a simple aggregate such that the multiagent will have a combined resource pool (material assets, liquid assets, children, etc.). This is represented in equation (6.3) below.

$$V_m + V_f = V_{m.f} \qquad (6.3)$$

So far, marriage consists of a combined resource set and the possibility of improvement in the agent's schemata. While obviously significant factors, the main variable of interest from the perspective of an evolutionary microeconomics will be the conjunction of the technology sets $\Sigma S(A)_m$ and $\Sigma S(A)_f$. The key point is that these do not combine in either an aggregative or partial manner, but enable the possibility of higher-level technologies that are not decomposable into contributions of either agent but are a property only of the multiagent. Such emergent combinations we term competence.

If the technologies of each agent are $n$-level systems then the competence of the multiagent, represented below by $S(A)_j$, is an $(n + 1)$-level system. From this knowledge-based perspective, a marriage is essentially a phenomenon of combination, as a commitment to the mutual development of competence at the level of the system.

$$S(A)_m + S(A)_f = [S(A)_m + S(A)_f] + S(A)_j \qquad (6.4)$$

The multiagent can be represented as such below.

$$u_m : \ <V_m : \Sigma S(A)_m> <X_m : P_m : Y_m> \qquad (6.5)$$
$$u_f : \ <V_f : \Sigma S(A)_f> <X_f : P_f : Y_f>$$
$$u_m + u_f = u_j$$
$$u_j : \ <V_{mf} : \Sigma S(A)_{m+f} + S(A)_j> <X_{m/f} : P_{m/f} : Y_{m/f}>$$

The term $S(A)_j$ is the emergent property of the multiagent, attainable only to the multiagent, not decomposable to either of the agents, and thus lost when the multiagent disaggregates. Thus $S(A)_j$ is a specifically combinatorial property, and associated with connections that can only be made between agent systems.

It has been suggested that love is such a connection, in that it is not a property of a free agent but minimally requires a bonded pair. Perhaps. But what I mean to encompass by this term are all technologies (in the sense of abilities to produce outcomes) that are attained by both agents cojointly but not possible to either agent individually. Sex is a good example, as is emotional and physical security. So too, in this respect, is emotional or physical violence (a negative competence). However I would not include, for example, domestic services, as such things are not emergent to the multiagent. In sum, the logic of the theory of the household in an evolutionary microeconomics is to hypothesize that multiagents form so as to build higher-level connections than attainable to any free agent. These connections—$S(A)_j$—are the basis of expectation formation regarding the decision to enter into marriage (generally, to enter a household arrangement), and, equally, the failure of these to materialize, or to materialize with negative value, would be the basis of the decision to annul a marriage. In the evolutionary microeconomics, a marriage as a household is a specific combinatorial product: a complex system.

The neoclassical theory of the household is different. Becker (1965, 1976, 1981) did not model marriage in such a combinatorial sense but rather in terms of exchange. In Becker's theory, each agent specializes in one form of production (market or non-market) and each then exchanges the services of one for the other as inputs into the joint household production function. The household production function is a given technology. There is nothing emergent to the union. As such, specialization can only be explained in terms of natural propensities. For instance, Becker suggests that women are naturally endowed for maternal care and thus would tend to specialize in non-market production. The point then is that the market mechanism, as it were, would tend to reinforce initial differences—whatever their origin, biological or otherwise—producing under optimal conditions complete specialization. Thus the crux of the logic is exchange and the gains from trade resulting from such exchange (Ben-Porath 1982: 61). The agents are otherwise fully independent (there is no joint product) but nevertheless contracted to exchange their services only with each other. It follows then that a marriage is explicable only in so far as it produces outcomes that cannot be achieved by any other means. So if the *raison d'etre* of marriage is to produce children, this is achieved by specialized production and bilateral exchange; which is of course equivalent in all salient respects to the orthodox theory of the market process.

For Becker, then, the distinction between a household and a firm is the production of, respectively, non-market and market goods. Thus a production function that produces market goods is nominally referred to as a firm, and a production function that produces non-market goods is referred to as a household. Becker's emphasis, however, is not on the concept of a generalized production system, but falls back entirely to the generalized concept of markets.

Households produce non-market goods, but the analysis treats these as if they were market goods. That is the purpose of the generalized production function, to set the context for the generalized application of market analysis.

Becker provides a theory of the choices made by a household, which is understood to be a preference function and a production function in one. The only act of choice, however, is the decision to form a household. It is this choice that Becker infers as marriage, and not the resultant system. Household formation is regarded as an expression of utility maximization, an act of rational choice in the context of a supposed market for mates. In the outcome of an optimal sorting, which invokes the usual field-theory assumptions, everyone maximizes their utility functions by marrying their uniquely perfect mate. Bürgenmeier (1992: 115) notes that, 'according to this interpretation, divorce is simply the result of imperfect market information'. Two further abstractions must also then be recognized: (1) there is no uncertainty, only potentially imperfect information, and (2) *de gustibus non est disputandum* (Stigler and Becker 1977), which in this case means that marriage changes nothing about the behaviour of the agents. These assumptions clearly spell out the nature of the household in the theory. For although Becker advances a model of what exists inside the black box, the integral assumption is still immutably retained. The unilateral rational decision to marry is a cost–benefit analysis to calculate the optimal allocation of resources into a set of all possible (non-market) production functions. The equilibrium outcome is this set of production functions, which, in the instance of perfect information, is what Becker calls an optimal sorting. The production functions are then presumably enacted. The household is a production function in the context of a field.

Becker prefixes his analysis of the household 'the economic approach'. I suggest that there are two 'economic approaches': the neoclassical analysis of household production functions in the context of a field; and the evolutionary analysis of production systems in the context of a non-integral space. These consider different aspects. The neoclassical framework is geared to study choices in terms of exchange relations in a timeless environment. The evolutionary framework is geared to study choices in terms of combinatorial relations in a turbulent environment.[6] However this model does not produce deductive conclusions that can be directly fitted against data. It is designed as a simulation model, intended to reveal dynamic properties associated with different settings on string values and sets of populations. Nevertheless we can attempt to rough fit the model to a set of stylized facts to close in upon the sorts of issues that may be illuminated.

**6.3.2 Stylized Facts**

There are a number of stylized facts and trends evident in marriage statistics in Western nations. Although the evolutionary microeconomics is not primarily intended to work with demographic data sets, or with aggregate data sets in general, we can nevertheless discern the key aspects that the model (as a simulation model) will need to explain.

First, there is a typically higher average age of marriage for those agents that have a higher educational component. For 1980 New Zealand data, which in this instance of differential is typical of Western demographic profiles, the mean age of marriage for males engaged in production, transport and labouring (accounting for 49 per cent of the total of first marriages) is 26.3 years, and is significantly lower than for professional, technical, administrative and managerial at 30.2 years (accounting for 31 per cent of first marriages). This differential is clearly evident in demographic statistics of New Zealand over the period 1881–1995 for both male and female.

Second, people now marry later and divorce more frequently. Furstenberg (1996: 35) explains (for US Census data)

> The median age of marriage has risen from a low of 20.3 for women and 22.8 for men in 1960, to 24.5 for women and 26.7 for men in 1994. The proportion of women never married by their late 20's tripled from a historical low of 11% in 1960 to a high of 33% in 1993. The divorce rate among ever-married women more than doubled between the early 1960's and the late 1980's.

Again, this trend is typical of Western nations.

Third, the middle-class nuclear family that is presently conceived as being under threat by the various social trends away from the formal institution of marriage has not always been the norm and is presently evolving. It became the norm in the developed nations in the 1950s as a stripped-down version of the extended families of previous decades. The incidence of extended families in the modern world is mostly confined to economic regions that have not followed the pace of Western economic development, for example, Polynesia, South-East Asia, China, India and suchlike. The extended family of past epochs has become the nuclear family, and while this is still the modal household type in the Western nations these marriages are typically starting later, finishing earlier, and less likely to be formally contracted.

Fourth, most people marry eventually. For American Census Bureau data, and in the case of women, Furstenberg (1996: 35) writes '[i]n 1960 94 percent of women had been married at least once by age 45. The share in 1994 was 91 percent. In other words, the vast majority of Americans are still willing to try marriage at some point.' For New Zealand, much the same demographic profile emerges with variations in the percentage over the course of the twentieth century but not beyond the 90–95 per cent range (NZ Census data). So it is clear from these demographic profiles that agents who actively choose not to marry or cohabit, at some stage in their lives, actually constitute only a small percentage of the population.

Fifth, a significant proportion of first marriages ends in divorce. In all Western demographic data, there is a high rate of remarriage for divorced persons, and greatest for the 25–34-year cohort. This suggests a change in the pattern of marital behaviour, in the direction of serial monogamy it would seem, rather than a rejection of the institution of marriage *per se*.

Sixth, there is an increasing proportion of ex-nuptial births in all Western nations. In the United States, for instance, the proportion of births occurring ex-nuptially has jumped from 5 per cent in 1960 to 31 per cent in 1993. The same Census Bureau data indicates that the number of children living with single parents has risen from 4 per cent in 1960 to 17 per cent in 1994. The standard economic explanation for this change has most often focused upon the rise in the market wage rate of women's labour, and therefore a fall in the quasi-wages for spousal labour, inducing a substitution from non-market to market work (for example, Grossbard-Shechtman 1995).

Seventh, there has been a large increase in the participation rate of women in the labour market (for New Zealand statistics, see Morrison 1995; for United Kingdom statistics, see Rees 1992). There has been an associated narrowing of the market wage differential between men and women (Lam 1997). And in consequence, the dual-career marriage is now approaching the modal form of the household (Sekaran 1986). According to 1996 US Bureau of Labor Statistics, the percentage of married couples in which both spouses work is now 60 per cent, and at the same time dual-career couples represent 45 per cent of the labour market.

Eighth, there has been a marked decline in what is known as 'the marriage premium', which is the statistical fact that married men earn higher wages than single men do (Daniel 1995). Married men are typically older, better educated and have more stable employment histories than single men, but these factors only partially explain the difference. It is argued that married men are more productive than single men; ergo, marriage raises men's productivity. But this premium is declining. Gray (1997: 487) explains, 'the fall in the marriage premium coincides with the apparent decline in specialization within households, as the mean labour market hours [of working American women] nearly doubled from 15 hours per week in 1976 to 28 hours per week in 1989'. He surmises that (ibid.: 501–2) 'studies attempting to explain the existence of the marriage premium argue that a state of marriage is associated with higher-levels of unobservable skills', so deducing that 'the fall in the marriage wage premium is attributable to declining productivity effects of marriage'. This is an important inference for our present theory.

So there are a number of definite demographic trends occurring simultaneously, all impacting on the nature of the household. Women are increasingly participating in the market sector; dual-career marriages are now approaching the norm; the household division of labour is far less dichotomous (and readily stereotyped); marriages occur later and dissolve more fluidly; the wage-rate differential between married and single men is narrowing; de facto relationships and single parenting accounts for an increasing proportion of households.

### 6.3.3 An Evolutionary Economic Reading of the Facts

Furstenberg (1996: 36) argues that

> The biggest stress on marriage in the late 20th century is a transition from a clear-cut gender based division of labour to a much less focussed one. The traditional bargain struck between men and women—financial support in exchange for domestic services—is no longer valid.

Reciprocal exchange and the division of labour no longer seem to be the dominant factors in the economic explanation of marriage. As such, I suggest that Becker's exchange and field-based theory does not provide a suitable ongoing basis for the analysis of the dynamics of the marriage institution. Given its foundation in combinatorial dynamics, the evolutionary framework is more appropriate.

But to make sense of such trends from this perspective we must recognize the context in which they are embedded. Broadly speaking, the economic environment over this same period has become more complex and more turbulent (Pryor 1996). Which is to say that the web of economic interactions and activities has become more densely connected. A marriage as a household is a complex system. The basic principle by which systems cope with an increase in the complexity of the environment is by structural decomposition: that is, by a reduction in internal connectedness. The evolutionary model locates these connections in the set $S(A)_j$, which are the high-level connections that define competence. The competence theory of marriage argues that these connections are the principal explication for the phenomenon of marriage. Agents enter into marriage to share in the benefits afforded by marriage. These benefits are synthesized by competence. Without this concept, theoretical explanation for any documented instability of marriage must ultimately reduce to information imperfections (Becker et al. 1977: 1143). The explanation is purely microfounded in integral space; the environment is not an explanatory factor.

Competence, so defined, is the locus of effect between the interior intentions of the agents and the conditions of the exterior environment. In a perfect world, the agents might construct within the marriage system a complete set of connections at the $S(A)_j$ level. They would fully become parts of a greater whole, sharing in the surplus of gains from trade and aspects emergent to the union. This perfect world is easy to define. We simply must disallow informational uncertainty and uninsurable risks. Becker et al. (1977) do this, and write as if these factors were mere technical problems, with solutions yet to be furnished by the market. But this misunderstands the cause and context of such phenomena. Uncertainty, information imperfections, uninsurable risks and suchlike are all necessarily defined in a non-integral space. Competence also can only be defined in a non-integral space. Environmental turbulence, in contrast to random exogenous shocks, is only defined in a non-integral space. The competence connections within a marriage are subject to the effects of such environmental turbulence. And it seems that with changing environmental conditions, the nature of competence has also changed. I cannot offer irrefutable conclusions, but only a way of making sense of these stylized facts in terms of a framework that describes what is actually changing and to suggest some reasons for why this change is occurring.

The hypothesis is a restatement of the general principles of complex systems theory. Systems adapt to environmental turbulence by weak connectivity, which is to reduce the causal connections between a subsystem and all other higher-level systems. Simon (1981) called this 'structural decomposition'. The exchange-based model of market and non-market specialization is a model of a rigid structure. A marriage, as a system, and like all adaptive systems in changing environments, needs to be flexible to survive. It must be capable of adaptation to a range of unforeseen contingencies.[7] Weak connectivity, or structural (topographic) complexity, is the general principle that enables this to occur most efficiently. Yet there are a number of dimensions to this, which we may relate back to our stylized facts.

One, it is a well-known principle of design that systems operating in parallel are much more robust to environmental contingencies than systems operating in series, which exhibit extreme sensitivity to disruption of critical connections. This is the primary risk associated with complete specialization and locked-in bilateral exchange: if one partner becomes unemployed, or is rendered unable to perform his or her contracted duty, the entire system is threatened. Dual-career marriages are instances of a system organized in parallel, such that in the event that one partner becomes unemployed he or she is effectively insured by the other partner, and the system as a whole is not threatened. The faster the pace of technological change and economic evolution in general, the greater the incidence of career volatility and thus the more likely we would be to witness dual-career marriages.

In a related manner, critical connections interior to the marriage, as associated with things such as sex, devotion and emotional intimacy, are connections that can be broken with catastrophic effect. As connections between the elements of the system that yield returns, these are identified as competencies. The competence will be lost if critical connections are either not made within the system (for example, lack of devotion or interest, emotional coldness) or are expressly made outside the system (for example, infidelity). When these relatively critical connections either fail to materialize or materialize in the wrong place, all other connections are threatened. Strategies to minimize such risks might involve prolonged search and periods of de facto living arrangements, as evidenced by the trend to later marriage and the increasing proportion of ex-nuptial births, but also strategies that effectively make such connections less critical. It is almost impossible to get reliable demographic profiles (celebrity profiles are another matter) on the extent of extra-marital affairs that do not end in divorce, of the incidence of open marriages, wife-swapping and such phenomena. The hypothesis would be that for lifestyles where both partners regularly come into contact with many other people (typical of affluent urban lifestyles) then the marriage system would adapt by making such connections relatively less critical and in doing so increasing the flexibility of the overall system.

Two, competence in relation to the non-market sector has been significantly affected by changes in the technology of consumer goods and services, and particularly since the 1950s. In effect, domestic or non-market production does not really require full-time specialization and is more akin to a luxury good, or perhaps even an article of conspicuous consumption. It is unclear, however, whether this implies resources freed up for the development of a specific other competence, or, on the other hand, whether the form of competence itself has evolved towards the management (rather than the labour) of a household system. In this respect, the stylized nuclear family was itself an adaptation made possible by the growth of wealth and technology, and there is no reason to suppose that the full effect is spent. The structural form of the household will be in significant part determined by available technologies, the techno-cultural milieu as it were, with the trend towards smaller more mobile household systems a reflection of the extant value of the flexibility afforded. These developments make possible different forms of competence, which is not the same thing as the loss of competence altogether.

Three, in the evolutionary microeconomics the process of selecting a mate is a mapping of schematic preferences to cooperation tag sequences. Each agent will display a set of characteristics in the $\Omega^+$ tag, and these will be mapped to $\Omega^-$ of another agent, which, as defined in Chapter 5, is actually a string in the set $P$. Most people eventually marry or cohabit, and therefore most will be engaging search routines with the aim of selecting a mate.

Consider the search problem. It is reasonable to suppose that each agent can only commit to a limited search for computational reasons and scarcity of resources that can be devoted to search. A trade-off, thus, is forced between a

wide and shallow search (over many potential mates but superficially) and a
narrow but deep search (undertaken over fewer partners, but revealing more
characteristics). Figure 6.4 illustrates this distinction.

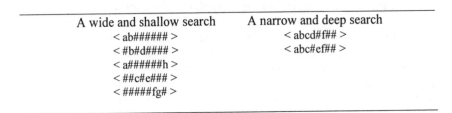

| A wide and shallow search | A narrow and deep search |
|---|---|
| < ab###### > | < abcd#f## > |
| < #b#d#### > | < abc#ef## > |
| < a######h > | |
| < ##c#e### > | |
| < ####fg# > | |

*Figure 6.4* Alternative learning strategies for schematic preferences

In both instances the agent acquires ten active sites, but in the first case the
agent has searched through the space of variety, and thus may have acquired
information on which characteristics are important, but he or she has less
information about how these characteristics combine. The other strategy has less
information about the variety of characteristics but more information about the
depth of combinations. Each strategy reveals different kinds of information. The
wide shallow search reveals the range of critical elements but nothing about how
they combine. The second strategy reveals the opposite. In practice, we would
expect agents to begin with wide shallow searches, then, once critical elements
are identified, to experiment with more in-depth searches based about such
characteristics. However, within this adaptive learning model it will not be
obvious when proficiency has actually been attained to make the decision.
Furthermore, if agents switch to the deep and narrow search too soon they may
be excluding many potential mates because they have not sufficiently learned to
recognize certain desirable characteristics. The problem here is not only tag
matching, but also tag interpretation. The same tag may be interpreted in many
different ways. For example, a Rolex watch may be a tag signalling a large
resource set, but then fakes are difficult to detect, and indeed others may well
interpret it as a tag for the characteristics of arrogance and self-indulgence. As
such, it is a plausible hypothesis to associate longer periods of search and the
increasing incidence of marriage annulment with the increasing difficulty of
interpreting the signs in a more heterogeneous population of rapidly changing
signals. For a more general consideration of search and learning in evolutionary
environments, see, for example, Dosi et al. (1997).

Such considerations of tag construction, matching and interpretation are not
unique to the 'marriage market', and are equally applicable more highly liquid
realms of interaction such as Blue-Chip stock markets. Indeed, it may well be
that it is the extent to which such markets have developed efficient and workable

tag construction, matching and interpretation institutions that is the essential feature that accounts for the liquidity (and therefore the function) of these markets.[8]

### 6.3.4 The Household System and the Complexity Constraint

The framework of evolutionary microeconomics allows us to confront new questions. An obvious one concerns the changes in the average size of the family in the context of technological change. The question is this. Why, given a vast increase in material wealth over the course of the twentieth century by the cumulative effect of the growth of technology, and thus by assumption increasing resources for the production of children, has fertility actually fallen? Why are families with more than five or six children so rare? This cannot be explained biologically. For although the sometimes expectation of annual births for many successive years is now mercifully, in most developed countries at least, a vestige of past centuries, this lowering of fertility is not a biological consequence but an exercise of choice. It is a choice, and therefore within the province of economics.

In the theory of markets, choice is constrained by scarcity such that for normal goods a shift outwards in the resource constraint monotonically increases the quantity of goods chosen. If children are just like durable goods, as Becker supposes, this theory does not make sense of the overarching fall in fertility over the twentieth century. I suggest that the prime determinant is not the material resource constraint (or a shift in preferences) but what we may term the 'complexity constraint'.

The complexity constraint is a hypothesis to the effect that beyond a certain point the complexity of the resultant system becomes too much to be viable. The evolutionary microeconomics suggests that the opposing (and in this domain, by implication, stronger) effect of wealth-creating technological progress is to shift the complexity constraint (threshold) to lower levels of fertility. The precise nature of the complexity constraint will of course vary according to circumstance. But the underlying topographic principle is clear. If we initially suppose that elements are family members, then as the number of elements ($n$) increases with the arrival of children the number of potential connections ($k$) within the system increases as a combinatorial function (see equation 3.4) and the number of distinct systems rises according to the equation $s = 2^n$. In simple terms, and ignoring for the moment issues of synergy and increasing returns, each extra dependant increases the potential complexity of the family system. This is in addition to the increase in elements brought by technological progress such as domestic appliances, vehicles, finance, leisure and health services, and so on. Technological change and the subsequent increase in per capita wealth has increased the number of elements that comprise the household system. Other things equal, the complexity of the household system has increased in its combinatorial aspect. It thus seems reasonable to hypothesize that the reduction in fertility in developed nations is a consequence of technological progress so as to maintain the household system within viable limits of internal complexity.

The difficulties of coordinating a large household are readily apparent. The logistics of child-care, shopping, health maintenance, ferrying to and from schools and extracurricular activities and suchlike are all made more complicated both by extra children and by a vastly increased range of services in this domain. Technological progress has certainly increased the quality of such services and support but at the same time it has, by increasing the number of elements in the household system, also increased the number of potential connections by a much greater factor. This increase in complexity must be paid for somewhere, and the immediate choice available to us is to reduce the number of elements in the system (see also Akerlof 1998). I suggest that this makes sense of two stylized facts: both the fall in the fertility rate (reduction in number of children), and the increasing proportion of single-parent families (reduction in the number of adults).

A curious counterpoint is that we do not often witness a reduction in the number of material elements, which would also be a strategy to reduce the complexity of the system. Why is this? It would seem that to do so effectively requires a mass coordination effort, something undertaken at the community or higher-level, due to the largely network nature of most goods. Communication services, media, health, education and so forth are all organized and coordinated on a scale that does not easily decompose. Laws prevent parents from opting out of the education or health systems, and media effects prevent parents from opting out of mass-marketed phenomena (think of the mass influences affecting choice of Christmas or Birthday presents). If you own a house or car, you are invariably locked into finance and insurance webs. In essence, it is almost impossible to individually pull out of the economic system's web and is seemingly only possible if done as a community movement (for example, communes of the late 1960s, for instance). The individual choices are in effect limited to a reduction in the number of people, either children or adults.

To explain the decline in the marriage premium, one need simply turn the argument around. It is single households that have become more efficient, in consequence of the fact that they are not usually near the face of the complexity constraint, and thus can often add new (productivity-enhancing) connections without overloading the system.

A microeconomic explanation of population dynamics and demographics is a potentially highly fruitful area for evolutionary microeconomics, and I believe there is much interesting work to be done in this area. In particular, connections are like investments over time, in that unlike normal goods (elements) for a connection to exist it must be continually reinvested in. This occurs in time, as for example, maintenance of connections within an extended family, or business community. When we commit time to the development and maintenance of such connections we forgo the opportunity to develop connections elsewhere (opportunity cost). Questions of interest arise regarding the competition between business and family connections and the formation of sub-culture affiliations (for example, gangs or clubs and suchlike). Such questions can be relatively easily posed in the language of an evolutionary microeconomics and are investigated by simulation techniques with differing initial distributions of connections and parameter settings on the entropy of connections.

### 6.3.5 Conclusion: The Competent Household?

The microeconomic framework of an evolutionary theory of the household is principally based about the existence of competence as system-level connections and the nature of the choice process leading to marriage is based about heuristic search and tag matching. The extent of environmental turbulence is a key parameter determining the structural form of the household system.

I suggest that we can define a research programme on the economics of the household in terms of the framework of an evolutionary microeconomics. The subject matter certainly overlaps with sociology. But so too with psychology, anthropology, law, heuristic decision processes, complex systems theory and the theory of the firm. We are interested in the same basic questions that motivated Becker to enter this domain: that is, to explain the choice process that leads to marriage and to explain phenomena connected to the gains from marriage. These are rightfully economic questions, but they can be approached with different economic frameworks. We can study the phenomenon of marriage from either an integral or a non-integral perspective. Becker's field-theory framework draws explicitly upon the theory of preferences and the presumption that a market for marriages exists. It is therefore geared to study questions relating to the allocation of the surplus from marriage and optimal pairings of agents (optimal sorting, *qua* market equilibrium) in the context of an integral space. By definition, it can tell us nothing about structure, emergent properties, the effects of different environments and the significance of uncertainty. This is the domain of evolutionary microeconomics, and in this section I have endeavoured to take some first steps towards a theoretical analysis.

This task will properly require simulation modelling of a population of agents as defined, with a variety of settings in the resource, technology and schemata strings. Such a model would be geared to understanding the relative range of flexibility of various systems, and the factors which are most likely to induce the formation of competence, and the conditions under which this is stable. Such models will flow most naturally from elaboration of the competence-based theory of the firm.

## 6.4   The Evolutionary Microeconomics of Knowledge Production

There is a certain abstract sense in which we can speak of a production function for knowledge. We may suppose that a quantity of researchers and equipment (labour and capital) will be expected to produce a certain output quantity of knowledge (inventions, design concepts, journal articles, patents and so forth). But those who have actually investigated the economics of corporate research and development (R&D) and the economics of innovation processes, rather than simply modelling it as a patent race, generally argue that things are much more complicated and subtle than that. In the study of technological change the black-box model of a firm as a production function has very little serious application. Such studies typically tend instead towards case-study methodology, or, more recently, evolutionary-based theory.

The reason why investigation into this production activity cannot make much use of production functions is simply that production functions exist in an integral space. In such a scheme, there lies before the agent a field of potential knowledge and the agent must decide upon the quantity of resources to spend upon its excavation. Expected benefits are balanced against expected costs and an optimal quantity of knowledge is produced. The irony is that research into such research is regarded as research. What must be realized instead is that both the tools or inputs of research (such as theories, paradigms, collaborations, data analysis) and the outputs of research are essentially objects in non-integral space.[9] A production function, and the marginal analysis it entails, is simply the wrong tool for elucidation of the dynamics of the process which, as Robert Solow alighted upon, is arguably the very seat of the material development of our economies. I suggest that the evolutionary microeconomics, with its conception of a production system, is a more appropriate framework under which to organize research on such questions.

Such research is already well under way, and there seem to have emerged three overarching issues: (1) that relating to the nature of the knowledge product; (2) that relating to scale and scope; and (3) that relating to strategic behaviour of the firm with respect to this product. The first issue turns on the fact that such knowledge is often either tacit or easy to replicate once discovered, both of which make property rights difficult to attach and enforce. Further to this, there are often major coordination issues associated with the establishment of standards (Hawkins et al. 1995). These issues largely relate to policy (Hall 1986). The second issue concerns the geometry of production, which is a characteristic concern of the Neo- and Post-Schumpeterian schools. The issue here is essentially whether size matters in terms of both the capabilities to produce new knowledge and also the incentive to do so. The third line is more directly concerned with how firms actually behave, and confronts issues such as first-mover advantages (compare, free-riding), learning curves, management and strategic alliances. If there is a major conclusion across such studies it is that the production of knowledge is conditional upon the firm building specific capabilities, or competence as it is now more commonly referred to, to handle that knowledge. This involves many factors, such as the gathering of complementary assets, the establishment of inter- and intrafirm coordination, appropriate management systems and generally things that in abstract amount to making the right connections. What we are referring to then is a knowledge production system. As such, if we frame the issue at this higher abstract level, then the evolutionary microeconomics can be applied. To make effective new connections (the output) the firm must first have in place a set of connections which we term competence. In other words, higher-level connections guide the development of lower-level connections. At this level of abstraction, the innovating firm is in the same class of dynamical objects as scientific research programmes.

Philosophers of science have drawn from the history of science theories about the nature of knowledge production in terms of high-level frameworks. The works of Thomas Kuhn (1962), Imre Lakatos (1978) and Paul Feyerabend (1978), in prime instance, are all essentially evolutionary theories that emphasize that the primary organization of the production of knowledge is in parallel. The overarching image here is of a set of productive enterprises (paradigms, research programmes), each using different technologies (theories, frameworks) to produce knowledge in the form of models that variously predict or explain. These are high-level connections guiding and constraining lower-level connections.

The connection between the growth of scientific knowledge and the behaviours of innovating and knowledge-creating firms has been made clear by Brian Loasby (1991). Loasby links these realms with the concept of connecting principles. He argues that knowledge production in general requires that knowledge be able to be coordinated, that it be commensurable, which is the function played by high-level theoretical frameworks in academic research. In so doing, Loasby is drawing emphasis to the crucial importance of coordinating webs or networks that are the necessary condition for the growth of knowledge to occur. Researchers studying innovating firms have recognized this in specific. The philosophers of science have argued this point in general. But as of yet there is seemingly no general theoretical framework with analytical bearing that can link all such understanding together. The framework of an evolutionary microeconomics is precisely adapted to represent these connections analytically, connecting principles or competence, and to examine the consequences of changes at the higher-level on the lower level or vice versa.

Consider the production of scientific knowledge. Let us suppose that the agents or elements in this process are individual researchers described by the general model below.

$$agent: <\Omega^+ : \Omega^- > < \pi^+ : \pi^- > < V : \Sigma S(A) > < X : P : Y >$$

$V$ represents the resource set, which in this case is the models and concepts and suchlike that the agent can access. Formal training would supply such stocks. $\Sigma S(A)$ is the technology of the scholar, his or her ability to make connections between these elements and also other elements (such as data). It is the making of these connections that constitutes knowledge and the discovery of new connections is the principal goal of the researcher. $X$ and $Y$ are the methods for generating new 'candidate solutions', by which agents search for such knowledge. The agents evaluate these with their schemata, $P$.

Agents can do one of two things to produce new knowledge. They can search the space interior to their own set $V$, seeking to make new connections between concepts, theories and data that they already possess, or they can seek to make connections between elements that they hold and elements in other agents' resource or technology sets.[10] The former is called the deductive method and proceeds by logically following the consequences of axioms (primitives in the set $V$). This produces knowledge. However seeking connections outside the set $V$ poses a major problem not faced by the deductive method, namely the problem of commensurability. The problem is: how do we know that we all mean the same thing when we refer to the same thing? It is here that the concept of a research programme or paradigm comes alive. A research programme is essentially a statement of the sorts of connections that can and cannot be made. It establishes the conduits, as it were, between elements and protects these by refusing entry to the network to any agent who does not agree to the principles by which the network is structured. These are the hard-core propositions. In terms of an evolutionary microeconomics, they are the competence connections, and occur at the $S(A)^{n+1}$ level of the production system. Scientific revolutions, or paradigm shifts, are abstractly a change in such connections; a reconfiguration of the geometry of research space, if you will.

There are many other aspects of such a model that may be considered, for instance we may inquire into the processes by which connections ossify or fragment (how does the hard core harden?) and the consequent affects on the dynamics of the growth of knowledge (what is the topographical nature of the attractor basins associated with different hard cores?). These are unanswered questions, but the point I make is that they can at least be posed within the framework of an evolutionary microeconomics in consequence of the key issues being essentially statements about the existence, structure, suitability or flexibility of connections. If there is ever to be a general theory of technological innovation or the production of scientific knowledge (or more ambitiously, a general theory of the growth of knowledge, corporate and academic) then we must first comprehend the systems nature of such an evolutionary process, which is essentially an interplay between distinct levels of connections.

## 6.5   Conclusion

This chapter has cut some first steps towards a general theory of production systems in terms of an evolutionary microeconomics. In this respect, it is parallel with and ultimately complementary to orthodox microeconomics, which defines a general theory of market exchange. I have endeavoured to emphasize the division of labour between the two general frameworks of microeconomics. And although I have not provided a definitive analysis that might demonstrate the theory, as the means of this is something that is still in the process of development, what I have outlined are the principles by which such simulation models will be constructed.

The main point I hope to have made clear is that at the centre of a general theory of production systems is the concept of complex competence. The analytical concept and mathematical framework of complexity are very new, as is the concept of competence in relation to the theory of the firm. In order to link these key theoretical concepts together we must define competence in a non-integral space. I have defined competence as the connections that can be realized and stabilized between the elements of a production system. For a production system to be efficient in terms of evolutionary dynamics the competence synthesized will be, by hypothesis, complex.

There remains much to be done before we have rigorous theory and useful models. There is little use here for aggregate data normally employed in econometric investigations. The data requirements for this programme are dis-aggregated micro studies of the units of analysis (for example, firms, households, research programmes) with particular attention to the nature of competence.

## Notes

[1] Demsetz (1997: 426) explains it thus: 'Neoclassical theory's objective is to understand price guided, not management guided, resource allocation. The firm does not play a central role in the theory. It is that well known "black-box" into which resources go and out of which goods come, with little attention paid to how this transformation is accomplished'. Which is to say that such theorists of the firm do not actually study firms—as Marshall suggested (1949: 218)—but rather a set of continuous and often linear mathematical forms called 'the theory of the firm'.
[2] For instance, in Witt's (1993a) edited volume *Evolutionary Economics*, of the 25 papers gathered, all but three are focused either directly or by leading examples and applications, about firms, technology, innovation, entrepreneurship or institutions. Hodgson's (1998) *Foundations of Evolutionary Economics 1890–1973* has similar statistics, with only one of the 22 texts addressed to consumer or distributional concerns.

[3] Compare Young (1928) on the effect of increasing returns (on the demand side) working through the division of labour simultaneously as industrial evolution and economic growth (see Groenewegen 1999).

[4] It will also be noted that a distinction between inputs as capital and inputs as commodities is also realized in the evolutionary theory of the firm.

[5] On the foundations of the competence perspective, see Lippman and Rumelt (1982), Demsetz (1988, 1997), Eliasson (1990), Prahlad and Hamel (1990), Langlois (1992, 1996), Dosi and Malerba (1996).

[6] It is perhaps prescient to note at this stage that the study of acquisition and merger in firms can be usefully thought of as a kind of marriage, and one that might proceed or not and subsequently succeed or fail or otherwise for essentially the same reasons as indicated here.

[7] As Becker et al. (1977: 1144) concede, 'the majority of divorces results from uncertainty and unfavorable outcomes and, therefore, would not occur in a world where outcomes could be anticipated'.

[8] Could it be that efficient markets have more to do with well-defined and institutionalized tag matching than the much lauded but little understood principle of universal free competition? See Lachmann (1986), Hodgson (1988), Burt (1992) and Callon (1997).

[9] A conference or discussion group, for instance, is a network object, connecting many researchers about a specific locus. By constraining the generation of variety to a specific subject matter or problem, or even to a specific way of looking at a problem, a steady focus is thereby achieved. It is important to keep in mind that science does not work by simultaneously connecting everything with everything else, but rather by quite deliberate and sometimes strenuous restriction to allow only a few things to be connected at once.

[10] In this way, and using the academic context, we can distinguish between journal articles as knowledge elements which can be acquired by agents for the cost of time and effort from the market, as it were, and phenomena such as conferences and collaborations, which are more akin to temporary marriages. Agents meet in such circumstances with the idealized purpose of forming potentially valuable higher-level connections that cannot be obtained otherwise. David Lodge's 'academic romance' *Small World* captures this idea elegantly.

# 7. The Theory of Expectations

> We must discontinue the practice of treating expectations as if they were ultimate data and treat them as what they are—variables which it is our task to explain.
>
> (Joseph Schumpeter 1939, Vol. 1: 55)

## 7.1 Introduction

Two elemental propositions now underpin the evolutionary microeconomics: (1) that the economic system is a complex open adaptive system; and (2) that the essential behaviour of this system is endogenous change and self-transformation (in historical time). For the greatest part, self-styled evolutionary economists have concentrated their attentions upon representation and analysis of the evolutionary dynamic, an approach complicit with the core Schumpeterian notion that in market-based capitalistic economic systems, change is the normal state of affairs. Given this, it is perhaps curious that the question of how agent behaviour then reacts to the possibility and indeed inevitability of such change has remained an issue mostly peripheral to the theoretical scheme. There is a conspicuous gap in the research programme—there is no definitive evolutionary theory of expectations. This chapter attempts to construct the first principles of an evolutionary theory of expectations, and one that will then link to an evolutionary macroeconomics.

The basic idea is twofold. From the perspective of the individual agent, we recognize that agents use internal models to process environmental signals into expectations. These production systems are represented in a multiagent simulation framework as schemata (Holland 1995, Epstein and Axtell 1996), which are sets of strings that operate as a kind of algorithmic suite. Agents are heterogeneous and capable of learning (Arthur 1993, Lettau and Uhlig 1999, Riechmann 1999). But an evolutionary theory of expectations involves more than just a refinement on the theory of agent learning to incorporate expertise. It must ultimately make sense of two deep but related insights, namely that preferences are themselves expectations and that expectation formation is a distributed process. (In this sense, the theory of knowledge production in the previous chapter leads into a theory of expectations as conjectural knowledge.) An evolutionary theory of expectations will also, when fully developed, become a theory of endogenous conjectural preferences. I do not achieve that ultimate synthesis here. Nevertheless, we can proceed with the initial notion that expectations form over a network ensemble as agents incorporate the expertise of selected other agents. The dynamics of expectations (and of preferences) are the dynamics of a complex distributed network process. Alan Kirman (1997c: 346–7) recently expressed the following view:

> What seems to me to be the most important factor to consider when studying economics in terms of networks is, not only how behaviour changes as agents interact through a network, but also how networks themselves evolve. What one wants is that links should be reinforced by good experience and weakened by bad. Very little has been done in this area in economics.

Expectations are an instance of a network structure *par excellence*. The attitudes, beliefs, hypotheses and conjectures, our world-views (or WORLD MODEL, as I will denote them here) and other such knowledge structures are products of local, discrete interactions. The standard approach is of course to conjure an information set with carefully defined set-theoretic and topological properties before endowing it upon the agent. It usually passes without remark that this imparts a degree of epistemic precision to expectations that is simply untenable. A major problem with the standard abstraction is that it fails to account for the fact that information always has a discrete and local origin: when we have information it is because someone or something communicated it to us (deliberately or otherwise). It is a small step from there to note that this process may well be highly complex, with many intermediate layers of filtering and amplification, all intermediated by schematic representation. The cognitive scientists assure us that this is indeed so.

An evolutionary microeconomic theory of expectations must therefore aim to synthesize this notion of complex heuristically defined, partially specialized agents situated in a variable network context. The crux of the framework that I propose is the notion that agents build internal models of the external environment. That much is orthodox. The heterodox spin is that these models are autonomous production systems that undertake many functions besides expectation generation. But to explore the implications of this, we need to first build a multiagent simulation model; I do not do this. The objective of this chapter is simply to consider some of the main issues in building such models with epistemic componentry. In Section 7.2, I shall consider the epistemic nature of expectations. Sections 7.3 and 7.4 will examine the relation between expectations and probability and between expectations and plans. In Section 7.5 the connection is made between expectations and expertise. In Sections 7.6 and 7.7, a proposal for modelling expectations as the distributed interaction of internal agent models is sketched. Section 7.8 concludes.

## 7.2  What are Expectations?

Expectations are of course a Swedish invention, and crucial to any understanding of the nature of money.[1] However there is more to expectations than the theory of Swedish money. Keynes (1936/1971, 1937) thought expectations important to explain mass movements in consumption and investment expenditure. Much of what Keynes said was subsequently assimilated into the mainstream (see Hicks 1939), but not his theory of expectations, which was doggedly misunderstood (see Townshend 1939 on this point). George Shackle (1958, 1972, 1979) thought that expectations presented a deep theoretical and epistemic challenge. But Shackle was always rather too much for many economists, who by and large preferred not to be challenged epistemically. And so his writings were largely ignored, except for the other occasions upon when they were misread (see Earl 1998 on this matter). Georgescu-Roegen's (1958, 1971) oblique study of expectations suffered similarly. Both clearly saw that the framework of positivism was ill-equipped to handle the epistemic and evolutionary-dynamic implications of expectations as cognitive byproduct. Katona (1951, 1960) thought expectations might be measured, but others quickly recognized that it would involve a lot of empirical survey work, and, nefariously, smelled a bit too much like sociology. Debreu (1959) had elegantly solved the problem anyway by assuming markets all the way to the end of the universe. Lucas (1972) saw that expectations are a property of agents, and thus argued that all macroeconomics must incorporate this: he folded macroeconomics back into microeconomics along the seam of expectations.

The problem with expectations is trying to figure what they are and where to put them in a scheme of analysis. There are a number of options; all perverse. If expectations are ignored completely, then economic analysis becomes hopelessly static. If they are treated as unambiguous data, then analysis becomes woefully deterministic. If they are fixed to rational agents, then macroeconomics collapses. If they are treated as conjectural inference, then optimization collapses. If they are supposed to be measurable, then positivism collapses. If they are permitted, then imagination, learning and novelty must also be permitted. If they exist, then a mechanism for generating them must also exist. If they exist *en masse*, then this implies some distributed network or field through which they are coordinated. This implies interdependence, which suggests self-organization and reflexivity. The point is this: the way in which expectations are treated is not an addendum to an otherwise well-defined analytical framework, but effectively determines the ultimate nature of that framework. For this reason, expectations are a subject matter deserving a much deeper consideration of their ontological and epistemic basis than is usually afforded. In other words, rather than beginning with a macroeconomics and then grafting a theory of expectations on to it, we shall instead begin with a theory of expectations and attempt to grow a macroeconomics from it.

The way that agent expectations have generally come to be treated in the standard conceptions of economic theory and modelling is simply to fit a further vector to the information set. Mathematically, this is a conventional and relatively unsophisticated treatment that does not affect the hard core of the research programme, or alter the formal perception of the geometry of economic space, which remains in $R^n$. This treatment is prima facie acceptable, as it takes the aspect we are sure of, namely that expectations are an input into the moment of choice, and suitably abstracts from the aspects we are not so sure of, which encompass the nature of the production system that constructs expectations, the inputs into this process, and the geometry of the total network of interactions.

In the standard mathematical treatment, an expectation is a construction built from elements of the theory of probability. The mathematical expectation of some variable $X$, denoted $E(X)$, is a weighted average of $n$ possible states of $X$ with probabilities $P_i$ used as weights, such that:

$$E(X) = \Sigma P_i X / n$$

At least three operations are required to map the concept of an expectation into economic theory. First, agents must construct a list space $(X)$, which defines the set of all possibilities. Second, each of these possibilities must be weighted $(P)$. Third, the array $E = P(X)$ must then be interpreted. From a computational perspective, this implies the existence of some creative/search operator that constructs $X$,[2] a rational/mathematical operator that subsequently constructs $P$, and a cognitive/heuristic operator that translates their product $(E)$ into the space of behaviour via some framework of interpretation.

The construction of $X$ is in an important sense unconstrained. For reasons of both bounded rationality and inductive insufficiency, it is impossible to ever know whether $X$ is a complete list. In consequence, the individual elements in $X$ need not actually have any formal relation to one another. However, some necessary logical structure is imposed upon $P$: (1) there must be as many elements in $P$ as there are in $X$; and (2) if expressed numerically, such that the weights are interpreted as probabilities, the elements in $P$ must sum to unity. When this occurs, the outcome is an expectational array that can enter into decision making (for example, as in subjective expected utility theory). Prior to this, we may delimit the various expectational schools of thought with respect to their definition of the two rudimentary constructs $P$ and $X$.

The standard approach is of course the New Classical theory of rational expectations, which is properly considered a development over the neoclassical theory of expectations, which originally orientated expectation formation with the assumption that the future value of a variable will be some function of past values of the variable in question. Fisher (1930) defined an expected inflation proxy as a distributed lag from past values. Cagan (1956) introduced the concept of adaptive expectations using an exponentially declining lag structure. This sort of approach was refined to account for such things as error correction (Meischelman 1962), and a variable lag structure (Friedman 1959). Muth (1961), and later Lucas (1972), introduced the concept of agents using current models to make projections about future variables. In this scheme, future values of a variable were now related not to past values of the variable, but to contemporaneous values of other economic variables within a closed-form model. The orientation changed but the basic presumptions have remained the same. The agent as such was assumed to use an econometric model to form expectations rather than merely using some technique of extrapolation. For the subjectivists (for example, Savage 1954) the weights are not actually attached to events or variables but rather to 'states of the world' (see Lawson 1988: 47). Nevertheless, in all such cases the list can be exhaustively constructed and weights (as probabilities) attached to something.

The rational expectations (RE) framework makes a number of simplifications. The essential assumption is that the construction of both $X$ and $P$ is a simple, costless, timeless, computable calculation of $E$. Furthermore, it is supposed that in the aggregate (and in the long run) all agents converge upon the same set of expectations. It is implicitly assumed that there is nothing fundamentally interesting to be said about how agents actually calculate expectations. (Many centuries ago, physicists made the same sort of presumption about how particles experience forces.) By this presumption, then, the nature of these constructive methods and cognitive computational operations remain entirely within the so-called black box (compare, Leibenstein 1979). RE is not a theory of how expectations are formed, but rather is the theoretical conjecturing of an *ex ante* data set consistent with the assumption of an exhaustive list of possible outcomes, each, ultimately, correctly weighted. The Austrian school and other Subjectivists deny that these weights are probabilities in the formal sense (for example, see Lachmann 1976) but instead something more closely corresponding to anticipation or subjective belief (because it is impossible to know the probability distributions). The Post-Keynesians, following Keynes (1937) directly on this matter, agree that these weights are not objective probability measures and also doubt whether an exhaustive list can ever be constructed (for example, Davidson 1982–3, 1991). For the Behavioural economists (see Earl 1990b), the impossibility of list construction is a direct consequence of bounded rationality. The extreme position on this is taken by Shackle (1949, 1972), who argues both that the list cannot be constructed and that weights cannot be meaningfully attached (also Loasby 1991). The theory of expectations thus ranges from the initial presumption that all possibilities can be defined (*X*) and weighted (*P*), to the suggestion that only *P* can be constructed, to the Shacklean argument that neither of these can be meaningfully constructed.

The evolutionary theory of expectations takes the Shacklean position with respect to list construction and weighting. The Shacklean posture is not a denial of the meaningfulness of forming expectations, but rather of the incorrectness of conceptualizing them in terms of well-defined (exhaustive, finite, linear) concepts of *X* and *P* (see Potts 2000). There is a simple reason for this. The real world, as that which agents are attempting to form expectations about, is informationally complex (see Collier and Hooker 1999) and continually changing, and consequently we should not presume that the formation of expectations is a trivial task.[3]

There is not, at present, a plausible and functionally defined theory of the way in which agents adapt their expectations to a continually changing environment. It is a mistaken view to suppose that either the RE theory (a theory of information updating, Muth 1961) or the Behavioural arguments (various theories of individual cognitive learning) provide, in themselves, a satisfactory theory of the evolutionary dynamics of expectations. The RE framework does not explain how expectations are formed or how this process may evolve with time. It is a framework that does nothing more than examine the consequences of functionally complete information (by assuming the expectation is an unbiased predictor). It does not consider how this might come to be, or whether it has any correspondence to the actual processes of information coordination. The Behavioural theories, while providing plausible accounts of processes, still lack a population perspective or account of how all expectations ultimately interact. The Post-Keynesian and Austrian treatments of expectations, with their mutual emphasis on fundamental uncertainty, realized as the impossibility of completing *X*, and problems of mass coordination do address the issues missing in the Behavioural analysis. But at the same time they lack an explicit treatment of what is actually going on inside the black box. An evolutionary theory of expectations is in this respect a highly synthetic approach, but one that ultimately ends up with an emergent product that is different from its components.

The essential point to recognize is that complex evolutionary systems (dynamical systems) of the sorts under consideration (agents, firms, governments and so forth) are autonomous anticipative adaptive systems (see Holland and Miller 1991). For Holland (1995), anticipative behaviour implies the existence of internal models of the external environment. These models form the basis and mechanism by which agents look ahead, and thus seek to adapt their behaviour to fit with the expected future environment. It is important, therefore, to distinguish between such things as short-term versus long-term adaptation (and by implication, short- versus long-term internal models), as well as to identify anticipations that are common to the population of agents and the level at which difference occurs. Yet in all such thinking one overarching point is clear: agents use models as the basis for anticipation or expectation. It follows that a general theory of expectations is necessarily a general theory of the nature of these internal models: of the way in which they are constructed; the heterogeneity and complexity of their population; and the way in which they change both individually and collectively. It is these models that we seek to understand, and the key point is that these models are complex evolving systems.

To summarize, the prime dimension of a theory of expectations is the construction of an array. This consists first of defining the set of possible events (constructed as either a finite set or on a continuum) and second, of weighting each of the possible events. The primary concerns that differentiate the different theoretical approaches to the theory of expectations (Neowalrasian, Neoclassical, Post-Keynesian, Austrian and Behavioural) are whether or not the array can be meaningfully defined as a closed set, and then either way, whether or not it can then be weighted in such a way that probabilities can be defined. The evolutionary theory of expectations takes the extreme view on this, and supposes that the set of possible events cannot be meaningfully defined as a closed set, and that it cannot be weighted in a way congruent with conventional probability measures. I shall defend this position in the subsequent section.

From an evolutionary perspective of algorithmically defined agents embedded in a variable lattice (about which they construct internal models), it is apparent that there are several dimensions missing from the theory of expectations. In my view, there are three: (1) time horizons; (2) the importance (or otherwise) of being correct; and (3) the geometry of the network of expectations.

First, how far ahead do agents look ahead into the future? Much study has been devoted to the measurement of lag structures and to analysis of the consequence of infinite horizons, but there has been seemingly little concern with the functional structure of horizons. The reason for this oversight is obvious: numerical data are not naturally generated by this hypothetical process. If it is sought it must be measured by the probing of intentions, which has no place in axiomatic models. The simplest conception of look-ahead horizons is to suppose that there are two different populations of expectations: short and long period. Short-period expectations are focused about the direction of movement of a single variable, and computationally involves solving a closed-form model. Long-period expectations are those that involve factoring into account changes in the constituents or nature of the economic system. Keynes warned against the treatment of these sorts of expectations in the same way as those of the short period, and preferred instead to think of them in a Jungian manner. Minsky (1975, 1982) developed this mass psychological posture as the locus of his financial instability hypothesis. However in the evolutionary framework, the functional difference between expectation horizons turns on whether expectations refer to either the elements or the connections of a system. That is, we distinguish between expectations about the movement of variables such as prices, and expectations about possible changes in the set of connections within the system.

A further consideration is the relative importance of being correct in forming expectations. It is apparent that the measure of this is the degree to which the behaviour (for example, the investment or contract) is reversible. Expectations matter most when decisions based upon them are irreversible in consequence of irrecoverable expenditure. Irreversibility calls forth strategic behaviours to deal with the possibility of expectations being confounded (for example, to increase the liquidity of the asset portfolio or to diversify the portfolio). However, another way of viewing this phenomenon is to consider the way in which different decisions (about the holding of assets, say) fit within the particular lattice structure of an economic lifestyle, which we define as a coordinated set of behaviours. This is an important issue for both consumers and firms (see Earl 1990). Again, this conception focuses concern on the existence of key elements, and in this sense is congruent with the lexicographic models of consumer choice (Earl 1986). The evolutionary microeconomic framework develops this one step further in abstraction, and considers the graphical structure of these complex systems. It becomes apparent that irreversibility, and hence the importance of the expectation decision, has a microeconomic explanation in addition to the degree of imperfection of the second-hand asset market or contingent contracting. This is the measure of centrality of the specific element in the system (or the graph, in the language of the theory).

To continue in this vein, we recognize that the density of connections in a network of expectations may vary over time, and, furthermore, that there may be frictions or costs associated with changing network connections. We generally conceive of activity in terms of measured output, so that during a recession there is less (growth in) economic activity. Does it follow that the connective geometry of the economic system, as the density of connections, changes during the course of fluctuations in economic output? I think this a reasonable hypothesis. It is suggestive of threshold effects, such that as growth rates of the economy accelerate (or decelerate) then existing activity is simply speeded up (slowed down) along the same lines, but beyond some threshold changes in the connective geometry of the system occur. The estimate of this threshold will be a function of the frictions involved in changing existing connections or the costs involved in establishing new ones. If so, this will presumably have significant implications for the structure of the web of expectations. The question is whether there is anything important to discover about the path and the dynamic properties of some measure of this density. This may be useful in understanding the interlinkage between phenomena such as growth and business cycles. We may suppose that recessions induce relatively low connectivity and prolonged booms have relatively high connectivity, then the implication would be that boom periods would be characterized by relatively more unstable expectational dynamics than periods of recession.

In sum then, what are expectations? If one is willing to accept the closure and transparency of all set concepts involved in the description of an economic system, then expectations are an array that may be appended to the information set possessed by each and all agents. If this total closure is not acceptable, due to problems of epistemic reflexivity and incompleteness, then expectations must be seen as the product of internal generative models of external networks which are themselves the product of these schematic models, and so on. And if it comes to pass that this is the essential structure of distributed expectations, then we must admit that classical probability theory has little to say on these matters.

## 7.3   Probability and Expectations

> There is no more common error than to assume that, because prolonged and accurate mathematical calculations have been made, the applications of the result to some fact of nature is absolutely certain.
>
> (Alfred North Whitehead *An Introduction to Mathematics*. 1911: 27)

In an excellent study of the prehistory of the modern probability concept, which arrives with Blaise Pascal and Pierre-Simon de Laplace, Hacking (1975) recounts how prior to around 1660 the meaning of the words probable and probability were associated with best opinion rather than best evidence. In this sense, the opinions of a good or approved authority (such as those of the Monarchy or the Church for instance) were more 'probable' to be correct than that of lesser opinion. Probability was a concept associated with 'who said what' rather than with what was actually said or presented. Modern probability emerged, according to Hacking (1975: 35), when the concept of internal evidence replaced that of situated opinion. Evidence, in this sense, was a product of the 'low sciences' of medicine, alchemy and suchlike, which could not by their nature furnish demonstrative proof, but instead appealed to 'signs' that signified evidence. In this respect, David Hume's 1739 *A Treatise of Human Nature*, which defined the problem of induction with reference to sequences of evidence, would not have been possible without this prior shift in the meaning of probability (degree of belief) from opinion to evidence. Similarly, the variants of the standard framework of mathematical expectations can be organized with respect to the different meanings attributed to the nature of the probability concept.

First, how does the concept of probability relate to knowledge? It is notable that there is no definitive taxonomy of forms of relation. Tony Lawson (1988: 40), for instance, makes two overarching categorizations—(1) probability as a property of an objective external reality; and (2) probability as a property of an agent's knowledge of this reality—by asking whether probabilities are to be understood as objects of knowledge, or merely as a form of knowledge. This distinguishes the subjectivists (for example, Bruno de Finetti, Leonard Savage, Frank Ramsey), who locate probability as a property of internal knowledge, from the objectivists (for example, Ludwig von Mises, proponents of the RE hypothesis), who locate probability as a property of external reality. This duality between an epistemological and an aleatory meaning has been long recognized by historians and philosophers of probability (Hacking 1975: 11ff.). Rudolf Carnap (1950: ch. 2) distinguished between what he termed *probability$_1$*, which refers to a logical relation between two sentences (hypothesis and evidence) interpreted as degree of confirmation, and *probability$_2$* which is the relative frequency in the long run of one property of some thing with respect to another. For Carnap, as for Keynes (1921), the first probability concept appeals to a logical analysis, the second probability concept appeals to an empirical analysis. The distinction turns upon whether probability is ultimately a logical or a mathematical relation.[4]

Both such interpretations are generally regarded as conforming to the formal laws of modern probability theory, which derives from the axiomatization of probability theory with measure theory (Kolmogorov 1933). (In all cases, probability refers to a measure over the unit interval.) Kolmogorov's treatment is based upon an abstract space of elementary events ($\Omega$, the probability space) and a $\sigma$-algebra of subsets of $\Omega$ (for example, see von Plato 1994: 21ff.). However, because both interpretations are consistent, the axiomatic approach effectively circumvents rather than addresses the question of the ontological nature of the probability concept. This issue is perhaps somewhat esoteric in the context of, say, quantum physics or statistical mechanics, whereby it is ultimately immaterial whether the probability measures be attached to the events themselves or the investigator's claim to knowledge of them. However, it is of more immediate relevance when we address the status of agent expectations in the economic context, where the subjectivist epistemic interpretation finds itself broadly consistent with introspection. Indeed, in the writings of George Shackle (particularly Shackle 1972) we find staked out a radical subjectivist position that effectively denies the logic of any form of objective probability concept that has any relevance to the economic context of expectation formation. This radical subjectivist position, ascribed to by both the Austrian and Post-Keynesian schools of thought, is based upon the notion that empirical knowledge of the external environment is incomplete (there exists fundamental uncertainty). It follows that if the probability space itself is undefined (unbounded) then it is meaningless (compare, impossible) to attach prior probabilities to imagined events. Shackle rejects the concept of probability and instates the concept of potential surprise, which is a non-additive and purely subjective measure that does not require the otherwise critical notion of closure that is imposed in any axiomatized scheme.

Nicolas Georgescu-Roegen (1971: 52ff.) argues that the various doctrines of probability 'all in fact have the same objective: to order expectations with the aid of some numerical coefficient which each doctrine calls "probability"'. He broadly distinguishes between the Subjectivistic, of which he is dismissive, and the Objectivistic, which defines the probability measure independent of the individual. He then insists, detailing the Frequentist and Classical formulations, that 'objective probability is basically a dialectical notion' of which the dialectical root is randomness. A dialectical concept is one which is 'surrounded by a penumbra within which they overlap with their opposites' (p. 45). Probability, as such, is not a discretely distinct concept but ranges continuously over the space between randomness and order.

This leads us to concern with the relation between probability and the nature of the (supposedly objective) world to which the concept refers. In this the crucial distinction is between an ergodic and a non-ergodic system. This moves us from concern with the *ex ante* nature of the space over which a system is defined to the *ex post* nature of a system's behaviour within that space. A collection of systems forms an ergodic ensemble if the modes of behaviour found in any one system from time to time resemble its behaviour at other temporal periods and if the behaviour of any other system chosen at random also is like the one system. (In statistics, ergodicity is called stationarity.) In contrast, a non-ergodic system (one whose behaviour is non-ergodic) is one that is in certain crucial respects incomprehensible through observation either for lack of repetition or for lack of stability. The *Web Dictionary of Cybernetic and Systems* defines that 'Evolution and social processes involving structural changes are inherently non-ergodic'. Paul Davidson (1982–3) distinguishes between ergodic and non-ergodic decision-making environments. This classifies environments into those in which the objective rules of probability do apply (a necessary condition is stationarity) and those in which they do not (a sufficient condition is non-stationarity). In a non-ergodic environment decisions are unique, irreversible, and potentially of crucial significance (Shackle 1972, Davidson 1991). In such circumstances, the ergodic laws of probability simply do not apply.

The Austrian and Behavioural schools dispense with a direct account of probability and proceed to expectations with uncertainty and bounded rationality leading to rule-governed behaviour. Expectations are then an application of such. The Austrian theory of expectations derives from the radical epistemic subjectivism of Hayek and Lachmann. For Dow (1985: 139–42), the Austrian theory of expectations is synonymous with Shackle (see also Lachmann 1976). However, Dow points out that while the Austrian conception contains an implicit argument in convergence and stability of expectations, Shackle's Kaleidic framework invokes no such presumption. It is also noteworthy that the Austrian economists did not distinguish a theory of expectations from a theory of knowledge (for example, Hayek 1945) until the 1970s. O'Driscoll and Rizzo (1985, 1986) distinguish between neoclassical spatialized Time and Subjectivist 'real' Time, a concept they associate with the thinking of Henri Bergson. The existence of uncertainty makes optimizing behaviour impossible, and thus agents standardize their behaviour in terms of rules (see Bausor 1983, Heiner 1983).

In consequence of the existence of fundamental uncertainty, the concept of probability is not a necessary corollary to the concept of an expectation. As O'Driscoll and Rizzo (1986: 258) note:

> The idea of genuine uncertainty implies both the endogeneity of the source of uncertainty and the perceived unlistability of all the potential outcomes of a course of action. Each of these features of uncertainty provides a basis for the adoption of rules.

Such rule-based (that is, algorithmic, heuristic) approaches to decision making have been simmering in the economics literature for some time now (Tversky and Kahneman 1974, Simon 1982) and have recently begun to flourish in the more mainstream literature (for example, Campbell and Mankiw 1990, Rosenthal 1993, Lettau and Uhlig 1999). This is certainly a welcome advance, in that it moves towards furnishing economic models with plausible (observable and testable) psycho-foundations. But if decision making can be comfortably and usefully perceived as heuristically generated (without reference to complete information sets or well-defined probability density functions), it seems reasonable to suppose that other internal cognitive actions can also be afforded such representation. In the following sections I submit that plans, expertise and expectation are all viably understood as the outcomes of constrained generating procedures (Holland 1998).

The economic agent in the multiagent setting is defined as an algorithmic suite of such functions. Some of these make decisions, others construct plans or embody expertise, and others still generate expectations. All such functions can be grouped together as a class and defined within an object-orientated design of an economic agent. In this setting expectations, decisions and other behaviours are generated rather than deduced, and so infer a procedural rather than substantiative rationality (Simon 1976). Within this setting, expectations are not necessarily related to an underlying probability construct.

## 7.4 Expectations and Plans

What do agents form expectations about, and for what purpose? The standard answer is that they form expectations about the probability distributions of future asset prices, and they use these to maximize subjective expected utility. But this misunderstands an important relationship, which George Richardson (1959: 224) has pointed out (see also Richardson 1953, 1960, 1971, 1972):

> It is obvious that no direct connection can exist between objective conditions and purposive activity; the immediate relationship is between *beliefs* about relevant conditions and *planned* activities which it may or may not prove possible to implement.

In the evolutionary microeconomics, we suppose that agents also form expectations over the space of connections in the economic system, and that they order these in relation to coordinated plans, which are of course proposals for future activity. The formation of expectations and the construction and coordination of plans are, in this way, two sides of the same coin. Hence, there are two reasons for constructing expectations. The first reason is as input data into calculation of optimal choice. Expectations of future prices serve this function, and serve to guide immediate actual activity. The other reason for forming expectations is to guide the coordination of plans for future actual or contingent activity. It is important to note that we (as economic agents) do not form expectations about everything. Equivalently, we do not make plans about everything. The demand for expectations comes from the need to construct plans (they are a derived demand), and in so far as plans are circumscribed, so too will be expectations.

Expectations and plans are interrelated constructs (they are both mental models), and each supposes the existence of the other. When the plans of individual agents are stable and widely known (or not), then it follows that expectations will also be stable (or not). Darley and Kauffman (1997) discuss this in the context of optimally complex (adaptively rational) models of other agent's behaviours. Similarly, when an agent is not able to form suitable expectations of other agents' behaviours, then he or she will likely restrict his or her own planning horizon as a means of protection. This will feed back into the system of expectations engendering even further instability. Why do agents form plans? Several answers might be given. An important one that we ought not to dismiss is their psychological value. To have a plan (or a goal) is to be acting with purpose, which, to some degree, is an end in itself. When businesses do this, it is called strategic planning (for example, writing mission statements and suchlike) and arguably serves much the same function. In general, though, a plan is a sequence of steps (conditionals) supposed sufficient to reach a target or goal or some such. These may be explicit and definite, as in contracts, or indefinite and unobservable as they exist in the minds of agents.[5] Expectations derive from plans, and plans are formalized as contracts. If we will move expectations to the centre of an evolutionary macroeconomics, then we must also centre contracts there as well (see Okun 1981).

Foster (1987, 2000) has argued at length that the foundations of an evolutionary macroeconomics mandate an explicit rejection of the notion of auction-markets as coordinating devices in favour of contracts. He further illustrates how this requires a reconception of the economic agent from *homo economicus*, who underpins the demand curve in auction markets, to *homo creativus*, who is a contracting unit. *Homo creativus* and *hetero economicus* are obviously close relatives (both exist in non-integral space), and point clearly towards Post-Keynesian, Institutional and self-organizational schools of macroeconomic thought to find a common ground in an algorithmic conception of agency within the evolutionary microeconomics. Much important work remains to be done here.

Expectations, plans and contracts are the threads of coordination that extend from a basis of agents having internal models of the world within which they structure internal goals and construct heuristic procedures for realizing these. This implies the existence of plans in the individual instance and contracts in the collective instance. The conjunction is a framework for action, which creates the demand for expectations over the space of the connections to which these refer.

## 7.5   Expectations and Experts

Expectations are a species of knowledge, which, in the evolutionary microeconomics, implies several things. First, there is the issue of the cognitive (Simon 1959) and epistemic (Shackle 1972) nature of this form of knowledge as an internal construct of the agent. Second, there is the issue of the distributed processing of a network of expectations (see Kirman 1997c). Third, we must recognize that the construction of expectations is an activity that involves, to some greater or lesser degree, skill or expertise. This realizes an important point. In many instances, when agents form expectations under conditions of informational complexity or uncertainty, they do so by looking to others (for example, Keynes 1937, Fleith and Foster 1999). In the case that the set of others is not chosen at random, and that there is some discrimination at work, we might suppose that the 'others' that agents look to are experts. But who are these so-called experts? From a Schumpeterian perspective, expertise defines the domain of the professional classes as those practising skills that are to some extent the product of reason (compare, Saul 1993). The expert, then, is an agent with specialized knowledge.

So what form does this take, and how might we hope to represent this within an abstract model? In the applied psychological literature on expertise (for example, Bédard and Chi 1992), the distinction is made between the expert and the novice. For instance: experts know more about their subject domain than novices; experts' knowledge is better organized (Einhorn 1973); they perform tasks better than novices in domain-related skills; and these skills often do not translate into unrelated domains (Wright and Bolger 1992). In the artificial intelligence literature, the eponymous instance is the expert-system, which is an application program that makes decisions or solves problems in a particular field by using knowledge and analytical rules defined by experts in the field. An expert-system is a program that combines databases, retrieval, interpretation and perception systems, knowledge representation schemes and inference engines. Expert-systems highlight the fact that expertise is not just data, but the selective interpretation and processing of it. Combining these two notions, I suggest that bit-strings can be employed as an abstract representation of expertise. Strings are also an easily computable and functionally transformable data structure. The agent will have a set of internal strings ('schemata', Holland 1995) that are the product of experience and learning.

Supposing, then, that expertise can be represented as a set of strings with specific functional definition, how does this relate to expectation? Expectation is the output of internal schemata (models), but we must recognize that some of the inputs are the outputs of other agents' schemata. It is a construction of expectations by means of expectations problem, if you will. But agents specialize, and as such while it may be useful to be an expert, it is equally useful to know how to find and identify one. Supposing this can be done, the computation of expectations involves the compiling of these distributed expert programs. In the multiagent simulation environment, such as *Swarm*, agents interact by sending messages to each other. This domain of message space defines the domain of interactions. The messages interact with what John Holland (1995) calls 'tags'. Tags are the external representation of the internal schemata.

To summarize. Expertise is represented as a bit-string that is developed by learning. These will be specialized, and hence require coordination. Agents signal to others their expertise via tags, which are also represented as bit-strings. Network structures of interaction will emerge, over which mass expectations flow. In this way, the structure of expectations in the evolutionary microeconomics consists of the distributed computation of subroutines of expertise.

## 7.6　On Populations of Model-Using Agents

The neowalrasian framework is of course based upon the implicit presumption that agents use internal models (and specifically ergodic econometric models) to form expectations. This is an idea carried over from the neoclassical theory of expectations, in which agents use some function of lagged variables as a generating mechanism. However there is no essential recognition that there exists a population of such agents, where each may differ in the model they use. By making use of the representative agent fiction, the issue of where this model actually exists (for example, within agents or between them or both) is cleverly evaded (see Davidson 1982–83, Kirman 1992). From this perspective, there is little to be said on such otherwise fundamentally important questions as, for instance, where the internal model came from, the processes by which it changes, and whether we indeed all have the same one. Similarly, the crucial importance of skill in forming expectations has no place in the framework.[6] At the other extreme is Shackle, who supposes that the process of expectation formation is a conjecture wrought by the faculty of imagination (compare, of deduction). Shackle recognizes that it is the ability and propensity of agents to actually build internal models that must be the fundamental basis of any theory of expectations. This same point is fully consonant with contemporary artificial intelligence research, in which it is widely agreed that autonomous artificial intelligence agents will of necessity have the capacity to create internal models of their environment. For instance, Herbert Simon (1959) makes much use of the distinction between the inner and outer environments. A population of such agents is naturally heterogeneous in respect of their internal models due to differences in experience.

In so far as expectations enter into the decision process, it must be recognized that there is a crucial difference between the information requirements of individual and collective decisions.[7] Loasby (1976) argues that the individual decision-making process employs expectations in a manner more analogous to Simon's collective coordination example rather than the expected utility arguments favoured by the orthodox theorists. In this, Loasby follows the psychologist George Kelly (1963), who frames cognition and behaviour as a systems process involving internal models as mental constructs or interpretive frameworks. From this perspective, expectations emerge as conjectured hypotheses that have the same form of relationship to the set of thought constructs as scientific hypotheses have to scientific research paradigms.

It is I think seriously misleading to conceive in this case of a representative agent with a representative internal model. For if we allow that agents have different internal models, this provides the sufficient conditions for a diversity of expectations irrespective of whether they have different input data or not. As such, it seems most reasonable to base our theorizing on the presumption that there will be a heterogeneous population of agents, each with different internal models. The key difference between such systems resides in their internal (and external) connectivity.

## 7.7 A Multiagent Framework

What is the relationship between the expectation, and the process by which the expectation is generated? Typically, expectations are defined as a class of information; specifically they are *ex ante* cognitive data. This of course presumes that there exists a method by which these are generated, but no explicit account is ever given (or required) in the theory. In the evolutionary microeconomics we use object-orientated programming techniques to shift our attention to the process that generates expectations. An expectation is defined as an object, which is a way of encapsulating both data and the functions (or methods) that operate on the data. The agent, *hetero economicus*, is a complex system composed of three sub-systems:

a set of resources and technology $\quad < V : \Sigma S(A) >$
a set of control algorithms and schemata $< X : P : Y >$
a set of tags for interaction $\quad\quad < \Omega^+ : \Omega^- > < \pi^+ : \pi^- > \rightarrow E(P)$

$$agent: < E(P) > < V : \Sigma S(A) > < X : P : Y >$$

This agent does, effectively, three things: (1) it explores the set of possible combinations that can be made with its current resource set; (2) it selects good combinations that can become building blocks in higher-level systems. It makes extensive use of abstraction to do so, and (3) it engages in exchange and combination interactions with other agents for the dual purposes of obtaining inputs into its current process system, and to integrate itself into higher-level systems. In other words, the agent identifies itself as an ensemble of resources ($V$). Specific combinations of these are technologies—$\Sigma S(A)$. The rules for making these structures become the fundamental dynamical operators in $P$. The system comes to life when $P$ is capable of internal self-adaptation ($X$). The algorithmic basis for interaction is furnished in $Y$, and with the set of tags serving as the conditionals that intermediate interaction. The same suite of algorithms that generates plans, expertise and other internal models generates expectations. This is a function of the internal control set $< X : P : Y >$ which consists of three operators:

$X = \{X_1, ..., X_q, ..., X_r\}$      //Operators defining change in strings
$P = \{P_1, ..., P_s, ...,P_t\}$      // Schematic preferences as strings

$Y = \{\text{LIST} : \text{CONSTRUCT} : \text{RANK} : \text{SELECT}\}$     // Platform of search algorithms

The static and operational basis of the control function is the set of schematic preferences $P$, which is the set (or population) of rules that are active in behaviour. The set $X$ is an internal system for modifying these rules. $Y$ is the set of processes engaged in search and evaluation. The set of schematic preferences is a population of high-level search rules (theories, as such) that enable the boundedly rational agent to cope with very large information sets (that contain redundancy) and/or novelty (see Holland 1975, 1995, 1998; Scarf 1989). Schematic preferences are made of schemata, which are rules for conditional acceptance of the IF–THEN} form. The individual rules (for example, $P_s$ in $P$) are symbol strings with combinations of specific and/or null sites. The symbol # represents the null sites, and thus enables agents to choose on the basis of partial mappings (as with incompletely specified, highly complex or novel situations). They enable agents to act in a changing, evolving world. (The extent to which schemata contain specific rather than null sites represents a measure of the expertise of the agent.) These rules are internally modified by a set of biomemetic (genetic) operators $X$. Learning occurs as $X$ acts on $P$.

The evolutionary microeconomic theory of expectations can be stated thus. Expectations are generated from a *WORLD MODEL*, which is constructed within the set $P$. Two classes of expectations are generated. The standard treatment is to presume that expectations are estimates of the probability distributions of a closed set of possible events. This is not the perspective taken here. Instead, expectations are estimates of the set of elements in the system, and the connections between them. Expectations are estimates (predictions) of the network geometry of the system. In this way, expectations are effectively statements about the stability, robustness, exhaustiveness and generality of the *WORLD MODEL*, and hence are epistemic objects that attempt to penetrate uncertainty. So it is not quite correct to say that expectations are generated with the *WORLD MODEL*, but, rather, the *WORLD MODEL* is the expectation. Furthermore, depending upon the performance of the *WORLD MODEL*, expertise is generated. How do we measure performance? Obviously, entrepreneurs test their own *WORLD MODEL* against reality. However, the problem is that they also need to evaluate other agents' models so as to value the output of those models. We can deal with this problem by supposing that agents signal their *WORLD MODEL* (expertise, expectations, plans) with representative tags.

## 7.8  Conclusion

In this chapter, I have proposed a theory of expectations as generated from the evolutionary microeconomics. The nature of the argument is this. First, we account for two primitive notions: (1) that economic agents build internal models with which they analyse and structure their economic actions; and (2) that agents are individually nodes in a network of information flows and interactions. Second, we recognize that the internal cognitive-processing systems and the external network systems are both complex systems, which invites us to rethink the economic meaning of the probability concept at the interface of these two systems. The classical probability framework is rejected (as is the Bayesian approach), and instead we suppose that decision making under uncertainty (including expectation formation) is achieved with rule-based production systems. Third, it is recognized that a theory of expectations must include the actions of the agents and the network, as well as the interactions between both levels.

The evolutionary microeconomic theory of expectations is framed within a multiagent simulation platform (for example, *Swarm*). Each agent consists of a set of behavioural heuristics plus a system for modifying these as a rule-governed production system (an algorithmic rationality, for example, Darley and Kauffman 1997). The agent uses this biomimetic algorithmic suite to perform such actions as production, trading, search, making plans, sending signals, monitoring and processing information, forming alliances and generating expectations. In the object-orientated programming environment, agents are self-contained objects that can transform themselves and interact with other agents. The environment is a partially connected lattice. Resources (in this case expertise and plans) are distributed over this network. Expectations then have three aspects. The first is the expert, which is a specialized agent that has developed highly effective subroutines for processing information relating to some dimension of the economic system. All agents face the task of either becoming themselves an expert, or of finding and connecting themselves to one. The second aspect is the construction of goals and plans, as the structure of behaviour. Expectations act to mark out the dimensionality of this behaviour. The superstructure that contains this process is termed a *WORLD MODEL*. The third aspect of expectations was the dynamic structure of the environment. Many of these ideas have their origins deep in heterodox thought. The purpose of this chapter has simply been to view these notions afresh through the lens of a multiagent simulation platform, which is a most expedient mode of analytical expression for the study of distributed emergent evolutionary processes. The task remaining to be done is to link this to an evolutionary macroeconomics.

# Notes

<sup>1</sup> See Wicksell (1898/1936), Cassel (1928), Myrdal (1939/1965) and Lindahl (1939).
<sup>2</sup> Foster's (1987) model of agency for evolutionary macroeconomics, *homo creativus*, explicitly recognizes the importance of this aspect.
<sup>3</sup> Consider Hicks's (1939: 124–5) qualifications to the treatment of expectations within his formal system: 'We generally interpret these expectations [of future prices] in a strict and rigid way, assuming that every individual has a definite idea of what he expects any price which concerns him to be in any future week. This method is of course excessively rigid, and actually errs in two different ways. For one thing, people's expectations are often not expectations of prices given to them from outside, but of market conditions, demand schedules for example. Second, and perhaps more importantly, people rarely have precise expectations at all'.
<sup>4</sup> There are of course other ways of parsing the probability concept. Pollock (1989), for instance, distinguishes between 'epistemic probability' (a measure of how good our reasons are for various beliefs, and is associated with subjective probability) and 'physical probability' (which concerns the structure of the physical world independent of knowledge or opinion, and is associated with objective probability).
<sup>5</sup> Hirschman (1970) has argued that the expression, by voice, of these unobservables plays an important role in market coordination. We might also suppose that local clusters within networks (clubs, trade associations, families, peer groups and so forth) play a similarly important role. See Hazledine (1998) and Fukuyama (1998) on the 'social capital' underpinnings of such. In the same sense, we must recognize that these local clusters will also be important forces in shaping expectations, as we draw upon the ideas and world views of others in forming our own expectations. As the other side of this coin, preferences will be interdependent about the same local clusters. Very little work has been done on this in economics.
<sup>6</sup> Frank Knight (1921) identified the entrepreneur as an agent who can cope with uncertainty when there is no procedure (as there always is in the neowalrasian framework) for expectation formation, a theme further pursued by Richardson (1953).
<sup>7</sup> Herbert Simon (1958: 57) points out that: 'Stability of Expectations can be so essential for decision making that it may be more important in some circumstances to have agreement on the facts than to be certain that what is agreed upon is really fact. Hence, we often find that the procedures for fact finding and for legitimating facts are themselves institutionalized. A crucial step in the innovative process is to secure legitimacy for the facts and expectations that justify the innovation'.

# 8. Conclusions

Complexity and change cannot be captured by that science dedicated
to the metaphor of the clockwork in the universe. If time is to be
considered, not as a simple parameter, a space coordinate or yet
another variable, but as real evolution, then a paradigmatic shift is
fully justified.

Francisco Louçã (1997: 102)

## 8.1 Amidst the shadows of economic theory

Thomas Kuhn (1962) once made a very Kantian claim about the nature of the
scientific enterprise: he argued that a paradigm cannot be seen from within
because a paradigm, rather, is how we see. This book has offered a fundamental
critique of the neowalrasian paradigm by showing, in effect, what it is not
seeing. The paradigm is exposed only by that which it is hiding, and what lies
hidden in the shadows of microeconomic theory, under the façade of integral
space and the analytics of a field, is specific local interactions and dynamic
microstructure—connections, in a word.

Instead, it is broadly the heterodox schools of economic thought—Austrian,
Behavioural, Evolutionary, Institutional, Post-Keynesian, Schumpeterian,
Resource-based theories of the firm, and in certain aspects of Game Theory—
that have recognized the existence of connections. But they have done so in a
rather disjointed manner, each finding their own species of connections, of
dynamic microstructure, but yet failing to notice that these may be particular
forms of something more general. In the same way, none of these schools has
yet furnished a coherent and general system of microeconomics, as a new
paradigm, for the study of the economy as an open complex adaptive system. In
this book I have argued that if we view each of these heterodox schools from the
more abstract perspective provided by a graph-theoretic ontology, we shall find
that they all rest upon a common foundation and thereby define a new paradigm
which I suggest we call the Evolutionary Microeconomics.

The evolutionary microeconomics is based upon an ontology of connections,
and squarely addresses the most fundamental criticism of the neowalrasian
paradigm: namely, its inability to account for the dynamics of such things as

181

institutions, technological change, and generally the concept of emergent systems. The overarching criticism has been that the paradigm is too narrow and that it could not be broadened without undermining its very essence. The proponents of the orthodox paradigm, however, did not seek to broaden the theoretical basis in order to account for such things but instead favoured the method of either outrightly denying their existence or cutting them to fit within the framework. They favoured a strong defence of the paradigm, and did so by supposedly integrating such concepts as knowledge (human capital theory), structure (industrial organization theory), coordination (the theory of the market), uncertainty (rational expectations theory), and history (neoclassical growth theory), among other things, into the framework. These were undeniably feats of technical and scholarly brilliance; they sharpened, flexed and displayed the power of the paradigm.

But criticism remained; indeed, intensified. It dawned that it was not so much that the neowalrasian paradigm could not consider such factors, but that the way it considered them abstracted from the very properties that were most of interest from a dynamic, evolutionary perspective. When organizational structure, knowledge, uncertainty, institutions and suchlike were read into an integral space, these concepts were denied their nature as complex webs of interactions, that is, as systems.

This was what the heterodox economics has revealed, in many different contexts and at many different levels. Heterodox economics comes together about a single point, that systems exist and that the crucial fact of their existence is structural incompleteness: that not every element is connected to every other. All the specific criticisms of method, abstractions and assumptions that have been volleyed against the neowalrasian paradigm ultimately reduce to a single criticism of the concept of an integral space. The ontological meaning of an integral space is that there exists connections between all elements and therefore any latent variation is of no conceptual significance. Furthermore, no energy is required to make these connections or to destroy them, and no local effects come of them. In short, there is no explanatory content in the connective structure, at any level, of the economic system. The acceptance of this hypothesis defines the neowalrasian microeconomics and its rejection defines the evolutionary microeconomics and is the ambit of the collective schools of heterodoxy. The heated methodological controversy that has erupted during the past few decades, the tremors of the so-called crisis in economic theory, can be plainly understood, I suggest, as the fractionation of economics along this ontological fault line.

Mounting dissatisfaction with the seeming lack of anything but heuristic progress in the theory project has been apparent for several decades now and drawn considerable energy into the tasks of diagnosis and reformulation. The avenues that have been suggested to 'bring life back into economics' (*à la* Hodgson 1993) display a remarkable consistency of prognosis.

First, the evolutionary metaphor, once carefully reconstructed, provides the basis for the study of economic change and process.[1] The interior detail is still engaged in debate, yet the metaphor is well established as a clear alternative to the equilibrium doctrine of mechanism.

Second, it is recognized that the mechanistic paradigm hid from view a fundamental question: what is the nature of order and coordination in a complex system? This question introduces concepts of complexity and self-organization into the fray, and, moreover, establishes the evolutionary metaphor as the heart of the analytical framework.

Third, and following from this, it is recognized that time is not simply another spatial dimension but fully an irreversible process. It is recognized, then, that the sequence of events matters to the course of events—history matters. This, fourthly, lends recommendation to a reinvestment in empirical-based work focused at the micro level, that is, gathering data about the actual behaviour of economic agents. This endeavour is being led by the Behavioural, Institutional, Game-theoretic and Post-Schumpeterian schools of thought.

Broadly speaking, the endeavour to reconstruct economics according to a new paradigm is indeed contemporaneously proceeding under the rubric of an evolutionary research programme. But the problem is and has been that this programme is not well defined, at least not so from first principles.

The objective of this book has been to reconstruct a framework of evolutionary microeconomics from first principles. The first cut was to distinguish the heterodoxy from the orthodoxy in terms of an analytical and ontological rudiment which I termed *the geometry of economic space*. This construct distinguishes between different primary forms of relationship attributed to a set of elements in terms of an integral and a non-integral space. This establishes the ontological foundations—the nature of existence of the economic system—necessary for the study of complex systems. Proceeding from this foundation, it is evident that the basic unit of analysis in all heterodox conceptions is a system.

A system is a set of elements and a set of connections between these elements, and is defined over a non-integral space. By definition, then, there are no systems interior to the neowalrasian framework, consisting only of a single system with each element connected to every other. In Chapter 3, I discussed the ontological and algebraic aspects of a graph-theory model of a system, and in Chapter 4 the domain of this geometry was defined over the regimes of state-space: order, complexity and chaos. This made a reinterpretation of the concept of efficiency. Dynamic efficiency is a property of a system realized by the coexistence of stability and flexibility, as a state of coordination achieved within a regime of state-space. Efficiency was thus recognized to have different meanings in integral and non-integral space. In Chapter 5, a model of the economic agent in the evolutionary microeconomics—*hetero economicus*—was outlined. This concluded the scheme of first principles. Chapter 6 then considered an application of the evolutionary microeconomics to the study of production systems in general. Chapter 7 considered the theory of expectations in the evolutionary microeconomics.

The economic process has two primary ontological dimensions, one of which has been systematically neglected. When we enter the domain of non-integral space we recover the concept of a connection, and with it the concept of a system. We may then bridge from microevolution to macroevolution by way of hyperstructure. Evolutionary dynamics are then equated with the dynamics of complex systems, and this may proceed at multiple levels of analysis. But the critical point is that complexity exists predominantly in the ontological dimension of connections. The cognitive dimension of the economic process exists as connections. The organization and coordination dimension exists as connections. The knowledge and institutional dimension exists as connections. The dimensions of ignorance, uncertainty and imagination are explicable only in the space of connections. The interface to the subjects of management, marketing, psychology, sociology, anthropology and geography requires an economics of connections. The evolutionary dimension of the economic process is changes in these connections. And the heart of the matter is that none of these concepts make any analytical sense until we can first establish that their building blocks exist. They exist only in non-integral space, which requires a paradigm shift at the foundation of microeconomic theory.

## 8.2  Prospects for evolutionary microeconomics

Some general conclusions are now in order.

This study has I hope made clear that the neowalrasian microeconomics involved two conceptual advances. The first was associated with the marginal revolution and inspired by positivist physics; the second was the entrenchment of axiomatic formalism and inspired by positivist mathematics. The first introduced the analytical technique of field theory. The second secured this with the mathematical formalisms of an integral space. We associate these steps with the neoclassical and the neowalrasian microeconomics, respectively, and from this we can observe two corresponding waves of heterodox dissension.

The first wave of American institutional economics and the theoretical concerns of Frank Knight, Ronald Coase, John Maynard Keynes, Joseph Schumpeter, Ludwig von Mises and suchlike were a clear response to the neoclassical microtheory, and sought to recognize that the field-theory framework excluded a number of dimensions, such as incompleteness (for example, uncertainty and bounded rationality), feedback and interdependence (for example, Keynesian expectations). These issues, however, were masterfully sidestepped by Hicks (1948) and Samuelson (1948) and then buried by Arrow and Debreu (1954) and Debreu (1959) in an appeal to the formal powers of integral space. And so it became that 'modern economic theory is mathematical. It has been described as a branch of pure mathematics, distinguished only by its origins,' as Backhouse (1997: 125) observes.[2]

This gave the neowalrasian paradigm axiomatic foundations and induced a second wave of heterodoxy (as first associated with Alchian, Hayek, Penrose, Simon and Georgescu-Roegen). The neowalrasian revolution was thus the formal setting of the integral space, and in consequence secured a victory for deductivism over empiricism. The nascent Austrian, Behavioural, Institutional, Schumpeterian, Post-Keynesian and Evolutionary schools were and remain, however, firmly based on empirical observation.[3] Yet such observations had no place in a framework committed to axiomatic formalism by way of an integral space because these observations were all ultimately claims that the geometry of economic space is not integral but composed of systems of specific connections. The conclusion we draw from this is that an evolutionary microeconomics can underpin the collective heterodoxy only by eschewing axiomatic foundations in an integral space. This is the principal methodological character of an evolutionary microeconomics. The ontological expression is the existence of this partial set of connections.

It does not follow, however, that because it is not mathematical in the deductive sense that it is not a microeconomics. An evolutionary microeconomics is a framework of connecting principles that interlink theory and empiricism, just as the neoclassical and neowalrasian microeconomics are also frameworks of connecting principles.[4] As such, the evolutionary microeconomics is a microeconomics in the sense that it expresses the concept of complexity and the model of a complex system formally as unifying connecting principles. Among evolutionary economists, such a singular point of focus has been difficult to discern. For instance, Witt (1993b: 91) remarks that, 'although there is a large variety of contributions now to what has come to be labelled evolutionary economics little agreement has been achieved as to what the basic features of this approach are'. Inevitably, an evolutionary economics is defined with respect to a definition of evolution. Witt suggests 'evolution can be defined as the self-transformation over time of a system under investigation'. Nelson (1995: 54) elaborates: 'the focus of attention is on a variable or set of them that is changing over time and the theoretical quest is for an understanding of the dynamic process behind the observed change; a special case would be a quest for understanding of the current state of a variable or a system in terms of how it got there'. But as Andersen (1994: 13) observes, 'the difficulties of evolutionary-economic theories are, not least, due to their attempt to account for the endogenous transformation of the knowledge applied in economic systems'. It is indeed the solution to this problem that is the basis of an evolutionary economics, which was that an evolutionary scheme of endogenous dynamics can be represented in terms of the dynamics of connections underpinning the emergence of the dynamics of systems.

A general theoretical framework requires a singular general principle. This is what the evolutionary framework lacks, and the concept of complexity is arguably the only serious candidate at this point. Other major candidates are the concepts of bounded rationality, disequilibrium and the growth of knowledge. Bounded rationality, however, is too narrow of focus, and can be interpreted as an aspect of complexity. The concept of disequilibrium has received much theoretical consideration but we must recognize that disequilibrium is the dual of equilibrium (Day 1999), both of which are in integral space. Disequilibrium frees theorizing from the implications of assuming continuous equilibria, but not from the assumption of integral space. It does not, as such, go far enough. Loasby (1991) has suggested 'the growth of knowledge' as a general connecting principle, but, as I have argued, this is too vague a concept in its ontological aspect and can be derived anyway as a special case within the hypothesis of evolution towards complexity. So I suggest that the concept of complexity can ultimately contain within its meaning a number of other high-level connecting principles that are prominent in heterodox theories.[5]

Furthermore, evolutionary economics suffers from an association with evolutionary biology that is largely misleading. The essence of the problem is that this draws too narrow a circumscription, as modern evolutionary economics is fully a synthesis of biological ideas plus non-equilibrium thermodynamics and systems theory, firm and organizational theory and theories of information processing and bounded rationality (Saviotti 1996). Evolutionary economics is an eclectic rubric centred about the paradigm of the complexity of open-system processes, and its basic substance is both more encompassing and more protean than a simple transferral of metaphor (Thoben 1982). The shift in metaphor is of course important in defining the nature of an evolutionary economics. Yet although it is well known that Alfred Marshall (1949: 637) defined economics as 'a branch of biology broadly interpreted' and somewhat surprising that Frank Hahn (1991: 48) recently predicted that in the next hundred years 'the subject will return to its Marshallian affinities to biology' we ought also to allow that affinities with biology may not necessarily mean that an evolutionary economics will be expressly of biology in its transmuted form.

The second conclusion of methodological sorts is that an evolutionary microeconomics de-emphasizes the subject domain demarcations forged by the respective schools of heterodoxy, and draws emphasis to a research programme dimensioned in terms of complex systems theory. The lines of this were sketched in Chapter 2, yet a clear expression of a unified research programme remains to be formulated. Towards this, I have gathered seven key areas of future research: (1) heterogeneity; (2) processes of adaptation; (3)

incompleteness; (4) complexity, criticality and turbulence; (5) complementarity and substitution; (6) the artifactual nature of choice; and (7), game theory and evolutionary economics.

### 8.2.1 Heterogeneity

Homogeneity of agents is a rudimentary assumption in the orthodox analysis, which does not require extant variety for the posited forces to work. In contrast, all evolutionary models require variation within the population of agents, or some such units, upon which the force of selection acts. In addition to this initial variety, 'there are also forces that continue to introduce new variety, which is further grist for the selection mill' (Nelson 1995: 54). Heterogeneity, thus, is the range of variation of a variable within a given selection environment at a particular time. Alchian (1950) and Friedman (1953) argued that although such variety is readily apparent, it could nevertheless be neglected for theoretical purposes because ultimately non-optimal variants will eventually be selected out. The problem with this argument is that it misunderstands the purpose of variety, as it were. Variety is necessary as contingency for environmental change. If ultimately nothing else changes, then eventually the sub-optimal variants will be selected out. But evolutionary theory does not presume other things equal, and regards variety and diversity as essential resources of a population.

Still, a number of basic issues remain cloudy. First, there have been no systematic studies of the range of diversity within populations of economic systems (commodities, agents, firms and so on) that attempts to correlate extant diversity with some index of the force of selection. Which is to say that we have no strong empirical basis for theorizing about the relationship between heterogeneity and the force of selection. Concomitantly, there does not exist theoretical explanation for the bandwidth of diversity. Second, there does not currently exist a satisfactory theory of the origins of diversity other than the standard presumption of random variation.[6] Third, and perhaps most important, there is no accord about what actually counts as diversity.

The framework of an evolutionary microeconomics gives analytical form to all three issues. Diversity is read from the set $E$, in which variables are binary (a connection does or does not exist), rather than the set $V$, in which they are continuous. This makes diversity at least in principle identifiable. Further, the origins of diversity can be understood from a perspective of changes in the set of connections, which can be modelled in a systematic manner from any point in state-space (as discussed in Chapters 4 and 5). In a related manner, the range of diversity can be theoretically related to the rate of change in the environment as a function of the relative position in state-space. Densely connected systems contain more variety but winnow it at a much faster rate than less densely connected systems.

Research investigating heterogeneity or model building that proceeds from the assumption of heterogeneity has been mostly concerned with variety in terms of technology and firms. There has also been important work done in terms of the diversity-driven evolution of sociocultural institutions (Boyd and Richerson 1980). The major area yet to be cultivated (or integrated) is in consumer theory, and on the diversity within a population of parallel decision rules. The scheme of this approach was defined in terms of schematic preferences and genetic algorithms in chapter five.

### 8.2.2 Processes of Adaptation

In contrast with convergence to equilibrium, an evolutionary microeconomics studies processes of adaptation. Both such schemes begin with some exogenous environmental disturbance, but the evolutionary theory then proceeds to track the actual processes by which a response occurs. The orthodox microtheory proceeds directly to the outcome (as comparative statics). An evolutionary investigation typically furnishes reasons why the erstwhile convergence might not occur or might be driven to other outcomes in terms of a series of processes, each of which depends upon the previous outcome as a kind of programme. This might be broken down, for instance, into recognition that something has changed, interpretation of that change, search for possible responses, execution of the triggered response, assessment of the outcome, and so forth sequentially. This applies to the behaviour of firms and consumers, both as agents. The modelling of such heuristic structure is well founded in the Behavioural research programme and largely ignored by the orthodox research programme, which cannot accommodate the necessary departures from an atemporal format, global rationality and unambiguous interpretation of events.

The study of adaptive processes is central to an evolutionary microeconomics, which further contributes a theoretical explanation for why some systems are more inherently capable of adaptation than others (see Dosi et al. 1999). Systems at or near the regime of complexity are structurally poised ready to adapt far more easily than those further in the ordered regime, in which change may not in fact even be possible. The research questions that remain open concern the way in which such systems actually achieve this poised state, the actual mechanisms of adaptation, and the implications this may have for prescriptions of dynamic efficiency. Furthermore, once free of the integral framework, it is reasonable to ask—adaptation to what? For instance, adaptation need not necessarily be entirely conceived in terms of quantity or price disturbances, but may be spurred by a perceived change in the scope of possibilities, broadly conceived. This, for instance, is what Kirzner's (1973) entrepreneur reacts to, characterized by alertness to such opportunity. This also seems key to the Post-Keynesian reading of expectation formation, which posits a kind of collective self-adaptation that is not necessarily hinged to any objective environmental circumstance. This is also known as self-organization (Foster 1997, Witt 1997). This research dimension, as such, overlaps significantly with management and organizational sciences and also psychology and the nascent field of experimental economics.

### 8.2.3 Incompleteness

A non-integral space is, with respect to the set of all possible connections, incomplete. A system within this space is not connected to all other systems, nor is it completely connected internally. Evolutionary microtheory suggests that this incompleteness is the very basis of the dynamic efficiency of any such system. This argument was presented in Chapter 4 and linked to theories of macroeconomic coordination (Leijonhufvud 1993, 1997), industry coordination (Richardson 1960, 1972), competence within the firm (Foss and Knudsen 1996) and, among other things, to bounded rationality (see Conlisk 1996).

I have shown how all heterodox economics is defined over a non-integral space, which means the space of incomplete connections. This makes sense of the characteristic heterodox concerns, variously with incomplete information, bounded rationality, uncertainty, organizational structure and suchlike. Research in this dimension has two main tasks. The first is a kind of empirical mapping, for instance addressing Herbert Simon's long-standing question: how bounded is bounded rationality? Such issues that relate to parameter settings have not been hitherto crucial because these parameters only figure usefully in algorithmic simulation models, few of which have been built. In Chapter 5 I introduced the theoretical scheme of a general class of such models, which are designed to represent this incompleteness in a computational way. A major research task is to provide some empirical mapping of this space.

The second task is to interpret these results. What we should be looking out for are characteristic structures, identifiable systems that are themselves composed of microinstitutions. Under examination is a wholesale test of complexity as a structural hypothesis, and it will be useful to first know where it plausibly fits and where it definitely does not. Hayek and Richardson suggested markets and industries, respectively. Schumpeter indicated the microeconomy and Keynes the macroeconomy. Georgescu-Roegen suggests that it applies everywhere. Herbert Simon suggested people and Brian Loasby, knowledge. Still, we need to refine these insights somewhat.

## 8.2.4 Complexity, Criticality, and Turbulence

The orthodox microeconomics presupposes a timeless world in which change does not occur to any significant degree. It is a model of a world several hundred years past in which uncertainty is for the greatest part a distant horizon and technological change was mostly negligible. The post-industrial world is different. It is a world of driving, incessant change. This is what Schumpeter, Hayek, Marx, Keynes and Georgescu-Roegen all understood: market capitalism is a system which is most crucially understood in terms of its dynamic properties rather than its static properties. The neoclassical analysis is of its static properties, and thus at best a partial explanation. Louçã (1997) has suggested that turbulence, as the metaphor for complexity, is a far more appropriate meta-theoretical basis than mechanism, which captures only the static aspect. The point is that the laws of motion of a complex dynamic self-transforming system embedded in a continuously changing environment (a complex system, for short) are very different from those descriptive of a linear determinant system superimposed upon an essentially static environment. There are several rudimentary principles, each of which forms a quasi-independent stream of research.

From the technical viewpoint, the strongest thread in the evolutionary microeconomics is its basis in non-linear dynamics (which has given rise to complexity theory, see Agliardi 1998, Rosser 1999). Richard Goodwin (1982, 1990) extracted such arguments from Schumpeter's analytical system, translating this into the language of dynamical attractors. These mathematical objects represent convergence of state trajectories but are not the same as an equilibrium. Small, and perhaps unmeasurably small, disturbances can escalate into wildly divergent trajectories. This is known as chaos, and is inherent in most systems of dynamically coupled variables. Such systems, curiously, are sometimes only mildly affected by (parametrically) large disturbances. In essence, the linear correlation between cause and effect is decoupled and the actual cumulation of causation depends critically upon the structure of feedbacks and structural decompositions within the system in question. This is a relatively new discovery to science (see Lorenz 1963) and has spurred investigation into punctuated equilibria, phase-transitions, path dependency and, broadly speaking, the importance of historical circumstance.

A major implication of these findings is the suggestion that much econometric work may be systematically flawed. Mandelbrot (1972) pointed this out a long time ago, but no one seemingly noticed. The crux of the matter relates to the meaning of the error term in any regression. As Louçã (1997: 201) indicates, complex mathematics

> . . .implies a whole reconceptualisation of random events, no longer defined as errors or unexplainable perturbations, but as being generated by the very system as unique

and unpredictable changes as well as by external influences, in such conditions that both origins are virtually indistinguishable: contingency and necessity are inseparable.

This point is wider than economics, as the physicist Laureate Philip Anderson (1997: 566) explains:

> Much of the real world is controlled as much by the 'tails' of distributions as by means or averages: by the exceptional, not the mean; by the catastrophe, not the steady drip; by the very rich, not the 'middle-class'. We need to free ourselves of 'average' thinking.

Average thinking is that which neglects the importance of small events subject to feedback, which is to say, of the importance of initial conditions and historical circumstance. Research in this direction aims to re-establish causality in terms more fitting to a complex adaptive system, where local microdynamics are superimposed over aggregate macrodynamics and vice versa (Delorme 1999).

Another seam of research relates to the concept of self-organized criticality and phase transitions between sub- and supercriticality. Although these issues provide less immediate scope for theoretical research in a well-defined sense, I nevertheless believe that this is the main research question in an evolutionary microeconomics. The question applies to the basic unit of analysis in an evolutionary microeconomics—a system—and asks where is this system in state-space? This is an empirical question that would establish a basis for inference about the sort of dynamics that we may expect to observe. There is a definite analogue between this concept and Keynes's schema, wherein the behaviour of the macrosystem, and thus the strategy of intervention, depends upon the position of the system relative to the benchmark of full employment. In other words, initial conditions matter. The same logic applies to a system in state-space, but here the benchmark is complexity. If the system is initially supposed to be more on the chaotic side (for whatever reason) then measures which increase the density of connections and interdependence will have completely different effects on the dynamics of the system than the same measures applied to a system on the ordered side of complexity. In short, reasonable intervention (the adding or removing of connections, thus including express non-intervention) must proceed from a knowledge of where that system is in a scheme of hyperstructure. The task of the evolutionary economist, then, is to make this identification.

A further application is to what we might call the microeconomics of macroeconomic reform or transition. There are contemporaneously occurring a number of real world experiments in intensive programmes of neoliberal market reform or as certain nations attempt the direct transition from central planning to market-based coordination. What is interesting here, from the scientific perspective, is that these experiments afford an excellent opportunity to study the structural, institutional and social underpinnings of how the market process works and what circumstances are conducive to it working well. There are large gaps in our understanding of such sociological factors as the importance of trust, reciprocity, empathy and forbearance in both the process of coordination and self-organization and in the transaction costs of market structures. Although it remains to be seen what can be done, the graph-theoretic framework and the string-theory model of interactions are certainly tools cut for the study of macroeconomic re-engineering on the premise that connections matter.

### 8.2.5 Complementarity and Substitution

In the orthodox scheme of microeconomics the principle of substitution is effectively universal. When change occurs the agent can, from the theoretical perspective at least, substitute one thing for another to achieve some comparable utility or profit outcome. This principle manifests in a number of ways, and in particular with respect to choice theory. Universal substitution implies a compensatory decision heuristic, where an agent can always compensate for less of one thing by having more of another. But this principle is not universal and in many cases provides a misleading abstraction for theorizing about system dynamics.

The evolutionary microtheory draws far more attention to the importance and structure of complements, and of the sensitivity of dynamical processes to changes in critical inputs (as elements). There are obvious linkages back to Sraffa's (1960) notion of a basic commodity. The scheme of hyperstructure may help to frame such issues.

Yet perhaps the most fertile research programme addressing this issue is coalescing under the rubric of the resource-based theory of the firm, and which is now being recast as the competence perspective. In this, the firm is modelled as a set of knowledge resources, implying that the connections within the firm are also resources of the firm. In other words, what is being investigated is the complementarity structure between the elements of production (compare, substitution in the neoclassical production function). In this way, managerial questions of strategy can enter naturally into economic concern with production efficiency.

### 8.2.6 The Artifactual Nature of Choice

The evolutionary microeconomics is in important ways a postmodern science. It proceeds from the basis that economic reality does not divide neatly between the objective world of quantities and prices and the subjective world of preferences defined over these objects. Instead, it is recognized that agents both construct their perceptions of the world about them, and thus the choice situation they perceive, and also the value the consequences attributed to potential actions (see Tamborini 1997). This is a much stronger meaning of subjectivity than that usually loaded onto preferences, in which case the meaning is that the theorist need not ask why. Indeed, it implies that there is a layer of investigation into the algorithmic basis of rationality, of event perception and other cognitive factors that contribute to the endogeneity of preferences and thereby the artifactuality of choice.

A crucial point too often overlooked is that agents learn by doing. That is, agents construct their models of the world, and gather the information they need to act within it, precisely by acting within it. Lane et al. (1996) have suggested that networks of such interactions, which they call *generative relationships*, will emerge and it is this structure that becomes the context for economic action.

In other respects, questions of this nature are sometimes considered the province of hermeneutics, and variously composed by the Austrian, Behavioural or Institutional economics. But such issues, far from being rarefied concerns of philosophy, are in fact pivotal to a multiagent framework. The basic research question concerns the way in which agents construct WORLD MODELS to interpret signals from the environment, and the role of interactions with other agents in this process. The evolutionary microeconomics is appropriately geared to this realm of investigation, in which an interpretive framework of constructs can be represented in graph-theoretical terms with signals and interfaces may be modelled using tags (see Stefansson (1997) on such applications in *Swarm*).

A further aspect of this is the question of how agents choose which other agents to interact with. This question relates not so much to the explanation of one-off interactions, but rather to the phenomenon of repeated semi-stable sorts of interactions, and of the type that characterize much of economic life. It is now being recognised that apart from generating benefits (or costs) capturable by the agents explicitly involved in the interaction, such stability acts to build what is termed 'social capital' (Bowles 1999) but of course is not 'capital' at all but self-organizing institutions. Again, there is much interesting and important territory here to explore.

### 8.2.7 Game Theory and Evolutionary Economics

I have in this book set the evolutionary microeconomics squarely and distinctly against the neowalrasian microeconomics, but what of game theory? Its theoretical basis is arguably more representative of the modern orthodoxy, and does game theory not deal with connections anyway? The quick answer to this is that it aims to, but so far it does not. Game theory and the neowalrasian framework were forged in effectively the same crucible (see Mirowski 2000) and have been alloyed ever since. In line with this partnership, game theory has more or less acquiesced and adapted itself to the same mathematical spaces that are a strict necessity for the neowalrasian framework.

Game theory is of course a method of studying strategies as actions. The space, or the substrate, over which the game is defined invariably assumes one of the two most analytically tractable forms: (1) games in which each agent interacts with all other agents under conditions of a cooperative game, or each agent interacts with all under non-cooperative conditions;[7] and (2) stochastic games, in which agents interact with a random set of others. These are respectively, the field model and the statistical mechanical model of actions. An evolutionary version of game theory, despite the name given to one such branch of the theory,[8] is still in fact yet to come. When this arrives, it will have two characteristics. First, it will be concerned with intermediate substrates involving interactions mostly with neighbourhood sites on a lattice but irregularly with other agents on a global scale (such as games on graphs in 'small worlds', Watts 1999). And second, the rules of the game will be endogenous and temporally irreversible (no refinement strategies permitted). This second condition is an essential requirement to define an 'evolutionary game' that encapsulates the Darwinian mechanisms of selection over a time-varying population (as in the extant so-called evolutionary game theory) but also the algorithmic logic of cumulative causation as an emergent hierarchy or hyperstructure (see Simon 1962, Dennett 1995).

In this way, game theory is in fact perfectly compatible with both systems of microeconomics—neowalrasian and evolutionary—because its potential substrate definition spans the integral and non-integral domains. My point here is to invite game theorists to consider the implications of exploring repeated games over non-integral spaces in irreversible time with hyperstructure. If that challenge can be met, then game theory may well usurp the evolutionary microeconomics too.[9]

## 8.3  Conclusion

When speaking of 'the continuous market, which is perpetually tending towards equilibrium without ever actually attaining it', Walras (1954: 380) suggested an analogy: 'For just as a lake is, at times, stirred to its very depths by a storm, so also the market is sometimes thrown into violent confusion by crises, which are sudden and general disturbances of the equilibrium'. In this metaphor, the lake is the market and the storm—the crisis—is an external and ultimately transitory event unrelated to the lake itself. When all transitory events have passed, the seeking and attainment of equilibrium is the basic character of the behaviour of the lake. It is a powerful and clear metaphor about market equilibrium.

Yet anyone who knows anything about lakes will know that they come from somewhere and they go somewhere. A lake is a stage in the natural cycle of water, which transforms between liquid, gas and crystal, variously manifesting lakes, rivers, precipitation, snow, clouds and suchlike. The lake stage is the most stable and tranquil of the cycle, all other stages being predominantly characterized by turbulence. Walras's lake and Walras's storm, which he so pointedly separates, are in fact different stages of the same process: the cycle of water transformation driven by solar flux. The lake does not of itself experience turbulence because it is not a driven system. Its state may be characterized by its equilibrium level, which is determined entirely by static parameters such as the contour of the valley in which it rests. The turbulence that Walras inferred is a completely transient and surface phenomenon that does not in the final analysis affect the position of the equilibrium. All other stages of the process, however, are substantially more turbulent because, principally, they are substantially more driven.

The evolutionary microeconomics is to the neowalrasian microeconomics what the river, say, is to the lake. In Heracletian terms the river is never the same, or, in the modern nomenclature, it is non-ergodic and time irreversible. The most immediate observation we can make, in distinction, is that the river flows. For much of the economic process the lake is the wrong metaphor. Technology, learning, institutional adaptation, resource depletion and discovery, innovation and entrepreneurship, imagination and conjecture, strategy, skills and competence, satiation and experimentation, and other such phenomena, these things drive the system. They are its gradient, the cause of its flow and inseparable from its being. A river, in this sense, is a far more appropriate metaphor.

From the almost imperceptible motion of a lake, the flow begins to quicken with the narrowing of the river and the phenomenon of turbulence then emerges. Without gradient, equilibrium is the basic character of a system; gradient arises as the system becomes driven, and as it is increasingly driven turbulence will be expressed and take over as the basic character of the system. For the greatest part of the history of economic systems the lake was indeed the appropriate metaphor because the flow of new information, structural and institutional reformation, technology and novelty was insufficiently steep to engender turbulence. The gradient existed, but it was the mild imperceptible gradient of a lake and could be effectively ignored (as in Marshall's *Principles*). One could speak of change, yet it was not an incessant, ubiquitous and driving change, but something more benign, less forceful. It could be reasonably abstracted from. Modern economic systems, and particularly the period since the Second World War, have, so to speak, entered the narrows.

Economic systems are driven from within to constant change: sometimes smoothly, sometimes more chaotically, but constantly to change. Radical uncertainty is fully an endemic feature of the contemporary economic decision. Is it no longer reasonably the case that other things will be equal. The most pressing fact of economic life is that other things, generally speaking, will not be equal. And hence what is now required, in the sense of what is clearly missing from the analytical and conceptual framework of microeconomic theory, are principles of abstraction cut to fit the supposition that there is always uncertainty, that change will always occur, that stability must be constructed, and that internal transformation is the natural state of an economic system.

In other words, dynamics in an integral space is simply statics plus another dimension; it is nothing more than higher-dimensional statics. The germane distinction is not between abstraction or inclusion of a temporal dimension (that is, statics and dynamics), but rather between abstraction or inclusion of the effects of time. Uncertainty, novelty, surprise, information, structure, coordination, organization and suchlike, these are the effects of time. The real effect of time, in the sense of a Realist framework, is to make space non-integral. The mathematical effect of time, in the sense of a Deductivist framework, is to add another dimension to integral space. Statics and Dynamics are not the fundamental categorizations of time's ontology, at least not in the context of an open system. Rather, the conceptual distinction occurs with respect to whether the subject of investigation is to be perceived as systematically dealing with the effects of time, or not. If uncertainty and suchlike exert systematic effects on the behaviour of the subject of investigation, then our framework transcends time as dimensional oblivion and apprehends its manifestation in the geometric properties of the subject of investigation. If our subjects are systems, then the effect of time is to push these systems into non-integral state-space. The presence of the effect of time is manifest in variety, in surprise, in contingency, but most generally as complexity. Time does not manifest in a dualistic way, either absent (statics) or present (dynamics) as is the nature of its Cartesian expression. Time is dialectic; in certain environments it may be suitably ignored and in others it presses much more forcefully and is veritably impossible to ignore. This distinction is important. Our inherited theoretical apparatus extends to include dynamics, but it does not yet extend to incorporate the effects of time. Moreover, it never can.

Consequentially, we must turn our investigation now to the study of turbulence, emergence and self-organization, and away from the study of equilibrium as the exclusive concern of analysis. From a metatheoretical perspective, our first reference point is that we need to free our thinking from the mathematically convenient but ontologically misleading domain of field-theory abstractions. And when our attention shifts to the study of local interactions rather than generalized actions, of distributed agents operating in parallel without centralized coordination, and of emergent structure and self-organization, then we will find that the integral or differential methods are not necessarily the most appropriate basis for microeconomic models. Instead, it would seem that graph theory, and combinatorics generally, provide a more appropriate mathematical foundation, and one that feeds directly into the burgeoning field of multiagent (and artificial life) simulation techniques.

Our second reference point is that the economic investigation is rightly concerned with the study of systems, and generally with the principles of the balance between stability and flexibility, which, in the non-integral context, is interpreted as the principles of dynamic efficiency. When the flow quickens, when the environment becomes more turbulent, the fundamental nature of optimization changes. Optimization means more than simply making the best use of current finite resources, expressed and solved purely as an allocation problem. In the midst of turbulence, our concern extends beyond the immediate hedonic moment to encompass scenarios of possible outcomes. These are within the domain of unknowledge, and cannot be apprehended in probabilistic terms, and therefore cannot (even in theory) be collapsed into the present. Turbulence is dealt with in the economic system in the same way it is dealt with in all other system domains, by structural complexity: order and chaos are melded, and this complex coexistence is the best that can be achieved given the effects of time; it is, in a word, efficient.

Our third point of reference is that systems are building blocks for building more systems. Systems are sets of things connected such that the combination synthesizes the emergence of a coherent whole, and which may then become part of another system. The flux and evolutionary processes within an economic system are those of the interaction, emergence and decomposition of systems.

The many species of system within an economic system can all be abstractly represented with the same analytical framework. This, I think, affords a much-needed clarity to the distinction between such phenomena as, for instance, knowledge, technology and capital. The Cartesian legacy has forced a strict conceptual distinction between material factors (capital as 'putty') and factors such as human skills, cognitive faculties or imagination. The former exists because it can be measured unambiguously, whereas the latter does not. Yet, as Simon (1982, 2: 144) has argued, 'a technology exists largely in the minds of its labour force', an insight similarly shared by the nascent competence-based theory of the firm (Penrose 1959, Foss and Knudsen 1996). The insight is that technology and competence are both systems. Nelson and Winter (1982) sparked what we may perhaps consider a renaissance of evolutionary economics by conceiving habits, routines and skills, as microinstitutions, or more generally as systems that are the building blocks of an evolutionary theory of the economic process. The common stream of heterodox thought, which I argue establishes the ontological and epistemological basis for a synthetic microeconomic coherence, is that all recognize systems. Equivalently, the common domain of heterodox economics is non-integral space.

Systems are the building blocks of the economic process and the rudimentary analytical abstraction of heterodox microeconomics. The different streams of heterodox thought come together about the ontological acknowledgement that systems exist, with each bringing a different understanding of how systems exist and knowledge of the properties of such systems. It is the reign of turbulence that has brought these latent systems into view. In equilibrium, these systems would not be readily apparent but in the boil of modern economic history the systems aspect has revealed itself to those who will care to look directly at the economic object as it occurs in real time. A number of economists of somewhat more orthodox stripes have arrived at much the same conclusion (for example, Arrow 1974, Hahn 1983, North 1990, Romer 1994, Stiglitz 1994).

My argument summarizes thus. Our economic actions are inseparable from their embeddedness in webs of systems. These systems are both internal to the agent, as for instance heuristic systems, and external, as say competence systems. Systems are characterized in their diversity not so much by what they are made of but by how they are connected together. A system is a set of connected elements. The evolutionary dynamics of the economic process, however, are to be mostly associated with the set $E$, the set of connections, and it is changes in these that explain changes in the set $V$, the set of things. From this perspective, it is the process of search, discovery, experimentation, investment, or, in general, choice over the set of connections that is descriptive of the evolutionary dynamics of the economic system. An evolutionary microeconomics, as the basis of a synthesis of heterodox thought, and which we may I suggest reasonably refer to as the evolutionary synthesis, is focused about the study of the set of connections that exist in an economic system. In essence, connections must be created—some elements are connected, some are not. Moreover, whether a connection exists or not, it matters. The evolutionary microeconomics is thus a new methodological paradigm and analytical framework for the study of the dynamics of connections in an economic system.

# Notes

[1] 'As interdisciplinary work and collaboration become increasingly common-place, economists of necessity must seek to extend their experiences outside of the preconceived confines of "the economy". And of course when evolution itself became recast as the playing out of the "genetic code" and biology captured the lion's share of scientific funding, was the reappearance of an evolutionary economics really such a bolt from the blue?' (Mirowski 1998: 938–9).

[2] An alternative conception, and one that I have given insufficient attention to in this book, is Mirowski's (2000) notion of *Cyborg economics*, which he identifies with the rise of strategic sponsorship of economic research driving the ascendancy of game theory, operations research, and computational economics from the 1950s onwards.

[3] See Hodgson (forthcoming).

[4] The most ubiquitous such connecting principle, for instance, is equilibrium. Reder (1982), for instance, argues that such a concept (as *tight prior equilibrium*) is the key to the Chicago School of

economics. In this way, it is axiomatics plus a high-level connecting principle (that is, equilibrium) that defines the orthodox system of microeconomics. Hausman (1992) makes precisely this argument.

[5] 'The use of formal evolutionary theory in economics is still new, and the proponents of evolutionary theory are struggling with both techniques and standards' (Nelson 1995: 85–6). Nelson then concludes his survey of recent evolutionary theorising thus. 'In my view economics would be a stronger field if its theoretical framework were expressly evolutionary. Such a framework would help us see and understand better the complexity of the economic reality. That, I think, is its greatest advantage. But it will not make the complexity go away'. Here complexity is the problem ('make the complexity go away'), the analytical focus ('the complexity of the economic reality'), and, by implication, the solution ('expressly evolutionary').

[6] An interesting aspect of this is the role of the producers in shaping perceptions of diversity through market media. This distinguishes, I think, two very different approaches to marketing. One the one hand, there is the field-theory model, which expresses product coordinates of the form 'this X at price p and located in the market at $(x, y, \ldots)$ coordinates.' This approach was typical of an earlier school of marketing, and in its information function is congruent with the field economics. On the other hand is something we tend to see more of in recent times, but is by no means a recent innovation: less emphasis on price, quantity and spatial coordinates, but more emphasis on associations. The message in many consumer-good advertisements is that product X is connected to some set $(A, B, C,...)$ of other products or attributes or some such. This is more congruent with the topographic evolutionary microeconomics, as the information disseminated is about the connections surrounding the element rather than the coordinates descriptive of the element. It may be argued that connections are far more subject to manipulation than elements.

[7] Strangely, game theorists refer to this situation, when agents cannot by definition know the moves that other agents will make, as one of *bounded rationality*. Evidently, they have never made sense of the distinction between substantiative and procedural rationality. They should read Herbert Simon (1976).

[8] Namely, evolutionary game theory (Weibull 1995).

[9] See, for instance, Weisbuch et al. (2000), Morris (2000) and Suk-Young Chwe (2000).

# References

Agliardi, E. (1998) *Positive Feedback Economics.* Basingstoke, Macmillan.

Akerlof, G. (1998) 'Men Without Children.' *Economic Journal.* **108**: 287–309.

Alchian, A. (1950) 'Uncertainty, Evolution and Economic Theory.' *Journal of Political Economy,* **58**: 211–22.

Alchian, A. (1953) 'Biological Analogies in the Theory of the Firm: A Comment.' *American Economic Review,* **43**: 600–603.

Alchian, A. and H. Demsetz (1972) 'Production, Information Costs, and Economic Organization.' *American Economic Review,* **62**: 772–795.

Aldrich, J. and R. McMelvey (1991) *Algorithmica* (Special Issue on Simulated Annealing), **6**.

Allen, P. (1988) 'Evolution, Innovation and Economics.' in Dosi et al. (eds) (1988) pp. 95–119.

Allen, P. (1993) 'Evolution: Persistent Ignorance from Continual Learning.' in Day and Chen (eds) (1993), pp. 101–112.

Andersen, E. (1994) *Evolutionary Economics: Post-Schumpeterian Contributions.* London: Pinter.

Anderson, P. (1997) 'Some Thoughts About Distribution in Economics.' in Arthur et al. (eds) (1997), pp. 565–6.

Anderson, P., K. Arrow and D. Pines (eds) (1988) *The Economy as an Evolving Complex System.* New York: Addison-Wesley.

Ansoff, H. (1968) *Corporate Strategy.* Harmondsworth, Penguin.

Aoki, M., B. Gustafsson and O. Williamson (eds) (1990) *The Firm as a Nexus of Treaties.* London: Sage.

Arecchi, F. (1997) 'Truth and Certitude in the Scientific Language.' in Schweitzer (ed.) (1997) pp. 3–20.

Arifovic, J. (1994) 'Genetic Algorithm Learning and the Cobweb Model.' *Journal of Economic Dynamics and Control.* **18**: 3–28.

Arrow, K. (1974) *The Limits of Organization,* New York: W.W. Norton.

Arrow, K. (1986) 'Rationality of Self and Others in an Economic System.' *Journal of Business,* **59**: 385–99.

Arrow, K. and G. Debreu (1954) 'The Existence of Equilibrium for a Competitive Economy.' *Econometrica,* **20**: 265–90.

Arthur, W. (1989) 'Competing Technologies, Increasing Returns and Lock-in by Historical Events.' *Economic Journal,* **99**: 116–31.

Arthur, W. (1991) 'Designing Economic Agents that Act like Human Agents: A Behavioural Approach to Bounded Rationality.' *American Economic Review, Papers and Proceedings*, **81**: 353–9.

Arthur, W. (1992) 'On Learning and Adaptation in the Economy.' Santa Fe Institute (Santa Fe, NM) Paper 92-07-038.

Arthur, W. (1993) 'On Designing Economic Agents that Behave like Human Agents.' *Journal of Evolutionary Economics*, **1**: 1–22.

Arthur, W. (1994) *Increasing Returns and Path Dependence in the Economy.* Ann Arbor: University of Michigan Press.

Arthur, W. (1997) 'Beyond Rational Expectations: Indeterminacy in Economic and Financial Markets.' in Drobak and Nye (eds) (1997) pp. 291–304.

Arthur, W., S. Durlauf and D. Lane (eds) (1997) *The Economy as a Complex Evolving System II.* New York: Addison-Wesley.

Baas, N. (1994) 'Emergence, Hierarchies, and Hyperstructure.' in C. Langton (ed.) *Artificial Life III: Santa Fe Institute Studies in the Science of Complexity.* New York: Addison-Wesley, pp. 515–37.

Baas, N. (1997) 'Self-Organization and Higher Order Structures.' in Schweitzer (ed.) (1997), pp. 53–62.

Backhouse, R. (1997) *Truth and Progress in Economic Knowledge.* Cheltenham: Edward Elgar.

Bak, P. (1996) *How Nature Works—The Science of Self-organized Criticality.* New York: Springer-Verlag.

Baranzini, M. and R. Scazzieri (eds) (1990) *The Economic Theory of Structure and Change.* Cambridge: Cambridge University Press.

Baumol, W. (1982) 'Contestable Markets: An Uprising in the Theory of Industry Structure.' *American Economic Review*, **72**: 1–15.

Baumol, W. and R. Quandt (1964) 'Rules of Thumb and Optimally Imperfect Decisions.' American Economic Review, **54**: 23–46.

Baumol, W., J. Panzar and R. Willig (1982) *Contestable Markets and the Theory of Industry Structure.* New York: Harcourt Brace Jovanovich.

Bausor, R. (1983) 'The Rational Expectations Hypothesis and the Epistemics of Time.' *Cambridge Journal of Economics*, **7**: 1–10.

Becker, G. (1965) 'A Theory of the Allocation of Time.' *Economic Journal*, **75**: 493–517.

Becker, G. (1976) *The Economic Approach to Human Behaviour.* Chicago: University of Chicago Press.

Becker, G. (1981) *A Treatise on the Family.* Cambridge, MA: Harvard University Press.

Becker, G., E. Landes and R. Michael (1977) 'An Economic Analysis of Marital Instability.' *Journal of Political Economy*, **85**: 1141–87.

Bédard, J. and M. Chi (1992) 'Expertise.' *Current Directions in Psychological Research*, **1**: 135–9.

Bedau, M., Snyder E. and N. Packard (1998) 'A Classification of Long-Term Evolutionary Dynamics.' in Adami et al. (eds) (1998) *Proceedings of Artificial Life VI*. Cambridge, MA: MIT Press.

Bell, D. and I. Kristol (eds) (1981) *The Crisis in Economic Theory*. New York: Basic Books.

Ben-Ner, A. and L. Putterman (eds) (1998) *Economics, Values, and Organization*. Cambridge: Cambridge University Press.

Ben-Porath, Y. (1982) 'Economics and the Family - Match or Mismatch? A Review of Becker's *A Treatise on the Family*.' *Journal of Economic Literature*, **20**: 52–64.

Bergson, H. (1911) *Creative Evolution*. New York: Henry Holt.

Bergstrom, T. (1996) 'Economics in a Family Way.' *Journal of Economic Literature*, **34**: 1903–34.

Bertalanffy, L. (1962) 'General Systems Theory—A Critical View.' *General Systems*, **8**: 1–20.

Best, M. (1990) *The New Competition: Institutions of Industrial Restructuring*. Cambridge MA: Harvard University Press.

Bianchi, M. (ed.) (1998) *The Active Consumer*. London: Routledge.

Bianchi, M. (1999) 'New Capabilities Embodied in New Products.' in Dow and Earl (eds) (1999) Vol. 1, pp. 119–38.

Biggiero, L. (1998) 'Sources of Complexity in Human Systems.' paper presented at *International Society for the Systems Sciences*, July 18–25 Atlanta, Georgia.

Birchenhall, C., N. Kastrinos, and S. Metcalfe (1997) 'Genetic Algorithms in Evolutionary Modelling.' *Journal of Evolutionary Economics*, **7**: 375–93.

Blatt, J. (1983) 'How Economists Misuse Mathematics.' in Eichner (ed.) (1983) pp. 166–86.

Blaug, M. (1978) *Economic Theory in Retrospect*. (3rd edn) New York: Cambridge University Press.

Boisot, M. (1995) *Information Space: A Framework for Learning in Organizations, Institutions and Culture*. New York: Routledge.

Börgers, T. (1996) 'On the Relevance of Learning and Evolution to Economic Theory.' *Economic Journal*, **106**: 1374–85.

Bossomaier, T., D. Green, S. Keen and R. Standish (eds) (1998) *Complex Systems 98*, Complexity On-Line. http://life.csu.edu.au/complex/

Boulding, K. (1966) 'The Economics of Knowledge and the Knowledge of Economics.' *American Economic Review*, **56**: 1–13.

Boulding, K. (1978) *Ecodynamics: A New Theory of Societal Evolution*. Beverly Hills, CA: Sage.

Boulding, K. (1989) 'Punctuationalism in social evolution.' *Journal of Social and Biological Structures*, **12**: 213–23.

204 *The new evolutionary microeconomics*

Boulding, K. (1991) 'What is Evolutionary Economics?' *Journal of Evolutionary Economics*, **1**: 9–17.

Bourbaki, N. (1968) *Theory of Sets*. New York: Addison-Wesley. (originally, *Éléments de Mathématique: Théorie des Ensemble*, 1966).

Bowan, M. (ed.) (1958) *Expectations, Uncertainty, and Business Behaviour*. New York: Social Science Research Council.

Bowles, S. (1999) 'Social Capital and Community Governance.' Mimeo, Department of Economics, University of Massachusetts at Amherst.

Boyd, R. and P. Richerson (1980) 'Sociobiology, Culture and Economic Theory.' *Journal of Economic Behaviour and Organization*, **1**: 97–121.

Brock, W. and S. Durlauf (1999) 'Interactions-based Models.' *SSRI Working Paper*. #9910, University of Wisconsin, Madison.

Brooks, D. and E. Wiley (1986) *Evolution as Entropy: Toward a Unified Theory of Biology*. Chicago: Chicago University Press.

Buchanan, J. and V. Vanberg (1991) 'The Market as a Creative Process.' *Economics and Philosophy*, **7**: 167–86.

Bunge, M. (1959) *Causality: The Place of the Causal Principle in Modern Science*. Cambridge, MA: Harvard University Press.

Bürgenmeier, B. (1992) *Socio-economics: An Interdisciplinary Approach*. Boston: Kluwer.

Burt, R. (1992) *Structural Holes: The Social Structure of Competition*. Cambridge, MA: Harvard University Press.

Cagan, P. (1956) 'The Monetary Dynamics of Hyper-inflation.' in M. Friedman (ed.) (1956) *Studies in the Quantity Theory of Money*. Chicago: University of Chicago Press.

Caldwell, B. (1990) 'Does Methodology Matter? How Should it be Practiced?' *Finnish Economic Papers*, **3**: 64–71.

Caldwell, B. and S. Boehm (eds) (1992) *Austrian Economics: Tensions and New Directions*. Boston: Kluwer Academic Publishing.

Callon, M. (ed.) (1997) *The Laws of the Markets*. Oxford: Blackwell.

Campbell, J. and N. Mankiw (1990) 'Permanent Income, Current Income, and Consumption.' *Journal of Business and Economic Statistics*, **8**: 265–79.

Carlson, M. (1997) 'Mirowski's Thesis and the "Integrability Problem" in Neoclassical Economics.' *Journal of Economic Issues*, **31**: 741–60.

Carnap, R. (1950) *Logical Foundations of Probability*. Chicago: University of Chicago Press.

Cassel, G. (1928) 'The Rate of Interest, the Bank Rate, and the Stabilization of Prices.' *Quarterly Journal of Economics*, **42**: 511–29.

Casson, M. (1982) *The Entrepreneur: An Economic Theory*. Oxford: Martin Robertson.

Chandler, A. (1962) *Strategy and Structure*. Cambridge, MA: MIT Press.

Chiaromonte, F. and G. Dosi (1992) 'The Microfoundations of Competitiveness and their Macroeconomic Implications.' in D. Foray and C. Freeman (eds) (1992) *Technology and Competitiveness*, London: Pinter.

Chick, V. (1998) 'On Knowing One's Place: The Role of Formalism in Economics.' *Economic Journal*, 108: 1859–69.

Choi, Y. (1993) *Paradigms and Conventions: Uncertainty, Decision-making, and Entrepreneurship*. Ann Arbor: University of Michigan Press.

Clark, N. and C. Juma (1987) *Long Run Economics: An Evolutionary Approach to Economic Growth*. London: Pinter.

Clarke, D. and J. Crossland (1985) *Action Systems: An Introduction to the Analysis of Complex Behaviour*. New York: Methuen.

Clower, R. (1965) 'The Keynesian Counterrevolution: A Theoretical Appraisal.' in F. Hahn and F. Brechling (eds) (1965) *The Theory of Interest Rates*. London: Macmillan.

Clower, R. (1994) 'Economics as an Inductive Science.' *Southern Economic Journal*, **60**: 805–14.

Clower, R. (1995) 'Axiomatics in Economics.' *Southern Economic Journal*, **62**: 307–19.

Clower, R. and P. Howitt (1997) 'Foundations of Economics.' in D'Autume and Cartelier (eds) (1997) pp. 17–34.

Coase, R. (1937) 'The Nature of the Firm.' *Economica*, **4**: 386–405.

Cohen, J. (1988) 'Threshold Phenomena in Random Structures.' *Discipline of Applied Mathematics*, **19**: 113–21.

Cohen, M. and R. Axelrod (1984) 'Coping with Complexity: The Adaptive Value of Changing Utility.' *American Economic Review*, **74**: 30–42.

Coleman, J. (1990) *Foundations of Social Theory*. Cambridge, MA: Harvard University Press.

Collier, J. and Hooker, C. (1999) 'Complexly Organised Dynamical Systems.' Mimeo, Department of Philosophy, University of Newcastle, Australia.

Commons, J. (1950) *The Economics of Collective Action*. New York: Macmillan.

Conlisk, J. (1996) 'Why Bounded Rationality?' *Journal of Economic Literature*, **34**: 669–700.

Coricelli, F. and G. Dosi (1988) 'Coordination and Order in Economic Change and the Interpretive Power of Economic Theory.' in Dosi et al. (eds) (1988) pp. 124–47.

Cowan, G., D. Pines and D. Meltzer (eds) (1994) *Complexity: Metaphors, Models and Reality*. Reading MA: Addison-Wesley.

Cowan, T. (1989) 'Are All Tastes Constant and Identical? A Critique of Stigler and Becker.' *Journal of Economic Behaviour and Organization*. **11**: 127–35.

Creedy, J. and V. Martin (eds) (1997) Nonlinear Economic Models: Cross-sectional, Time Series and Neural Network Applications. Cheltenham: Edward Elgar.

Crutchfield, J. (1994) 'The Calculi of Emergence: Computation, Dynamics and Induction.' *Physica D*, **75**: 11–54.

Cyert, R. and J. March (1963) *A Behavioural Theory of the Firm*. Englewood Cliffs, NJ: Prentice-Hall.

D'Autume, A. and J. Cartelier (1997) *Is Economics Becoming a Hard Science?* Cheltenham: Edward Elgar.

Dallago, B. and L. Mittone (eds) (1996) *Economic Institutions, Markets and Competition: Centralization and Decentralization in the Transformation of Economic Systems*. Cheltenham: Edward Elgar.

Daniel, K. (1995) 'The Marriage Premium.' in Tommasi and Ierulli (eds) (1995) pp. 113–25.

Darley, V. and S. Kauffman (1997) 'Natural Rationality.' in Arthur et al. (eds) (1997) pp. 45–80.

Davidson, P. (1982-83) 'Rational Expectations: A Fallacious Foundation for Studying Crucial Decision-making Processes.' *Journal of Post-Keynesian Economics*, **5**: 182–98.

Davidson, P. (1991) 'Is Probability Theory Relevant for Uncertainty? A Post Keynesian Perspective.' *Journal of Economic Perspectives*, **5**: 129–43.

Davidson, P. (1996) 'Reality and Economic Theory.' *Journal of Post Keynesian Economics*, **18**: 479–508.

Dawkins, R. (1976) *The Selfish Gene*. New York: Oxford University Press.

Dawkins, R. (1999) *The Extended Phenotype: The Long Reach of the Gene*. (1st edn 1983) [Afterword by Daniel Dennett]. Oxford: Oxford University Press.

Day, R. (1994) *Complex Economic Dynamics, Vol. 1: An Introduction to Dynamical Systems and Market Mechanisms*. Cambridge, MA: MIT Press.

Day, R. (1999) 'Economics, the State, and the State of Economics.' in Dow and Earl (eds) (1999). Vol. 2, pp. 306–21.

Day, R. and P. Chen (eds) (1993) *Nonlinear Dynamics and Evolutionary Economics*. Oxford: Oxford University Press.

Day, R. and G. Eliasson (eds) (1986) *The Dynamics of Market Economies*. Amsterdam: North Holland.

De Uriarte, B. (1990) 'Free Will and Rational Agents.' *Journal of Post-Keynesian Economics*, **12**: 605–17.

De Vree, J. (1997) 'Self-Organization in Social Systems: The Process of Integration.' in Schweitzer (ed.) (1997) pp. 343–54.

Debreu, G. (1959) *Theory of Value*. New York: Wiley.

Debreu, G. (1984) 'Economic Theory in a Mathematical Mode.' *American Economic Review*, **74**: 267–78.

Debreu, G. (1986) 'Theoretic Models: Mathematical Formalism and Economic Content.' *Econometrica*, **54**: 1259–70.

Debreu, G. (1991) 'The Mathematization of Economics.' *American Economic Review*, **81**: 1–7.

Defoe, D. (1719) *The Life and Adventures of Robinson Crusoe*. Republished (1954) London: Frederick Warne Co. Ltd.

Delorme, R. (1999) 'Complexity and Evolutionary Theorising in Economics.' paper presented at *Workshop on Evolutionary Economics*, University of Queensland, July.

Demsetz, H. (1968) 'Why Regulate Utilities?' *Journal of Law and Economics*, **11**: 55–66.

Demsetz, H. (1988) 'The Theory of the Firm Revisited.' *Journal of Law, Economics and Organization*, **4**: 141–62.

Demsetz, H. (1997) 'The Firm in Economic Theory: A Quiet Revolution.' *American Economic Review: Papers and Proceedings*, 87: 426–29.

Dennett, D. (1995) *Darwin's Dangerous Idea: Evolution and the Meanings of Life*. New York: Simon & Schuster.

Depew, D. and B. Weber (1985) *Evolution at the Crossroads: The New Biology and the New Philosophy of Science*. Cambridge, MA: MIT Press.

Donaldson, P. (1984) *Economics of the Real World*. Harmondsworth: Penguin.

Dopfer, K. (1991) 'Towards a Theory of Economic Institutions: Synergy and Path Dependency.' *Journal of Economic Issues*, **25**: 535–50.

Dopfer, K. (1994) 'The Phenomenon of Economic Change: Neoclassical vs. Schumpeterian Approaches.' in Magnusson (ed.) (1994) pp. 125–71.

Dopfer, K. (2000) 'History Friendly Theories in Economics: Reconciling Universality and Context in Evolutionary Analysis.' in Foster and Metcalfe (eds) (2000), pp. 147–70.

Dosi, G., R. Aversi, G. Fagiolo, M. Meacci and C. Olivetti (1999) 'Cognitive Processes, Social Adaptation and Innovation in consumption Patterns.' in Dow and Earl (eds) (1999) pp. 139–72.

Dosi, G., C. Freeman, R. Nelson, G. Silverberg and L. Soete, (eds) (1988) *Technical Change and Economic Theory*. New York: Pinter.

Dosi, G. and R. Nelson (1994) 'An Introduction to Evolutionary Theories in Economics.' *Journal of Evolutionary Economics*, **4**: 153–72.

Dosi, G. and F. Malerba (1996) *Organisation and Strategy in the Evolution of Enterprise*. London: MacMillan.

Dosi, G., L. Marengo and G. Fagiolo (1997) 'Learning in Evolutionary Environments' *Working Paper, IIASA*, Laxenburg, Austria.

Dow, S. (1985) *Macroeconomic Thought: A Methodological Approach*. Oxford: Basil Blackwell.

Dow, S. and P. Earl (eds) (1999) *Economic Knowledge and Economic Coordination: Essays in Honour of Brian J. Loasby*. 2 Vols. Aldershot: Edward Elgar.

208 *The new evolutionary microeconomics*

Dow, S. and J. Hillard (eds) (1995) *Keynes, Knowledge and Uncertainty*. Aldershot: Edward Elgar.

Downie, J. (1958) *The Competitive Process*. London: Duckworth.

Doyle, P. (1976) *Every Object is a System*. Surrey: Unwin

Drobak, J. and J. Nye (eds) (1997) *The Frontiers of the New Institutional Economics*. San Diego: Academic Press.

Durlauf, S. (1993) 'Non-ergodic Economic Growth.' *Review of Economic Studies*, **60**: 349–66.

Durlauf, S. (1996) 'Statistical Mechanics Approaches to Socioeconomic Behaviour.' *SSRI Working Paper* #9617. University of Wisconsin, Madison.

Earl, P. (1986) *Lifestyle Economics: Consumer Behaviour in a Turbulent World*. Brighton: Wheatsheaf Books Ltd.

Earl, P. (ed.) (1988) *Behavioural Economics*. 2 Vols. Aldershot: Edward Elgar.

Earl, P. (1990a) *Monetary Scenarios: A Modern Approach to Financial Systems*. Aldershot: Edward Elgar.

Earl, P. (1990b) 'Economics and Psychology: A Survey.' *Economic Journal*. **100**: 718–55.

Earl, P. (1998) 'George Richardson's Career and the Literature of Economics.' in Foss and Loasby (eds) (1998) pp. 14–43.

Ebeling, W. and H. Ulbricht (eds) (1989) *Irreversible Processes and Self-organization*. Leipzig: Teuber.

Edmonds, B. (1999) 'Appendix 1. A brief overview of some existing measures of complexity.' http://www.cpm.mmu.ac.uk/~bruce/thesis

Edwards, S. and P. Anderson (1975) 'The Theory of Spin-glasses.' *Journal of Physica F*, **5**: 965.

Eichner, A. (ed.) (1983) *Why is Economics Not Yet a Science?* Armonk, NY: Sharpe.

Eigen, M. and P. Schuster (1979) *The Hyper-cycle: A Principle of Natural Self-organization*. New York: Springer-Verlag.

Einhorn, H. (1973) 'Expert Judgement: Some Necessary Conditions and an Example.' *Journal of Applied Psychology*, **59**: 562–71.

Einstein, A. (1953) Foreword to *Concepts of Space*, M. Jammer (1954) Cambridge, MA: Harvard University Press.

Eldredge, N. and S. Gould (1977) 'Punctuated Equilibria: The Tempo and Mode of Evolution Reconsidered.' *Paleobiology*, **3**: 115–51.

Eliasson, G. (1990) 'The Firm as a Competent Team.' *Journal of Economic Behaviour and Organization*, **13**: 275–98.

Eliasson, G. (1991) 'Deregulation, Innovative Entry and Structural Diversity as a Source of Stable and Rapid Economic Growth.' *Journal of Evolutionary Economics*, **1**: 49–63.

Elster, J. (1983) *Explaining Technological Change: A Case Study in the Philosophy of Science*. Cambridge: Cambridge University Press.

Emery, F. (ed.) (1969) *Systems Thinking*. Harmondsworth: Penguin.

Endres, A. (1997) *Neoclassical Microeconomic Theory: The Founding Austrian Version*. London: Routledge.

Enke, S. (1951) 'On Maximizing Profits: A Distinction between Chamberlin and Robinson.' *American Economic Review*, **41**: 566–78.

Epstein, J. and R. Axtell (1996) *Growing Artificial Societies: Social science from the bottom Up*. Cambridge, MA: MIT Press.

Erdos, P. and A. Renyi (1959) *On the Random Graphs 1*. Vol. 6. Institute of Mathematics, University of Debreceniens, Hungary.

Erdos, P. and A. Renyi (1960) *On the Evolution of Random Graphs*. Institute of Mathematics, Hungarian Academy of Sciences. 5.

Etzioni, A. (1985) 'Opening the Preferences: A Socio-economic Research Agenda.' *Journal of Behavioural Economics*, **14**: 183–205.

Etzioni, A. (1986) 'The Case for a Multiple Utility Conception.' *Economics and Philosophy*, **2**: 159–84.

Etzioni, A. (1988) *The Moral Dimension: Toward a New Economics*. New York: Free Press.

Faber, M., R. Manstetten and J. Proops (1996) *Ecological Economics: Concepts and Methods*. Cheltenham: Edward Elgar.

Fenzl, N. and W. Hofkirchner (1997) 'Information Processing and Evolutionary Systems.' in Schweitzer (ed.) (1997).

Feyerabend, P. (1978) *Science in a Free Society*. London: New Left Books.

Finch, H. (1995) *Wittgenstein*. Rockport, MA: Element.

Fisher, I. (1930) *The Theory of Interest*. New York: MacMillan.

Fleith, B. and J. Foster (1999) 'Interdependent Expectations.' Mimeo, Department of Economics, University of Queensland.

Foss, N. (1993) 'Theories of the Firm: Contractual and Competence Perspectives.' *Journal of Evolutionary Economics*, **3**: 127–44.

Foss, N. (1994) 'The Biological Analogy and the Theory of the Firm: Marshall and Monopolistic Competition.' *Journal of Economic Issues*, **28**: 1115–36.

Foss, N. (1996) 'The Emerging Competence Perspective.' in Foss and Knudsen (eds) (1996) pp. 1–12.

Foss, N. (1997) 'Evolutionary Economics and the Theory of the Firm: Assessments and Proposals for Research.' in Reijnders (ed.) (1997) pp. 69-107.

Foss, N. (1999) 'Incomplete Contracts and Economic Organization: Brian Loasby and the Theory of the Firm.' in Dow and Earl (eds), Vol. II, pp. 40–66.

Foss, N. and C. Knudsen (eds) (1996) *Towards a Competence Theory of the Firm*. London: Routledge.

Foss, N. and B. Loasby (eds) (1998) *Economic Organization, Capabilities and Co-ordination: Essays in Honour of G.B. Richardson*. London: Routledge.

Foster, J. (1987) *Evolutionary Macroeconomics*. London: George Allen Unwin.

Foster, J. (1993) 'Economics and the Self-organization Approach: Alfred Marshall Revisited.' *Economic Journal*, **103**: 975–91.

Foster, J. (1994) 'The Self-organization Approach in Economics.' in S. Burley and J. Foster (eds) (1994) *Economics and Thermodynamics: New Perspectives on Economic Analysis*. Boston: Kluwer. pp. 183–202.

Foster, J. (1997) 'The Analytical Foundations of Evolutionary Economics: From Biological Analogy to Economic Self-organization.' *Structural Change and Economic Dynamics*, **8**: 427–51.

Foster, J. (2000) 'The Emergence of Organized Complexity in Economic Systems: The Role of Transaction Costs.' Paper presented at conference of Pacific Rim Allied Economic Organisations, Sydney, January.

Foster, J. and J. Metcalfe (eds) (2000) *Frontiers of Evolutionary Economics: Competition, Self-organization and Innovation Policy*. Cheltenham: Edward Elgar.

Frey, B. (1997) *Not Just for the Money: An Economic Theory of Personal Motivation*. Cheltenham: Edward Elgar.

Friedman, M. (1953) 'The Methodology of Positive Economics' in M. Friedman (1953) *Essays in Positive Economics*. Chicago: University of Chicago Press, pp. 3–43.

Friedman, M. (1959) 'The Demand for Money: Some Theoretical and Empirical Results.' *Journal of Political Economy*, **67**: 327–51.

Fukuyama, F. (1995) *Trust: The Social Virtues and the Creation of Prosperity*. New York: Free Press.

Fukuyama, F. (1998) *The Great Disruption: Human Nature and the Reconstitution of Social Order*. London: Profile Books.

Furstenberg, F. (1996) 'The Future of Marriage.' *American Demographics*, **18**: 34–39.

Gell-Man, M. and S. Lloyd (1996) 'Information Measures, Effective Complexity and Total Information.' *Complexity*, **2**: 44–52.

Georgescu-Roegen, N. (1958) 'The Nature of Expectation and Uncertainty.' in Bowan (ed.) (1958) pp. 11–29.

Georgescu-Roegen, N. (1970) 'The Economics of Production.' *American Economic Review*, **60**: 1–9 (1969 Richard T. Ely Lecture).

Georgescu-Roegen, N. (1971) *The Entropy Law and the Economic Process*. Cambridge, MA: Harvard University Press.

Georgescu-Roegen, N. (1975) 'Energy and Economic Myths.' *Southern Economic Journal*, **41**: 347–81.

Georgescu-Roegen, N. (1984) 'Feasible Recipes versus Viable Technologies.' *Atlantic Economic Journal*, **12**: 21–31.

Gilbert, N. and K. Troitzsch (1999) *Simulation for the Social Scientist*. Buckingham: Open University Press.

Gleick, J. (1987) *Chaos: The Making of a New Science*. New York: Penguin.

Goldberg, D. (1989) *Genetic Algorithms in Search, Optimization and Machine Learning*. Reading, MA: Addison-Wesley.

Goodwin, R. (1982) *Essays in Economic Dynamics*. London: Macmillan.

Goodwin, R. (1990) *Chaotic Economic Dynamics*. Oxford: Clarendon Press.

Gowdy, J. (1985) 'Evolutionary Theory and Economic Theory: Some Methodological Issues.' *Review of Social Economy*, **43**: 316–24.

Gowdy, J. (1992) 'Higher Selection Processes in Evolutionary Economic Change.' *Journal of Evolutionary Economics*, **2**: 1–16.

Gowdy, J. (1994) *Coevolutionary Economics: The Economy, Society and the Environment*. Norwell, MA: Kluwer.

Gray, J. (1997) 'The Fall in Men's Return to Marriage.' *Journal of Human Resources*, **32**: 481–504.

Green, D. (1994) 'Connectivity and the Evolution of Biological Systems.' *Journal of Biological Systems*, **2**: 91–103.

Green, D. (1996). 'Towards a mathematics of complexity.' in R. Stocker et al. (eds) (1996) *Complex Systems - from Local Interactions to Global Behaviour*. Amsterdam: IOS Press. pp. 97–105.

Greenhut, M. (1995) *Spatial Microeconomics: Theoretical Underpinnings and Applications*. Aldershot: Edward Elgar.

Groenewegen, P. (1999) 'Perfect Competition, Equilibrium and Economic progress: That Wretched Division of Labour and Increasing Returns.' in Dow and Earl (eds) (1999) Vol. I, pp. 225–38.

Grossbard-Shechtman, S. (1995) 'Marriage Market Models.' in Tommasi and Ierulli (eds) (1995) pp. 92–112.

Grossman, S. and O. Hart (1986) 'The Costs and Benefits of Ownership: A Theory of Lateral and Vertical Integration.' *Journal of Political Economy*, **94**: 691–719.

Hacking, I. (1975). *The Emergence of Probability: A Philosophical Study of Early Ideas about Probability, Induction and Statistical Inference*. Cambridge: Cambridge University Press.

Hackl, P. and A. Westlund (eds) (1991) *Economic Structural Change: Analysis and Forecasting*. Berlin: Spinger-Verlag.

Hahn, F. (1970) 'Some Adjustment Problems.' *Econometrica*, **32**: 1–17.

Hahn, F. (1981) 'General Equilibrium Theory.' in Bell and Kristol (eds) (1981) pp. 123–38.

Hahn, F. (1982) 'Stability.' in K. Arrow and M. Intriligator (eds) (1982) *Handbook of Mathematical Economics*, Vol. II. New York: North-Holland, pp. 745–93.

Hahn, F. (1984) *Equilibrium and Macroeconomics*. Oxford: Basil Blackwell.

Hahn, F. (1991) 'The Next Hundred Years.' *Economic Journal*, **101**: 47–50.

Hall, P. (ed.) (1986) *Technology, Innovation and Economic Policy*. Oxford: Phillip Allan.

212 *The new evolutionary microeconomics*

Hall, R. and C. Hitch (1939) 'Price Theory and Business Behaviour.' *Oxford Economic Papers*, **2**: 12–45.

Hamilton, D. (1991) *Evolutionary Economics: A Study in Change in Economic Thought*. 3rd edn New Brunswick: Transaction.

Harman, P. (1982) *Energy, Force and Matter*. Cambridge: Cambridge University Press.

Harper, D. (1994) 'A New Approach to Modelling Endogenous Change and Endogenous Learning Processes in Economic Theory.' *Advances in Austrian Economics*, **1**: 49–79.

Harper, D. (1996) *Entrepreneurship and the Market Process—An Inquiry into the Growth of Knowledge*. London: Routledge.

Hart, O. (1995) *Firms, Contracts and Financial Structure*. Oxford: Clarendon Press.

Hart, O. and J. Moore (1990) 'Property Rights and the Nature of the Firm.' *Journal of Political Economy*, **98**: 1119–58.

Hartley, J. (1997) *The Representative Agent in Macroeconomics*. New York: Routledge.

Hausman, D. (1992) *The Inexact and Separate Science of Economics*. Cambridge: Cambridge University Press.

Hawkins, R., R. Mansell and J. Skea (eds) (1995) *Standards, Innovation and Competitiveness: The Politics and Economics of Standards in Natural and Technical Environments*. Cheltenham: Edward Elgar.

Hayek, F. (1933) 'The Trend of Economic Thinking.' *Economica*, **13**: 121–37.

Hayek, F. (1945) 'The Use of Knowledge in Society.' *American Economic Review*, **35**: 519–30.

Hayek, F. (1952) *The Counter-revolution in Science: Studies in the Abuse of Reason*. New York: Free Press.

Hayek, F. (1969) 'The Primacy of the Abstract.' in Koestler and Smythies (eds) (1969), pp. 309–23.

Hayek, F. (1974) 'The Pretence of Knowledge.' in Hayek (1978) pp. 23–34.

Hayek, F. (1978) *New Studies in Philosophy, Politics, Economics and the History of Ideas*, London: Routledge & Kegan Paul.

Hayek, F. (1991) 'Spontaneous ("grown") Order and Organized ("made") Order.' in Thompson et al. (eds) (1991) pp. 293–305.

Hazledine, T. (1998) *Taking New Zealand Seriously: The Economics of Decency*. Auckland: Harper Collins.

Heertje, A. and M. Perlman (eds) (1990) *Evolving Technology and Market Structure: Studies in Schumpeterian Economics*. Ann Arbor: University of Michigan Press.

Heilbroner, R. and W. Milberg (1995) *The Crisis of Vision in Modern Economic Thought*. New York: Cambridge University Press.

Heiner, R. (1983) 'The Origin of Predictable Behaviour.' *American Economic Review*, **73**: 560–95.

Hesse, H. (1969) *The Glass Bead Game (Magister Ludi)*. translated from the original *Das Glasperlenspiel* (1943) by Richard and Clara Winston. New York: Holt, Rinehart & Winston, Inc.

Hey, J. (1982) 'Search for Rules of Search.' *Journal of Economic Behaviour and Organization*, **3**: 65–81.

Hicks, J. (1948) *Value and Capital*. (first published 1939) Oxford: Clarendon Press.

Hicks, J. (1986) 'Is Economics a Science?' in M. Baranzini and R. Scazzieri (eds) (1986) *Foundations of Economics*. Oxford: Blackwell, pp. 91–101.

Hirschman, A. (1970) *Exit, Voice and Loyalty*. Cambridge, MA: Harvard University Press.

Hodgson, G. (1988) *Economics and Institutions: A Manifesto for a Modern Institutional Economics*. Cambridge: Polity Press.

Hodgson, G. (1993) *Economics and Evolution: Bringing Life back into Economics*. Cambridge: Polity Press.

Hodgson, G. (1996) 'The Ubiquity of Habits and Rules.' *Cambridge Journal of Economics*, **21**: 663–84.

Hodgson, G. (ed.) (1998) *The Foundations of Evolutionary Economics: 1890-1973*. Vols. I and II. Cheltenham: Edward Elgar.

Hodgson, G. (1999) *Evolution and Institutions: on Evolutionary Economics and the Evolution of Economics*. Cheltenham: Edward Elgar.

Hodgson, G. (forthcoming) *How Economics Forgot History: The Problems of Historical Specificity in Social Science*.

Holland, J. (1975) *Adaptation in Natural and Artificial Systems: An Introductory Analysis with Applications to Biology, Control, and Artificial Intelligence*. Ann Arbor: University of Michigan Press.

Holland, J. (1995) *Hidden Order: How Adaptation Builds Complexity*. New York: Helix Books.

Holland, J. (1998) *Emergence: From Chaos to Order*. Oxford: Oxford University Press.

Holland, J. and J. Miller (1991) 'Artificial Adaptive Agents in Economic Theory.' *American Economic Review: Papers and Proceedings*, **81**: 365–70.

Hollis, D. and E. Nell (1975) *Rational Economic Man: A Philosophical Critique of Neo-Classical Economics*. London: Cambridge University Press.

Horgan, J. (1995) 'From Complexity to Perplexity.' *Scientific American*, **272**: 74–9

Houthakker, H. (1952) 'Changes in quantities and qualities consumed.' *Review of Economic Studies*, **19**: 155–63.

Jammer, M. (1969) *Concepts of Space: The History of Theories of Space in Physics*. (2nd edn) Cambridge, MA: Harvard University Press.

Jantsch, E. (1980) *The Self-organizing Universe: Scientific Implications of the Emerging Paradigm of Evolution*. Oxford: Pergamon.

Kahneman, D. and A. Tversky (1979) 'Prospect theory: An Analysis of Decision Under Risk.' *Econometrica*, **47**: 263–91.

Katona, G. (1951) *Psychological Analysis of Economic Behaviour*. New York: McGraw-Hill.

Katona, G. (1960) *The Powerful Consumer: Psychological Studies of the American Economy*. New York: McGraw-Hill.

Kauffman, S. (1969) 'Metabolic Stability and Epigenesis in Randomly Constructed Genetic Nets.' *Journal of Theoretical Biology*, **22**: 437–67.

Kauffman, S. (1988) 'The Evolution of Economic Webs.' in Anderson et al. (eds) (1988) pp. 117–46.

Kauffman, S. (1993) *The Origins of Order: Self-organization and Selection in Evolution*. Oxford: Oxford University Press.

Kauffman, S. (1995) *At Home in the Universe: The Search for the Laws of Self-organization and Complexity*. New York: Oxford University Press.

Kauffman, S. (1996) 'Investigations: The Nature of Autonomous Agents and the Worlds they Mutually Create.' an unpublished preprint, http://www.santafe.edu/sfi/People/kauffman/Investigations.html

Kay, J. (1993) *Foundations of Corporate Success*. Oxford: Oxford University Press.

Kay, N. (1982) *The Evolving Firm*. London: Macmillan.

Kay, N. (1984) *The Emergent Firm: Knowledge, Ignorance and Surprise in Economic Organisation*. London: Macmillan.

Kay, N. (1997) *Pattern in Corporate Evolution*. Oxford: Oxford University Press.

Kelly, G. (1963) *A Theory of Personality*. New York: Norton.

Keynes, J. (1921) *Treatise on Probability*. reprinted in *Collected Works*, Vol. VIII.

Keynes, J. (1937) 'The General Theory of Employment.' *Quarterly Journal of Economics*, 51: 209–23.

Keynes, J. (1971) *Collected Works*, Vols. I–XXX. London: Macmillan, Cambridge University Press (for the Royal Economic Society).

Khalil, E. (1991) 'Natural Complex vs. Natural System.' *Journal of Social and Biological Structures*, **14**: 9–31.

Kirkpatrick, S., C. Gelatt, and H. Vecci (1983) 'Optimization by Simulated Annealing.' *Science*, **220**: 671–7.

Kirman, A. (1983) 'Communication in Markets: A Suggested Approach.' *Economics Letters*, **12**: 101–8.

Kirman, A. (1987a) 'Combinatorics.' in J. Eatwell, M. Milgate and P. Newman (eds) (1987) *The New Palgrave: A Dictionary of Economics*. Vol. 1. London: Macmillan, p. 493.

Kirman, A. (1987b) ''Graph Theory.' in J. Eatwell, M. Milgate and P. Newman (eds) (1987) *The New Palgrave: A Dictionary of Economics*. Vol. 2. London: Macmillan. pp. 558–9.

Kirman, A. (1989) 'The Intrinsic Limits to Modern Economic Theory: The Emperor Has No Clothes.' *Economic Journal*, **99**, supplement: 126–39.

Kirman, A. (1992) 'Whom or What Does the Representative Individual Represent?' *Journal of Economic Perspectives*, **6**: 117–36.

Kirman, A. (1993) 'Ants, Rationality and Recruitment.' *Quarterly Journal of Economics*, **8**: 137–56.

Kirman, A. (1994) 'Economies with Interacting Agents.' *Working Paper 94-05-030*. Santa Fe, NM: Santa Fe Institute.

Kirman, A. (1997a) 'The Evolution of Economic Theory.' in D'Autume and Cartelier (eds) (1997) pp. 92–107.

Kirman, A. (1997b) 'The Economy as an Interactive System." in Arthur et al. (eds) (1997) pp. 491–530.

Kirman, A. (1997c) 'The Economy as an Evolving Network.' *Journal of Evolutionary Economics*. **7**: 339–53.

Kirzner, I. (1973) *Competition and Entrepreneurship*. Chicago: Chicago University Press.

Kirzner, I. (1981) 'The "Austrian" Perspective on the Crisis.' in Bell and Kristol (eds) (1981) pp. 111–22

Kirzner, I. (1997) 'Entrepreneurial Discovery and the Competitive Market Process: An Austrian Approach.' *Journal of Economic Literature*, **35**: 60–85.

Kirzner, I. (1999) 'Rationality, Entrepreneurship, and Economic "Imperialism".' in Dow and Earl (eds) (1999) pp. 1–13.

Klamer, A. and D. McCloskey (1995) 'One Quarter of GDP is Persuasion.' *American Economic Review*, **92**: 191–5.

Klamer, A., D. McCloskey and R. Solow (eds) (1988) *The Consequences of Economic Rhetoric*. New York: Cambridge University Press.

Knight, F. (1921) *Risk, Uncertainty and Profit*. Boston: Houghton Mifflin.

Koestler, A. (1969) 'Beyond Atomism and Holism—The Concept of the Holon.' in Koestler and Smythies (eds) (1969) pp. 192–216.

Koestler, A. (1975) *The Act of Creation*. London: Picador Books.

Koestler, A. (1978) *Janus: A Summing Up*. London: Hutchison.

Koestler, A. and J. Smythies (eds) (1969) *Beyond Reductionism: New Perspectives in the Life Sciences*. London: Hutchinson.

Kollman, K., J. Miller and S. Page (1997) 'Computational Political Economy.' in Arthur et al. (eds) (1997) pp. 461–90.

Kolmogorov, A. (1933) *Grundbergriffe der Wahrscheinlichkeitrechnung*. Berlin.

Kornai, J. (1971) *Anti-equilibrium: An Economic Systems Theory and the Tasks of Research*. Amsterdam: North-Holland.

Kornai, J. (2000) 'What the Change of System From Socialism to Capitalism Does and Does Not Mean.' *Journal of Economic Perspectives*, **14**: 27–42.

Krugman, P. (1994) 'Complex Landscapes in Economic Geography.' *American Economic Review*, **84**: 412–6.

Krugman, P. (1997) 'How the Economy Organizes Itself in Space: A Survey of the New Economic Geography.' in Arthur et al. (eds) (1997) pp. 239–62.

Kuhn, T. (1962) *The Structure of Scientific Revolutions.* Chicago: University of Chicago Press.

Kwasnicki, W. (1996) *Knowledge, Innovation and Economy: An Evolutionary Exploration.* Cheltenham: Edward Elgar.

Lachmann, L. (1976) 'From Mises to Shackle: An Essay on Austrian Economics and the Kaleidic Society.' *Journal of Economic Literature*, **14**: 54–62.

Lachmann, L. (1986) *The Market as an Economic Process.* Oxford: Basil Blackwell.

Lakatos, I. (1978) *The Methodology of Scientific Research Programmes.* (From articles 1963–1976). Cambridge: Cambridge University Press.

Lam, D. (1997) 'Demographic Variables and Income Inequality.' in M. Rosenzweig and O. Stark (eds) (1997) *Handbook of Population and Family Economics.* Amsterdam: Elsevier Science Publishers, pp. 1015–59.

Lancaster, K. (1966) 'Change and innovation in the technology of consumption.' *American Economic Review*, **56**: 14–23.

Lane, D., F. Malerba, R. Maxfield and L. Orsenigo (1996) 'Choice and Action.' *Journal of Evolutionary Economics*, **6**: 43–76.

Langlois, R. (1988) 'Economic Change and the Boundaries of the Firm.' *Journal of Institutional and Theoretical Economics*, **144**: 635–57.

Langlois, R. (1992) 'Transaction Cost Economics in Real Time.' *Industrial and Corporate Change*, **1**: 99–127.

Langlois, R. (1998) 'Capabilities and the Theory of the Firm.' in Foss and Loasby (eds) (1998) pp. 183–203.

Langlois, R. (1999) 'Scale, Scope and the Re-use of Knowledge.' in Dow and Earl (eds) (1999) pp. 239–54.

Langlois, R. and P. Robertson (1995) *Firms, Markets and Economic Change: A Dynamic Theory of Business Institutions.* London: Routledge.

Langton, C. (ed.) (1995) *Artificial Life: An Overview.* Cambridge, MA: MIT Press.

Lavoie, M. (1992) *Foundations of Post-Keynesian Economic Analysis.* Aldershot: Edward Elgar.

Lawson, T. (1988) 'Probability and Uncertainty in Economic Analysis.' *Journal of Post Keynesian Economics*, **11**: 38–65.

Lawson, T. (1995) 'A Realist Perspective on Contemporary Economic Theory.' *Journal of Economic Issues*, **29**: 1–32.

Lawson, T. (1997) *Economics and Reality.* London: Routledge.

Leamer, E. (1983) 'Lets take the Con out of Econometrics.' *American Economic Review*, **73**: 31–43.

Leibenstein, H. (1976) *Beyond Economic Man.* Cambridge, MA: Harvard University Press.

Leibenstein, H. (1979) 'A Branch of Economics is Missing: Micro–Micro Theory.' *Journal of Economic Literature,* **17**: 477–502.

Leijonhufvud, A. (1968) *On Keynesian Economics and the Economics of Keynes.* New York: Oxford University Press.

Leijonhufvud, A. (1973) 'Effective Demand Failures.' *Swedish Journal of Economics,* **75**: 27–48.

Leijonhufvud, A. (1981) *Information and Coordination: Essays in Macroeconomic Theory.* Oxford: Oxford University Press.

Leijonhufvud, A. (1993) 'Towards a Not-Too-Rational Macroeconomics.' *Southern Economic Journal,* **60**: 1–13.

Leijonhufvud, A. (1997) 'Macroeconomics and Complexity: Inflation Theory.' in Arthur et al. (eds) (1997), pp. 321–36.

Leontief, W. (1971) 'Theoretical Assumptions and Nonobserved Facts.' *American Economic Review,* **61**: 1–7.

Leontief, W. (1982) Letter in *Science,* **217**: 104–7.

Lettau, M. and H. Uhlig (1999) 'Rules of Thumb versus Dynamic Programming.' *American Economic Review,* **89**: 148–74.

Levy, S. (1992) *Artificial Life: The Quest for a New Creation.* New York: Pantheon Books.

Lewin, P. (1994) 'Knowledge, Expectations and Capital: The Economics of Ludwig M. Lachmann.' in P. Boettke and M. Rizzo (eds) (1994) *Advances in Austrian Economics,* Vol. 1. London: JAI Press Inc, pp. 233–56.

Leydesdorff, L. (1994) 'New Models of Technological Change.' in Leydesdorff and Van Den Besselar (eds) (1994), pp. 180–92.

Leydesdorff, L. and P. Van Den Besselaar (eds) (1994) *Evolutionary Economics and Chaos Theory: New Directions in Technology Studies.* London: Pinter.

Lindahl, E. (1939) *Studies in the Theory of Money and Capital.* London: Allen & Unwin.

Lippman, S. and R. Rumelt (1982) 'Uncertain Imitability: An Analysis of Inter-firm Differences in Efficiency under Competition.' *Bell Journal of Economics,* **13**: 418–38.

Loasby, B. (1976) *Choice, Complexity and Ignorance.* Cambridge: Cambridge University Press.

Loasby, B. (1978) 'Whatever Happened to Marshall's Theory of Value?' *Scottish Journal of Political Economy,* **25**: 1–12.

Loasby, B. (1986) 'Organization, Competition and the Growth of Knowledge.' in R. Langlois (ed.) (1986) *Economics as a Process.* Cambridge: Cambridge University Press.

Loasby, B. (1989) *The Mind and Method of the Economist: A Critical Appraisal of Major Economists of the Twentieth Century.* Aldershot: Edward Elgar.

218     *The new evolutionary microeconomics*

Loasby, B. (1991) *Equilibrium and Evolution: An Exploration of Connecting Principles in Economics*. Manchester: Manchester University Press.

Loasby, B. (1995) 'Acceptable Explanations.' in S. Dow and J. Hillard (eds) (1995) *Keynes, Knowledge and Uncertainty*. Aldershot: Edward Elgar, pp. 6–24.

Loasby, B. (1996) 'The Organization of Industry.' in Foss and Knudsen (eds) (1996) pp. 38–53.

Loasby, B. (1998a) 'The Concept of Capabilities.' in Foss and Loasby (eds) (1998) pp. 163–82.

Loasby, B. (1998b) 'The Organization of Capabilities.' *Journal of Economic Behaviour and Organization*, **35**: 139–60.

Loasby, B. (2000) 'Market Institutions and Economic Evolution.' *Journal of Evolutionary Economics*, **10**: 297–309.

Lorenz, E. (1963) 'Deterministic Nonperiodic Flow.' *Journal of Atmospheric Science*, **20**: 130–41.

Louçã, F. (1997) *Turbulence in Economics: An Evolutionary Appraisal of Cycles and Complexity in Historical Processes*. Cheltenham: Edward Elgar.

Lucas, R. (1972) 'Expectations and the Neutrality of Money.' *Journal of Economic Theory*, **4**: 103–24.

Lucas, R. (1975) 'An Equilibrium Model of the Business Cycle.' *Journal of Political Economy*, **83**: 1113–44.

Magnusson, L. (ed.) (1994) *Evolutionary and Neo-Schumpeterian Approaches to Economics*. London: Kluwer.

Magnusson, L. and J. Ottosson (eds) (1997) *Evolutionary Economics and Path Dependence*. Cheltenham: Edward Elgar.

Mainzer, K. (1996) *Thinking in Complexity: The Complex Dynamics of Mind, Matter and Mankind*. Berlin: Springer-Verlag.

Mäki, U., B. Gustafsson and C. Knudsen (eds) (1993) *Rationality, Institutions and Economic Methodology*. London: Routledge.

Mandelbrot, B. (1972) 'Statistical Methodology for Non-Periodic Cycles.' *Annals of Economic and Social Measurement*, **1**: 259–90.

Mandelbrot, B. (1987) 'Towards a Second Stage of Indeterminism in Science.' *Interdisciplinary Science Reviews*, **12**: 117–27.

Marshall, A. (1949) *The Principles of Economics*. 8th (reset) edn (1st edn 1890), London: Macmillan.

Mas-Colell, A. (1985) *The Theory of General Economic Equilibrium: A Differentiable Approach*. New York: Cambridge University Press.

Meischelman, D. (1962) *The Term Structure of Interest Rates*. Englewood Cliffs, NJ: Prentice-Hall.

Ménard, C. (1995) 'Markets as Institutions versus Organizations as Markets?' *Journal of Economic Behaviour and Organization*, **28**: 169–82.

Metcalfe, J. (1994) 'Evolutionary Economics and Technology Policy.' *Economic Journal*, **104**: 918–31

Metcalfe, J. (1995) 'Technology Systems and Technology Policy in an Evolutionary Framework.' *Cambridge Journal of Economics*, **19**: 25–47.

Metcalfe, J. (1997) 'Evolutionary Concepts in Relation to Evolutionary Economics.' *Queensland University Discussion Paper*, 226.

Metcalfe, J. (1998) *Evolutionary Economics and Creative Destruction*. London: Routledge.

Miller, G. (1956) 'The Magic Number Seven Plus or Minus Two: Some Limits on our Capacity for Processing Information.' *Psychological Review*, **63**: 81–97.

Minsky, H. (1975) *John Maynard Keynes*. New York: Columbia University Press.

Minsky, H. (1982) 'The Financial instability Hypothesis: Capitalist Processes and the Behavior of the Economy.' in C. Kindleberger and J. Laffergue (eds) (1982) *Financial Crises: Theory, History, and Policy*. Cambridge: Cambridge University Press.

Mintzberg, H. (1979) *The Structuring of Organizations*. Englewood Cliffs, NJ: Prentice-Hall.

Mirowski, P. (1988a) *Against Mechanism: Protecting Economics from Science*. Totowa, NJ: Rowman & Littlefield.

Mirowski, P. (1988b) 'Energy and Energetics in Economics: A Review Essay.' *Journal of Economic Issues*, **22**: 811–32.

Mirowski, P. (1989) *More Heat Than Light: Economics as Social Physics*. New York: Cambridge University Press.

Mirowski, P. (1990) 'From Mandelbrot to Chaos in Economic Theory.' *Southern Economic Journal*, 57: 289–307.

Mirowski, P. (1991a) 'Postmodernism and the Social Theory of Value.' *Journal of Post Keynesian Economics*, **13**: 565–82.

Mirowski, P. (1991b) 'When Games Grow Deadly Serious: The Military Influence on the Evolution of Game Theory.' *History of Political Economy*, **23**: 227–60.

Mirowski, P. (ed.) (1994) *Natural Images in Economic Thought: Markets Red in Tooth and Claw*. New York: Cambridge University Press.

Mirowski, P. (1998) Review of *Is Economics Becoming a Hard Science?'* D'Autume and Cartelier (1997), *Journal of Economic Literature*, **36**: 937–9.

Mirowski, P. (2000) *Machine Dreams: Economics Becomes a Cyborg Science*. New York: Cambridge University Press. Forthcoming.

Mirowski, P. and K. Somefun (1998) 'Markets as Evolving Computational Entities.' *Journal of Evolutionary Economics*, **8**: 329–56.

Mises, L. von (1949) *Human Action: A Treatise on Economics*. New Haven: Yale University Press.

Mitchell, M. (1998) *An Introduction to Genetic Algorithms*. Cambridge MA: MIT Press.

Mokyr, J. (1990) *The Lever of Riches*. New York: Oxford University Press.

Mongiovi, G. (1994) 'Capital, Expectations, and Economic Equilibrium: Some Notes on Lachmann and the so-called "Cambridge School".' in P. Boettke and M. Rizzo (eds) (1994) *Advances in Austrian Economics*, Vol. 1. London: JAI Press Inc, pp. 257–77.

Monod, J. (1972) *Chance and Necessity: An Essay on the Natural Philosophy of Modern Biology*. London: Collins.

Montgomery, C. (1995) *Resource Based and Evolutionary Theories of the Firm: Towards a Synthesis*. Boston: Kluwer Academic Publishers.

Morowitz, H. and J. Singer (eds) (1995) *The Mind, The Brain, and Complex Adaptive Systems*. New York: Addison Wesley Longman.

Morris, S. (2000) 'Contagion.' *Review of Economic Studies*, **67**: 57–78.

Morrison, P. (ed) (1995) 'Labour, Employment and Work in New Zealand.' Victoria University, Wellington: Mimeograph.

Moss, S. (1984) 'The History of the Theory of the Firm from Marshall to Robinson and Chamberlin: The Source of Positivism in Economics.' *Economica*, **51**: 307–18.

Muth, J. (1961) 'Rational Expectations and the Theory of Price Movements.' *Econometrica*, **29**: 315–35.

Myrdal, G. (1965) *Monetary Equilibrium*. (first published 1939) New York: Kelley.

Nell, E. (1996) *Making Sense of a Changing Economy: Technology, Markets and Morals*. New York: Routledge.

Nelson, J. (1994) 'I, Thou, and Them: Capabilities, Altruism and Norms in the Economics of Marriage.' American Economic Review: Papers and Proceedings, **84**: 126–31.

Nelson, R. (1994) 'The Role of Firm Differences in an Evolutionary Theory of Technical Advance.' in Magnusson (ed.) (1994) pp. 231–42.

Nelson, R. (1995) 'Recent Evolutionary Theorizing About Economic Change.' *Journal of Economic Literature*, **33**: 48–90.

Nelson, R. and S. Winter (1982) *An Evolutionary Theory of Economic Change*. Cambridge, MA: Harvard University Press.

Nicolis, G. and I. Prigogine (1977) *Self-organization in Non-equilibrium Systems*. New York: Wiley.

Nicolis, G. and I. Prigogine (1989) *Exploring Complexity*. New York: Freeman.

Norgaard, R. (1987) 'Economics as Mechanics and the Demise of Biological Diversity.' *Economic Modelling*, September: 107–21.

North, D. (1990) *Institutions, Institutional Change and Economic Performance*. Cambridge: Cambridge University Press.

O'Driscoll, G. and M. Rizzo (1985) *The Economics of Time and Ignorance*. Oxford: Basil Blackwell.

O'Driscoll, G. and M. Rizzo (1986) 'Subjectivism, Uncertainty and Rules.' in I. Kirzner (ed) (1986) *Subjectivism, Intelligibility and Economic Understanding.* London: Macmillan. pp. 252–67

Okun, A. (1981) *Prices and Quantities: A Macroeconomic Analysis.* Oxford: Basil Blackwell.

Padgett, J. (1997) 'The Emergence of Simple Ecologies of Skill: A Hypercycle Approach to Economic Organization.' in Arthur et al. (eds) (1997), pp. 199–221.

Parsons, T. (1940) 'The Motivation of Economic Activities.' *Canadian Journal of Economics and Political Science,* **6**: 187–203.

Penrose, E. (1959) *The Theory of the Growth of the Firm.* Oxford: Basil Blackwell.

Peters, E. (1986) 'Marriage and Divorce: Informational Constraints and Private Contracting.' *American Economic Review,* **76**: 437–54.

Pettersson, M. (1996) *Complexity and Evolution.* Cambridge: Cambridge University Press.

Pirisg, R. (1991) *Lila: An Inquiry into Morals.* London: Corgi.

Poincaré, H. (1963) *Mathematics and Science: Last Essays.* New York: publisher unknown [cited in Georgescu-Roegen 1971: 25].

Polanyi, M. (1967) *The Tacit Dimension.* Garden City, NY: Doubleday Anchor.

Pollock, J. (1989) *Nomic Probability and the Foundations of Induction.* New York: Oxford University Press.

Popper, K. (1965) *Conjectures and Refutations: The Growth of Scientific Knowledge.* New York: Harper & Row.

Potts, J. (1999) 'Choice, Complexity and Connections.' in Dow and Earl (eds) (1999) Vol. 2, pp. 287–305.

Potts, J. (2000) 'Uncertainty, Complexity, and Imagination.' in P. Earl and S. Frowen (eds) (2000) *Economics as an Art of Thought: Essays in Memory of G.L.S. Shackle.* London: Routledge, pp. 162–84.

Powell, W. (1991) 'Neither Market nor Hierarchy: Network Forms of Organization.' in Thompson et al. (eds) (1991). pp. 265–76.

Prahlad, C. and G. Hamel (1990) 'The Core Competence of the Corporation.' *Harvard Business Review,* **66**: 79–91.

Prigogine, I. (1976) 'Order Through Fluctuation: Self-organization and Social Systems.' in Jantsch and Waddington (eds) (1976) pp. 93–133.

Prigogine, I. (1993) 'Bounded Rationality: From Dynamical Systems to Socio-economic Models.' in Day and Chen (eds) (1993) pp. 3–13.

Prigogine, I. and I. Stengers (1984) *Order out of Chaos: Man's New Dialogue with Nature.* Toronto: Bantam Books.

Pryor, F. (1996) *Economic Evolution and Structure: The Impact of Complexity on the U.S. Economic System.* New York: Cambridge University Press.

*The new evolutionary microeconomics*

Quddus, M. and S. Rashid (1994) 'The Overuse of Mathematics in Economics: Nobel Resistance.' *Eastern Economic Journal*, **20**: 251–65.

Radner, R. (1992) 'Hierarchy: The Economics of Managing.' *Journal of Economic Literature*, **30**: 1382–415.

Radner, R. (1996) 'Bounded Rationality, Indeterminacy, and the Theory of the Firm.' *Economic Journal*, **106**: 1360–73.

Radzicki, M. (1990) 'Institutional Dynamics, Deterministic Chaos and Self-organizing Systems.' *Journal of Economic Issues*, **24**: 57–102.

Reder, M. (1982) 'Chicago Economics: Permanence and Change.' *Journal of Economic Literature*, **20**: 1–38.

Rees, T. (1992) *Women and the Labour Market*. London: Routledge.

Reijnders, J. (ed.) (1997) Economics and Evolution. Cheltenham: Edward Elgar.

Richardson, G. (1953) 'Imperfect Knowledge and Economic Efficiency.' *Oxford Economic Papers*, **5**: 136–56.

Richardson, G. (1959) 'Equilibrium, Expectations and Information.' *Economic Journal*, **69**: 223–37.

Richardson, G. (1960) *Information and Investment*. Oxford: Oxford University Press.

Richardson, G. (1971) 'Planning *Versus* Competition.' *Soviet Studies.* **22**: 443–57. (reprinted in G. Richardson (1998) *The Economics of Imperfect Knowledge*, Cheltenham: Edward Elgar. pp. 128–42.)

Richardson, G. (1972) 'The Organisation of Industry.' *Economic Journal*, **82**: 883–96.

Riechmann, T. (1999) 'Learning and Behavioral Stability: An Economic Interpretation of Genetic Algorithms.' *Journal of Evolutionary Economics*, **9**: 225–42.

Robinson, D. (1966) 'Moments on a Graph.' *New Zealand Mathematics Magazine*, **3**(3): 88–93.

Robinson, J. (1962) *Economic Philosophy*. London: Watts.

Romer, P. (1990) 'Endogenous Technological Change.' *Journal of Political Economy,* **98** Supplement: 71–101.

Romer, P. (1992) 'Two Strategies for Economic Development: Using Ideas and Producing Ideas.' *Proceedings of the World Bank Annual Conference on Development Economics—1992*, Washington, DC: World Bank.

Romer, P. (1994) 'The Origins of Endogenous Growth.' *Journal of Economic Perspectives*, **8**: 3–22.

Romer, P. (1996) *Changing Tastes: How Evolution and Experience Shape Economic Behaviour*. New York: Cambridge University Press.

Rosenthal, N. (1993) 'Rules of Thumb in Games.' *Journal of Economic Behaviour and Organization*, **22**: 1–13.

Rosser, J.B. (1991) *From Catastrophe to Chaos : A General Theory of Economic Discontinuities*. Boston: Kluwer.

Rosser, J.B. (1992) 'The Dialogue between the Economic and the Ecological Theories of Evolution.' *Journal of Economic Behaviour and Organization*, **17**: 195–215.

Rosser, J.B. (1999) 'On the Complexities of Complex Economic Dynamics.' *Journal of Economic Perspectives*, **13**: 169–92.

Rosser, J.B. (2001) 'Uncertainty and Expectation.' in *A New Guide to Post Keynesian Economics*, R. Holt and S. Pressman, (eds) (2001) London: Routledge.

Rothschild, M. (1992) *Bionomics: The Inevitability of Capitalism*. London: Futura.

Rutherford, M. (1994) *Institutions in Economics: The Old and the New Institutionalism*. Cambridge: Cambridge University Press.

Sah, R. and J. Stiglitz (1986) 'The Architecture of Economic Systems: Hierarchy and Polyarchy.' *American Economic Review*, **76**: 716–27.

Salthe, S. (1985) *Evolving Hierarchical Systems*. New York: Columbia University Press.

Samuelson, P. (1938) 'A Note on the Pure Theory of Consumers' Behaviour.' *Economica*, **5**: 61–71.

Samuelson, P. (1948) *Fundamentals of Economic Analysis*. Cambridge, MA: Harvard University Press.

Samuelson, P. (1956) 'Social Indifference Curves.' *Quarterly Journal of Economics*, **70**: 1–22.

Santarelli, E. (1995) 'Directed Graph Theory and the Economic Analysis of Innovation.' *Metroeconomica*, **46**: 111–26.

Sargent, T. (1993) *Bounded Rationality in Macroeconomics*. Oxford: Clarendon.

Saul, J. (1993) *Voltaire's Bastards.* London: Penguin Books.

Savage, L. (1954) *The Foundations of Statistics*. New York: Wiley.

Saviotti, P. (1996) *Technological Evolution, Variety, and the Economy*. Cheltenham: Edward Elgar.

Scarf, H. (1989) 'Mathematical Programming and Economic Theory.' *Cowles Foundation Discussion Paper*, No. 930, Yale University, Connecticut.

Scheinkman, J. and M. Woodford (1994) 'Self-Organized Criticality and Economic Fluctuations.' *American Economic Review*, **84**: 417–21.

Scherer, F. and M. Perlman (eds) (1992) *Entrepreneurship, Technical Innovation and Economic Growth: Studies in the Schumpeterian Tradition*. Ann Arbor: University of Michigan Press.

Schumpeter, J. (1939) *Business Cycles*. Vols. I and II. New York: McGraw Hill

Schumpeter, J. (1951) 'The Historical Approach to the Analysis of Business Cycles.' in. R. Clemence (ed.) (1951) *Essays on Economic Topics*. Port Washington, NY: Kennikat.

Schumpeter, J. (1954) *Capitalism, Socialism and Democracy*. 4th edn (1st edn 1942) London: George Allen & Unwin.

Schweitzer, F. (ed.) (1997) *Self-organization of Complex Structures: From Individual to Collective Dynamics*. Amsterdam: Gordon & Breach.

Scitovsky, T. (1976) *The Joyless Economy*. New York: Oxford University Press.

Scitovsky, T. (1986) *Human Desire and Economic Satisfaction*. Brighton: Wheatsheaf.

Scitovsky, T. (1993) *Welfare and Competition*. Aldershot: Gregg Revivals. (First published 1952, London: George Allen & Unwin.)

Sekaran, U. (1986) *Dual Career Families*. San Francisco: Jossey-Bass.

Sen, A. (1973) 'Behaviour and the Concept of Preference.' *Economica*, **40**: 241–59.

Shackle, G. (1949) *Expectation in Economics*. Cambridge: Cambridge University Press.

Shackle, G. (1958) 'Expectation and Liquidity.' in Bowan (ed.) (1958), pp. 30–44.

Shackle, G. (1967) *The Years of High Theory: Invention and Tradition in Economic Thought 1926–1939*. Cambridge: Cambridge University Press.

Shackle, G. (1972) *Epistemics and Economics: A Critique of Economic Doctrines*. Cambridge: Cambridge University Press.

Shackle, G. (1979) *Imagination and the Nature of Choice*. Edinburgh: Edinburgh University Press.

Shackle, G. (1983) 'The Bounds of Unknowledge.' in Wiseman (ed.) (1983) pp. 28–37.

Shiner, J. (1997) 'Self-Organization, Entropy and Order in Growing Systems.' in Schweitzer (ed.) (1997), pp. 21–35.

Silverberg, G. (1997) 'Is there Evolution after Economics?' in Schweitzer (ed.) (1997), pp. 415–23.

Simon, H. (1957) *Models of Man*. New York: Wiley.

Simon, H. (1958) 'The Role of Expectations in an Adaptive or Behaviouristic Model.' in Bowan (ed.) (1958), pp. 49–58.

Simon, H. (1959) 'Theories of Decision-making in Economics and Behavioral Science.' *American Economic Review*, **49**: 253–83.

Simon, H. (1962) 'The Architecture of Complexity.' *Proceedings of the American Philosophical Society*, **106**: 476–82.

Simon, H. (1965) *Administrative Behavior*. New York: Free Press.

Simon, H. (1976) 'From Substantive to Procedural Rationality.' in S.J. Latsis (ed.) (1976) *Method and Appraisal in Economics*. Cambridge: Cambridge University Press.

Simon, H. (1979) 'Rational Decision Making in Business Organizations.' *American Economic Review*, **69**: 493–513.

Simon, H. (1981) *Sciences of the Artificial*. 2nd edn (1st edn 1968). Cambridge, MA: MIT Press.

Simon, H. (1982) *Models of Bounded Rationality*. 2 Vols. Cambridge, MA: MIT Press.

Simon, H. (1991) 'Organizations and Markets.' *Journal of Economic Perspectives*, **5**: 25–44.

Sklar, L. (1974) *Space, Time, and Spacetime*. Berkeley: UCLA Press.

Smale, S. (1966) 'Structurally Stable Systems are not Dense.' *American Journal of Mathematics*, **88**: 491–6.

Smale, S. (1980) *The Mathematics of Time: Essays on Dynamical Systems, Economic Processes and Related Topics*. Berlin: Springer Verlag.

Smith, V. (1991) 'Rational Choice: The Contrast Between Economics and Psychology.' *Journal of Political Economy*, **99**: 877–97.

Sober, E. (1993) *The Nature of Selection: Evolutionary Theory in Philosophical Focus*. (1st edn 1984) Chicago: University of Chicago Press.

Sraffa, P. (1960) *The Production of Commodities by Means of Commodities: A Prelude to a Critique of Economic Theory*. Cambridge: Cambridge University Press.

Starr, R. (1997) *General Equilibrium Theory: An Introduction*. New York: Cambridge University Press.

Stefansson, B. (1997) '*Swarm*: An Object Orientated Simulation Platform Applied to Markets and Organizations.' in P. Angeline et al. (eds) (1997) *Evolutionary Programming VI*. New York: Springer-Verlag.

Steindl, J. (1952) *Maturity and Stagnation in American Capitalism*. Oxford: Blackwell.

Stigler, G. and G. Becker (1977) '*De gustibus non est disputandum.*' *American Economic Review*, **67**: 76–90.

Stiglitz, J. (1994) *Whither Socialism?* Cambridge, MA: MIT Press.

Stocker, R., H. Jelinek, B. Durnota and T. Bossomaier (eds) (1996) *Complex Systems: From Local interactions to Global Phenomena*. Amsterdam: IOS Press.

Stonier, R. and X. Yu (eds) (1994) *Complex Systems: Mechanisms of Adaptation*. Amsterdam: IOS Press.

Sugden, R. (1989) 'Spontaneous Order.' *Journal of Economic Perspectives*, **3**: 85–97.

Suk-Young Chwe, M. (2000) 'Communication and Coordination in Social Networks.' *Review of Economic Studies*, **67**: 1–16.

Swann, P. (1999) 'Marshall's Consumer as an Innovator.' in Dow and Earl (eds) (1999) Vol. I, pp. 98–118.

Tamborini, R. (1997) 'Knowledge and Economic Behaviour: A Constructivist Approach.' *Journal of Evolutionary Economics*, **7**: 49–72.

Teece, D. (1992) 'Competition, Cooperation and Innovation: Organizational Arrangements for Regimes of Rapid Technological Progress.' *Journal of Economic Behaviour and Organization*, **18**: 1–25.

Terna, P. (1998) 'Simulation Tools for Social Scientists: Building Agent-Based Models with *Swarm.*' *Journal of Artificial Societies and Social Simulation,* **1**(2) http://www.soc.surrey.ac.uk/JASSS/1/2/4.html\

Thoben, H. (1982) 'Mechanistic and Organistic Analogies in Economics Reconsidered.' *Kyklos,* **35**: 292–306.

Thom, R. (1975) *Structural Stability and Morphogenesis: An Outline of a General Theory of Models.* Reading, MA: Benjamin.

Thompson, A., J. Frances, R. Levacic, J. Mitchell (eds) (1991) *Markets, Hierarchies and Networks.* London: Sage.

Tisdell, C. (1998) 'Diversity and Economic Evolution.' *Department of Economics Discussion Paper* 239, University of Queensland.

Tommasi, M. and K. Ierulli (eds) (1995) *The New Economics of Human Behavior.* Cambridge: Cambridge University Press.

Townshend, H. (1939) 'Liquidity Premium and the Theory of Value.' *Economic Journal,* **47**: 157–66.

Trost, J. (1975) 'Married and Unmarried Cohabitation: The Case of Sweden.' *Journal of Marriage and the Family,* **37**: 677–82.

Tversky, A. and D. Kahneman (1974) 'Judgement Under Uncertainty: Heuristics and Biases.' *Science,* **185**: 1124–31.

United Nations (1992) *Patterns of Fertility in Low Fertility Settings.* Sales No. E.92.XIII.11.

United Nations–Population Division (1996) 'Fertility Trends among Low Fertility Countries.' http://www.undp.org/

Van Daal, J. and A. Jolink (1993) *The Equilibrium Economics of Léon Walras.* New York: Routledge.

Vanberg, V. (1986) 'Spontaneous Market Order and Social Rules: A Critical Examination of F.A. Hayek's Theory of Cultural Evolution.' *Economics and Philosophy,* **2**: 75–100.

Veblen, T. (1898) 'Why is Economics not an Evolutionary Science?' *Quarterly Journal of Economics,* **12**: 373–97.

Veblen, T. (1899) *The Theory of the Leisure Class.* (republished 1934) New York: Modern Library.

Veblen, T. (1919) *The Place of Science in Modern Civilization and other Essays.* (reprinted 1990, with introduction by W. Samuels.) New Brunswick: Transaction Books.

Velupillai, K. (1994) 'Rationality and Learning in a Computable Setting—Part I: Computable Rationality.' UCLA Center for Computable Economics Discussion Paper Series, #15, University of California, Los Angeles.

Velupillai, K. (1995a) *Computable Economics: The Fourth Arne Ryde Lectures.* Oxford: Oxford University Press.

Velupillai, K. (1995b) 'The Computable Approach to Economics.' Working Paper of the Center for Computable Economics: UCLA.

Vriend, N. (1996) 'Rational Behaviour and Economic Theory.' *Journal of Economic Behaviour and Organization*, **29**: 263–85.

Vriend, N. (1999) 'Was Hayek and ACE?' Working Paper 403, Queen Mary and Westfield College, University of London.

Vriend, N. (2000) 'An Illustration of the Essential Difference between ndividual and Social Learning.' *Journal of Economic Dynamics and Control*, **24**: 1–19.

von Plato, J. (1994) *Creating Modern Probability: Its Mathematics, Physics, and Philosophy in Historical Perspective*. Cambridge: Cambridge University Press.

von Tunzelmann, G. (1995) *Technology and Industrial Progress: The Foundations of Economic Growth*. Aldershot: Edward Elgar.

Vromen, J. (1995) *Economic Evolution: An Inquiry into the Foundations of New Institutional Economics*. London: Routledge.

Waddington, C. (ed.) (1972) *Towards a Theoretical Biology*. Edinburgh: Edinburgh University Press.

Waldrop, M. (1992) *Complexity: The Emerging Science at the Edge of Order and Chaos*. New York: Simon and Schuster.

Walras, L. (1954) *Elements of Pure Economics, or The Theory of Social Wealth*. (1st edn 1874) trans. W. Jaffe. New York: Augustus Kelly.

Watts, D. (1999) *Small Worlds: The Dynamics of Networks between Order and Randomness*. Princeton: Princeton University Press.

Weibull, J. (1995) *Evolutionary Game Theory*. Cambridge, MA: MIT Press

Weintraub, E. (1979) *Microfoundations: The Compatibility of Microeconomics and Macroeconomics*. Cambridge: Cambridge University Press.

Weintraub, E. (1985) *General Equilibrium Analysis: Studies in Appraisal*. Cambridge: Cambridge University Press.

Weintraub, E. and P. Mirowski (1994) 'The Pure and the Applied: Bourbakism comes to Mathematical Economics.' *Science in Context*, **7**: 245–72.

Weisbuch, G., A. Kirman, and D. Herreiner (2000) 'Market Organisation and Trading Relationships.' *Economic Journal*, **110**: 411–436.

Wernerfelt, B. (1984) 'A Resource-based View of the Firm' *Strategic Management Journal*, **5**: 171–80.

Whitehead, A. (1929) *Process and Reality: An Essay in Cosmology*. Cambridge: Cambridge University Press.

Whyte, D. (1990) *Dating, Mating, and Marriage*. New York: Aldine de Gruyter.

Wicken, J. (1986) 'Evolutionary Self-organisation and Entropic Dissipation in Biological and Socioeconomic Systems.' *Journal of Social and Biological Structures*, **9**: 261–73.

Wicksell, K. (1936) *Interest and Prices: A Study of the Causes Regulating the Value of Money*. London : Macmillan. (First published 1898, *Geldzins und Guterpreise*).

Wigner, E. (1969) 'The Unreasonable Effectiveness of Mathematics in the Natural Sciences.' in T. Saaty and F. Weyl (eds) (1969) *The Spirit and Uses of the Mathematical Sciences*. New York: McGraw-Hill, pp. 123–40.

Williams, L. (1966) *The Origins of Field Theory*. New York: Random House.

Williamson, O. (1975) *Markets and Hierarchies: Analysis and Anti-trust Implications*. New York: Free Press.

Williamson, O. (1996) *The Mechanisms of Governance*. Oxford: Oxford University Press.

Wilson, R. (1985) *An Introduction to Graph Theory*. 3rd edn, Essex: Longman.

Wiseman, J. (1983a) 'Dream and Reality.' in Wiseman (ed.) (1983b) pp. 13–27.

Wiseman, J. (ed.) (1983b) *Beyond Positive Economics?* New York: St Martin's Press.

Wiseman, J. and S. Littlechild (1990) 'Crusoe's Kingdom: Choice Cost and Political Economy.' in S. Frowen (ed.) (1990) *Unknowledge and Choice in Economics*. New York: St Martin's Press. pp. 96–128.

Witt, U. (ed.) (1993a) *Evolutionary Economics*. Cheltenham: Edward Elgar.

Witt, U. (1993b) 'Emergence and Dissemination of Innovations: Some Principles of Evolutionary Economics.' in Day and Chen (eds) (1993) pp. 91–100.

Witt, U. (1997c) 'Self-Organization and Economics—What is New.' *Structural Change and Economic Dynamics*, **8**: 489–507.

Wolfram, S. (1994) *Cellular Automata and Complexity*. Reading, MA: Addison-Wesley.

Wright, G. and F. Bolger (eds) (1992) *Expertise and Decision Support*. London: Plenum Press.

Young, A. (1928) 'Increasing Returns and Economic Progress.' *Economic Journal*, **38**: 527–42.

Ziman, J. (1998) *Technological Innovation as an Evolutionary Process*. Cambridge: Cambridge University Press.

# Index

Quality 95
Quandt, R. 45
Quddus, M. 28

Radner, R. 29
Radzicki, M. 53
Ramsey, F. 170
Random Boolean networks 87, 90, 92
Random graphs 66, 81
Randomness 84, 171, 190
Rashid, S. 28
Rational
  behaviour 48
  expectations (see *Expectations, rational*)
  mechanics 24
Rationality
  assumptions 40, 42, 103, 172, 193
  bounded 28, 31, 41, 67, 98, 120, 133,
    164–165, 178, 184, 186, 189, 199
  perfect 28, 142
Real field 9, 11, 27, 52
Realism, critical 25, 32, 38, 54
Realist ontology 40, 196
Reality, of existence and change 39
Reality, representation of 7, 14
Recession 168
Recontracting 116
Reder, M. 198
Reductionism 103
Rees, T. 147
Reflexivity 163
Regime of complexity (description) 90–91
Regimes of dynamical behaviour 89, 183
Regular system (k-regular) 62
Renyi, A. 66–67
Repeated trading relationships 79
Replication, mechanism of 101
Representative agent 6, 16, 40, 43, 132, 176
Research and development 155
Research programmes 8–9, 21, 156, 176
Residual control 100
Resource-based theory of the firm 136ff.,
  181
Resources of the firm 58
Reversible behaviour 168
Richardson, G. 16–17, 41, 45, 94, 102, 104,
  114, 137, 173, 180, 189
Richerson, P. 188
Riechmann, T. 133, 161
Ring, commutative 27–28, 53
Rizzo, M. 17, 23, 172
Robertson, P. 45, 60, 73, 97
Robinson J. 66, 73, 96

Romer, P. 48, 58, 119, 122, 198
Rosenthal, N. 172
Rosser, J.B. 84, 88–89, 110, 190
Rothchild, K. 53
Routine nature of social life 39
Routines 59, 68–69, 118, 137, 197
Rules 39, 120–121, 133
Rumelt, R. 159
Rutherford, M. 44

Sah, R. 45
Salthe, S. 34
Samuelson, P. 18, 33, 37, 98, 136, 142, 185
Santa Fe Institute 75
Sargent, T. 113
Saul J.R. 174
Savage, L. 165, 170
Saviotti, P. 48, 80, 96, 186
Scale and scope 155
Scarcity 113–114
Scarf, H. 121, 178
Scazzieri, R. 46
Scenario planning 89
Scheinkman, J. 110
Schematic preferences 120ff., 161, 178
Schmoller, G. 7
Schumpeter, J. 3–4, 47, 54, 94, 102, 112,
  184, 189–190
Schumpeterian economics 30, 137, 161,
  174, 181
Schuster, P. 110
Schweitzer, F. 53, 101, 110
Scientific legitimacy 37
Scientists 1
Scitovsky, T. 54, 60, 74, 131
Scope, economies of 77
Search 65, 108, 113, 115, 120–121, 133,
  141, 150, 178
Second-hand market 168
Sekaran, U. 147
Selection 34–36, 92, 95, 187, 194
Self-organization 4, 37, 47, 80, 84, 93, 101–
  105, 163, 183, 189–192, 196
Self-organized criticality 191
Sen, A. 34
Sentiments of human behaviour 112
Set, definition of 71
Shackle, G. 3, 16, 19, 23, 37, 42, 47–49, 60,
  95, 104, 134, 163, 165, 170–172, 174,
  176
Shaw, G.B. 141
Shiner, J. 84
Signal 41